The Role of the Pension Fund Trustee

The Role of the Pension Fund Trustee

Fourth edition

Written by
John Cunliffe

Partner, McKenna & Co, Solicitors

LAW & TAX

In association with the National Association of Pension Funds

© Pearson Professional Limited 1997

John Cunliffe has asserted his right under the Copyright, Designs and Patents Act 1988 to be identified as the author of this work.

ISBN 07520 0462 X

Published by FT Law & Tax
21–27 Lamb's Conduit Street
London WC1N 3NJ

A Division of Pearson Professional Limited

Associated Offices
Australia, Belgium, Canada, Hong Kong, India, Japan, Luxembourg, Singapore, Spain, USA.

First published 1989.

A CIP catalogue record for this book is available from the British Library.

Printed in Great Britain by Biddles, Guildford.

Contents

Preface

The last edition of this book appeared in April 1994. Since then the pensions world has undergone a sea change. We have had:

- six judgments from the European Court of Justice, culminating in the *Coloroll* case, on various aspects of sex equality;
- the government's White Paper on pension law reform;
- the Pensions Act; and
- not least the Act's brood of subsidiary legislation.

The Pensions Act is the largest piece of legislation relating to occupational pensions ever to have been enacted. It covers 187 pages, sets up a new regulator—OPRA, equalises State pension ages, changes the rules for SERPS and contracting-out and makes some long overdue headway in tackling the problems caused by the loss of pension rights on divorce.

This edition has been substantially re-written to take account of all these changes and reflects the position as at 1 March 1997. The book ends with four appendices which contain a glossary of terms frequently used, a summary of the duties and sanctions imposed by the Pensions Act, a checklist of actions to be taken to comply with the Act and details of the new rules for the selection of member-nominated trustees.

First time readers of the Lawyer's Tales, which illustrate the text, may be forgiven for bafflement because the Tales are arranged in order of the subject, rather than chronologically. Archie Smithers and David—the heroes, if that is the right word, of the Tales—started life by working, surely a misnomer if ever there was one, for the Magnificent Mutual Life Assurance Society, running its docs department. When their lack of industry was discovered, they arranged a buy out. Sadly in 1991 there was a parting of the ways. David was head hunted by PEPS—Pan European Pension Consultants. Archie and the rest of the team went to Megalaw, a City law factory.

My thanks are due to:

- my friends from those halcyon days at the Magnificent Mutual and in particular Steve Mingle, Keith Boughton, Bob Folley and Doug Hamilton;
- the NAPF and especially Colin Steward (until recently an employee of the NAPF) for his direction and guidance on each edition of the book;
- the successive editors of *The Role of the Pension Fund Trustee* for their tolerance of my eccentricities;
- my long suffering secretary Donna Jacobs who can read my mind as well as my writing;
- my loving wife, who fleetingly appears under the name Bella from time to time;
- Andrew Bayliss, the original of David in the Lawyer's Tales;
- Mark Kowalik, whose idea the book was in the first place and who, with Andrew Bayliss, formed the original team; and
- last but not least all my colleagues, past and present, who have been a source both of education and inspiration and who are gently lampooned from time to time in the Lawyer's Tales. Alas they are now too numerous to thank individually but their names should be recorded—in alphabetical order—to show my appreciation:
Mark Atkinson
Iain Batty
Mark Grant
Simon Jeffreys
Mark Kowalik
Nigel Moore
Simon Pilcher
Kevin Pither
Michael Salters
Neil Smith and
Keith Webster.

John Cunliffe
March 1997

Foreword

It is three years since the third edition of *The Role of the Pension Fund Trustee* was published—and eight years since the publication of the first edition.

Any Act of Parliament containing 181 clauses and 7 schedules will be far from insignificant. The Pensions Act 1995, with its main *raison d'etre* being the introduction into law of the majority of the recommendations of the Pension Law Review Committee (under Professor Roy Goode's Chairmanship) endorses the concept of trust law as the foundation for occupational pension schemes. It has strengthened the security of occupational schemes, including increases in the power, duties and responsibilities of trustees. In addition, most occupational schemes now are legally required to have member-nominated trustees—unless the majority of the members of any particular scheme agree otherwise.

As a result, major changes have had to be made to the third edition. Furthermore, a reader comparing the fourth edition with the first would wonder at the changes in the law affecting occupational schemes which have taken place in a mere eight years.

The NAPF played a major role in the representations made to the Department of Social Security and to Social Security Ministers during the passage of the Bill which was to become the Pensions Act 1995 and during the preparation of all the Regulations which comprise the secondary legislation.

The Role of the Pension Fund Trustee provides an admirably clear guide to the underlying principles as well as the implications of all the changes.

Tom Ross, Chairman
National Association of Pension Funds
March 1997

ix

Chapter 1

Trusts

What is a trust?

A trust is simply an arrangement under which one person or group of people called trustees hold property—the assets of the trust—for the benefit of others, called beneficiaries. Trustees are so called because they are trusted by the person who sets up the trust to administer the trust assets, not for their own benefit, but for the benefit of the beneficiaries. An occupational pension scheme is a good example of a trust. The trustees hold the assets for the benefit of the members and pensioners. Another example is a village hall where the people in the village have the right to use the hall in accordance with its rules. The legal title to the hall is vested in the trustees who administer it, pay the caretaker and allow people to use it in accordance with the rules.

Contract and trust

A personal pension is a half-way house. An individual enters into a contract with a pension provider that, in return for the payment of the contributions, the provider will pay a pension to the individual at a selected age. But the provider must also enter into enforceable obligations to third parties. Thus any widow, widower or other person who becomes entitled to any payment under the scheme, which gives effect to protected rights, must be able to enforce that entitlement. A trust is one method of achieving this. A contract creates personal rights which cannot be enforced by anyone who is not a party to it. A trust creates rights which are enforceable by third parties and does not, unlike a contract, require the person enforcing the rights to give consideration or something in return. Accordingly a pension scheme which is set up as a trust can be enforced by members who were not even alive when it was established. Thus one of the reasons for using a trust to set up a pension scheme is to enable the beneficiaries to enforce their rights.

Reasons for a trust

There are, however, two other reasons for a trust. The first is that the assets of the trust are separated from the employer's property. This is so even if the employer is the sole trustee of the pension scheme. He or she will hold the scheme assets in a separate legal capacity. They are therefore not available to the employer's creditors; so if the employer goes into liquidation, the liquidator cannot claim the pension scheme's assets for the benefit of creditors. This legal separation of the pension scheme assets is a valuable protection to the members whose accrued benefits are, at least to the extent of the assets, secured. It also means that the assets are invested to produce a return for the scheme. The alternative would be for the contributions to be used by the employer in the business and pensions are then simply paid out of revenue when they become due. This would deprive the members of the independent security of an asset backing for their benefits.

Inland Revenue requirements

The second reason for having a trust is that it is a condition of Inland Revenue approval. If a pension scheme is set up under irrevocable trusts and various other conditions are satisfied, the Inland Revenue will approve it. This means that various valuable tax breaks are given. An employee's contributions are tax deductible. Not only are the employer's contributions allowed as a trading expense, they are not taxable as a benefit in kind in the employee's hands. The investment income and capital gains of the scheme are largely free from tax. The pensions ultimately payable are taxed as earned income and a tax free cash sum can be paid to the member on retirement, and to his or her dependants on death in service. It is the giving of tax approval that confers these advantages.

How a trust is established

Except where land is concerned, there are no formalities needed to establish a trust. It can be done by word of mouth. In the case of land a written document is necessary. But in practice trusts are always created by a written document. Imagine the problems if you tried to set up a pension scheme by word of mouth. Who would remember all the details and for how long?

Signed and delivered

For that practical reason, therefore, the trusts of a pension scheme are written down. A deed is not legally required but is almost invariably used. This means that instead of simply signing the document, a person signs and delivers it. Signing needs no explanation. Delivering the deed means that the person concerned intends to be legally bound by it and delivers or hands over the document to someone else as proof of this.

Pension schemes are sometimes set up by resolution of a company's board of directors. A number of personal pension schemes were established in this way. Occupational pension schemes, however, are usually set up by a deed. Two kinds of document are used for this purpose—an interim trust deed and a definitive trust deed and rules. What is the difference between them?

Interim deeds

An interim trust deed is a document that is used to get a pension scheme going in a short time span. It is a short deed containing the basic trust provisions relating, for example, to transfers in and out, investment, appointment and removal of trustees and winding up. Attached to it will be an announcement or booklet setting out the essential features of the scheme such as contributions and benefits. This procedure enables the scheme to be established with a minimum of delay. The Inland Revenue will not grant the scheme full tax approval before the definitive trust deed and rules, which sets out the constitution of the scheme in full, is entered into. But the Revenue will grant provisional relief from tax on employees' contributions and will not charge to tax as benefits in kind the employer's contributions.

Definitive trust deed and rules

A definitive trust deed and rules then has to be prepared within a two year period, which can be extended with the Revenue's consent. This is a lengthy document which contains full details of all the scheme benefits, company and members' contributions, all the provisions required by legislation relating to preservation, Inland Revenue limits on maximum benefits, contracting-out and the like. Essentially, pension schemes can be very simple, but successive waves of legislation relating to early leavers, compulsory transfer rights, revaluation of preserved benefits and contracting-out have made the drafting of definitive trust deeds and rules a complex job. The document has to be read and approved, with or without amendments, by both the employer and the trustees. It then has to be approved by the Pension Schemes Office of the Inland Revenue before full tax approval is granted, resulting largely in freedom from income and capital gains tax on the investments of the scheme. It is a long process and often takes the two years allotted for the task. In practice it would usually be impossible to set up a pension scheme from scratch using a definitive trust deed and rules; it would simply take too long.

'The Lawyer's Tale: Over-egging the Pudding', which follows this chapter illustrates how trust deeds can be drafted to protect members' interests.

The Lawyer's Tale: Over-egging the Pudding

'This is the life' remarked Archie to his friend David sipping champagne as their plane taxied to the runway and the engines revved up for take-off. Sadly it was only the Manx Airlines early morning flight to Douglas.

They had been summoned to a meeting of the trustees of the Manx Building Society. The Manx was way down the building society league table in size. It was currently being courted by one of the UK clearing banks and also by one of the overseas banks that found its UK branch network a readymade solution to its problems. The Society's management had decided that it was not sensible to continue to go it alone.

As Sir Giles Templewood, the Chairman, said: 'Big is beautiful, at any rate in financial services. If we merged with either of our suitors, we could expand into Europe and take the world by storm.'

All this was of course familiar to Archie and David from the pages of the *FT*. David looked up and said to Archie:

'If you ask me, Sir Giles, like you, is off his trolley. Doesn't he realise that we're in Europe already. Plus he and his pals are going to get swallowed up by the sharks in the City. The only place he'll expand to is his sunset home.'

The stewardess brought their steaming hot breakfast of scrambled eggs and kippers and freshened their champagne.

'I don't suppose Sir Giles is going to consult us about that. I had imagined that we were being asked for our pensions expertise' Archie commented sarcastically.

'Right' replied David.'It's all in that file that I biked to you yesterday. As you obviously haven't read it, I'd best tell you the story. The Board have decided to put the Society up for auction. But they're worried about the staff and the pension scheme. The scheme is very generous and the next valuation is just about ready. We're due to meet the trustees and the actuary, Colin Bell, today. You and Colin are old foes, Archie. Colin told me he reckons they've got a surplus on the Government Actuary's basis so something will have to be done. They want advice about how to protect the members after the takeover or, should I say, 'merger'. So you'd best eat up, stick to the coffee and read the trust deed and rules. Meanwhile I'll go back to the sports pages.'

An hour later they touched down on a brilliant summer morning at Ronaldsway. They were met by a peak-capped chauffeur who sped them to Douglas in a stretch Mercedes to meet the trustees. Sir Giles was an imposing figure, with white hair and a full, rich voice. His co-trustees were Vera Fothergill and Ron Smith, the Society's chief accountant, a mousy little man who was completely ignored by his co-trustees and never said anything. Vera was the Society's personnel manager. She wore a vivid purple ensemble with outsize gold earrings, pink hair, orange makeup and the brightest red lips Archie had ever seen. The other member of the party was the actuary Colin Bell, who wore a sharp check suit and a flashy bow tie. He looked more like a bookie than an actuary. There was not much difference. Both professions calculated the odds and got them wrong. But bookies charged less for their mistakes.

'Sit down, gentlemen' boomed Sir Giles. 'Let's get down to brass tacks. Our depositors will get an excellent deal when the Society is merged. Our job today is to make sure that the members of the pension scheme do as well. We don't want any of those smart Alecs from the City to have our surplus. First, Colin, you'd better tell us the financial position of the scheme.' He then sat back, twiddling his thumbs in his braces.

'There's more than enough in the scheme, you'll be glad to know' started Colin in a warm Lancastrian accent 'The pensioners won't be shivering this winter. The Society could have a contribution holiday for at least the next five years and you'd still be in trouble with the Revenue. On my preliminary figures you've got a £75 million surplus on the prescribed basis. Knock off £20 million for the Society's contribution holiday; that leaves £55 million to be spent on benefit improvements or a repayment to the Society or a bit of both; otherwise you'll start losing tax relief on part of the scheme's investment income. But I don't suppose you want to make a refund to the Society.'

'Certainly not; it's not their money' Vera broke in. 'We want to ensure that all of that £55 million is spent on benefit improvements. And we want to make sure that we're all safe when these dreadful banking people take us over. It's no use Sir Giles pretending it's a merger; it's not. Whatever shall we do?'

Everyone looked at Archie. 'Well, for starters, Colin should draw up a list of suggested benefit improvements. But to protect the rights and expectations of the members you need to do four things:

    (1) To convert all discretionary benefits—early retirement on enhanced terms, pension increases and the like—into rights.

At the moment pension increases are discretionary, although for years you have given increases in line with the RPI. Anyone made redundant over the age of 50 is given an unreduced pension. But this requires the Society's consent, which may not always be forthcoming.

(2) To ban any kind of self-investment. One of the quickest ways for sticky fingers to get their hands on the money is for the scheme to buy some of the Society's branches. Even though self-investment is limited to 5 per cent, in a scheme of your size that's still a lot of money.

(3) You should require the company to contribute to the scheme at the rate fixed by the trustees after taking the advice of their actuary.

(4) Last and for good measure, you should change the rules to give any powers and discretions to the trustees alone rather than to the company alone or jointly with the trustees. So the company couldn't take a refund or remove the trustees and appoint new ones in their place.'

'Capital, capital' cried Vera, earrings flashing.

'Hold on, Archie' said David, 'if you do all that, no employer could live with the scheme. Any right minded company would simply walk away and leave the members to drown in their own honey well. When they come up gasping for air and levying a company contribution for tomorrow's manna, they'll be met with a blank refusal. You can't make a company continue to pay contributions.'

'Eh, you are a daft haporth, Archie!' cried Colin. 'That's all well and good for the pensioners but how are the active members going to go on earning gold-plated benefits if the new employer won't play ball.'

'I think I see a half-way house' interjected Sir Giles. 'While the present directors are in office, there is, of course, no problem. We don't need to make any of these changes. It's only when the new brooms come in from Wall Street or Singapore or, even worse, Lombard Street, that we need to pull up the drawbridge. And so if you agree, we'll commission Smithers to draw up a deed changing the rules conditionally on a change in control of the Society.'

'But' said David, 'you can't do that. If Archie's recommendations are a good thing, then they're just as good whether you're running the Society, Sir Giles or some sharp suited yuppies from EC2. Also as directors of the Society you should look after the interests of the depositors as well as the staff. You can't have poison pills which would deter a takeover—er, merger—of the Society, can you, Archie?'

'Up to a point, David' replied Archie. 'But the directors are not doing this to frustrate the merger; rather the reverse. They're going to do their best for the depositors, but at the same time they're going to look after the staff. I'm not suggesting poison pills to deter a takeover bidder. That's not the object, is it Sir Giles?'

'Quite right, Smithers. Why are you two making such a meal of this?' he growled at David and Colin.

'It's all quite simple really' replied David. 'How many pensioners, deferreds and actives have you got, Sir Giles?'

'The membership is about equally split' replied Colin.

'Well then,' David returned to the fray, 'if on a change in control of the Society, you trigger Archie's gold plated benefits, that's fine for the pensioners and deferreds. They will get their index linked pensions fully guaranteed. It's also fine for anyone made redundant who is over the hill, like Archie. They'll get an unreduced pension as of right, even though it costs a fortune. But even that's a mixed blessing. It might in fact encourage the butcher's knife. But what about those poor souls who are left in employment? Archie will have spent all the surplus. Who is going to pay for their future service benefits?'

The faces of Sir Giles and the other trustees clouded. Colin thought it was time to draw the meeting to a conclusion.

'There's no mad rush, is there?' he said. 'Why don't I complete my valuation, draw up a list of benefit improvements and ask David and Archie to advise on their further recommendations. We could then meet again in a couple of weeks time and knock it on the head.'

'Excellent' replied Sir Giles.

'What about having an independent trustee' interposed David, 'that's certainly one of the options you ought to consider. I look after one scheme where an independent trustee was appointed when the company got taken over. When the predator found out, he was incandescent with rage. That sounds like a good advertisement to me for an independent trustee.'

Back at the airport Archie couldn't resist buying a half-stone box of frozen Manx kippers, despite Colin and David's protests.

They had a smooth flight home on a lovely hazy warm summer evening, landing at Heathrow an unheard of ten minutes early.

'You get carried away sometimes, Archie' said Colin as David piloted them skilfully through the busy M25 traffic in his silver

Porsche. 'A pension scheme is a delicate balance between the rights of the employer and the rights and expectations of the members. Both have to be protected. The Pension Law Review Committee saw that all right, but I wonder if you do, you old clothhead. In the last resort your job as well as your pension depends on the goodwill of your employer. Predator protection requires a lot more thought than you seem capable of.'

As they ground to a halt in the rush hour traffic David quietly remarked 'You must have been joking about the trustees fixing the company contribution rate, Archie. That's really over-egging the pudding. Plus you've forgotten something, haven't you, Archie? What about surplus on winding up; you'd best make sure that belongs to the members. And there's something else you've forgotten. You left your kippers on the plane. I bet it stinks to high heaven by now!'

The Pensions Act is here: responsible, impartial stewardship of pension funds – always an ideal – has now been legally backed by legislation.

BESTrustees: a proactive and constructive ...

Can you be confident of your grasp of the complex issues surrounding trusteeship?

Can you be sure that you are asking all the right questions?

Do you understand the complexities of pension fund investment?

Do you have effective safeguards in place to protect beneficiaries, trustees and the sponsoring company?

... part of your team

Now you can have the confidence and assurance of a highly professional and independent trustee working alongside you.

Appointed by schemes as diverse as the pensions industry itself, BESTrustees is well-established and respected for its wealth of experience and quality of personnel.

BESTrustees provides an independent and objective service to pension schemes, their trustees and pension managers, working with them to protect their interests and those of their scheme members.

For more information, contact Clive Gilchrist on 0171-623 3600.

BESTRUSTEES

An approach beyond reproach

BES Trustees plc, The Cannon Centre, 78 Cannon Street, London EC4N 6HH   Telephone: 0171-623 3600

Chapter 2

Trustees

Appointment and removal

The first trustees of the scheme are appointed by the interim trust deed. This deed will also usually give the employer power to remove the trustees and appoint others in their place. There is no upper or lower limit on the number of trustees and the employer can be either the only trustee or one of the trustees of the scheme. However, the trust deed often specifies a maximum and minimum number of trustees. The practice of having the employer as the sole trustee of the scheme causes conflict of interest and, although not unlawful, it is not regarded as good practice.

Statutory provisions

If the trust deed does not deal with the appointment and removal of trustees, the matter is regulated by the Trustee Act 1925. The Act gives the power to appoint trustees to the person, if any, nominated in the trust deed; in the absence of such a power the trustees are given the power to appoint new trustees. There is no power given by the Trustee Act to remove a trustee and so this power has to be given in the trust deed. The Pensions Act provides for member-nominated trustees. This is dealt with below.

Resignation of trustees

A trustee cannot simply resign or retire. Either a new trustee has to be appointed in his or her place or at least two individual trustees or a corporate trustee (a trust corporation) must remain in office and give their consent. Because this can be a nuisance, scheme rules usually confer a power of removal on the employer. This gets over the difficulty which arises when a trustee, who is an employee of the company, gives in his or her notice and resigns as a trustee. Alternatively the employee may assume that, having left, he or she is no longer a trustee. This is not the case and a properly worded power of appointment and removal in the rules will avoid these problems.

Types of trustee

There are various types of trustee. First there are individual trustees who may or may not be employees of the company concerned. Individual trustees need no further explanation. They will be reimbursed their expenses but are not usually paid for their services. Then there are corporate trustees. Here a company is appointed as the sole trustee or one of the trustees. Such a company is usually a subsidiary of, or controlled by, the principal employer. Its directors will take the place of individual trustees. This is a change of form rather than substance but does avoid the need for numerous deeds of removal and appointment when the individuals cease to hold office. If they are individual trustees, usually a deed will be needed; this is not the case if they are directors of a corporate trustee, who can be changed by a board resolution.

Member trustees

The trustees must ensure that arrangements are made for some of the trustees to be nominated and selected by the members. But this does not apply to some schemes, principally one member schemes, unapproved schemes and small self-administered schemes. Nor does it apply if the employer has proposed alternative arrangements which are put to the members for approval. If less than 10 per cent of the members (or 10,000 members, if less) object, the proposals will be treated as approved. It is important to understand that there are no restraints on what the employer can put forward. There is complete freedom so long as the arrangements pass muster with the members.

If the employer either does not put forward alternative proposals or they are rejected, then the trustees must ensure that the number of member-nominated trustees is at least two or (if the scheme has less than 100 members) at least one, and at least one third of the trustees.

A member-nominated trustee cannot be removed without the consent of the other trustees and will normally remain in office for not less than three and no more than six years, although he can be re-elected. A non-member cannot be selected by the members unless the employer approves.

Trustees can put forward selection rules to suit the circumstances of their scheme. Members from different locations may wish to have trustees chosen from each site; some schemes may want to have a pensioner trustee. Any of these options is possible so long as they are not rejected by the members. For this purpose members includes not just the active members but pensioners and such of the deferred pensioners as the trustees decide to consult. The trustees might, for example, decide not to consult those deferred pensioners with whom they have lost contact. But they must not pick and choose capriciously which of them should be consulted.

If less than 10 per cent of the members (or 10,000 members, if less) object either to the employer's proposals for alternative arrangements or to the trustees' proposals, they will be treated as approved. If they are rejected, either the employer or the trustees can think again and re-present or there will have to be a ballot. If there is a ballot, a simple majority of the members who vote prevails.

If neither the employer nor the trustees put forward proposals or their proposals are rejected, there are statutory rules of last resort, in which only the active members are involved.

The arrangements will normally last for six years or, if it is earlier, when new rules are approved. But if there is a bulk transfer or a change in participating employers or one of the participating employers is taken over by an outside company and the trustees consider that it would be wrong for the current arrangements to continue, the existing approval will lapse.

Further details of the complicated rules for the selection of member-nominated trustees are contained in Appendix 4.

Trust corporations

A trust corporation is a particular kind of corporate trustee, usually a bank or an insurance company with experience of managing large trusts and pension schemes. A trust corporation has to have an issued share capital of £250,000 of which not less than £100,000 is paid up. Such a corporation can act as sole trustee where otherwise the scheme might need two individuals. A trust corporation will require to be paid for its services.

Custodian trustees

A custodian trustee is simply a trustee appointed to have safe custody of the scheme's assets, for example share certificates and the like. A custodian trustee acts on the instructions of the ordinary trustees, who are then in this situation often called managing trustees. Custodian trustees (as opposed to custodians) have rather gone out of favour. They need to be paid and can only be got rid of by applying to the court for a removal order. Custodians, on the other hand, are usually subsidiaries of banks and are sometimes appointed to hold the assets of the scheme on behalf of the trustees. Custodians, who are independent of the employer, are usually seen to be an additional protection for the security of members' interests.

Pensioneer trustees

Pensioneer trustees are special trustees approved by the Inland Revenue. Certain small pension schemes have to have a pensioneer trustee as one of the trustees. This ensures that the tax breaks given to approved schemes are not abused. A self-administered pension scheme—as opposed to an insured scheme—with less than 12 members will normally, as a condition of Revenue approval, be required to have a pensioneer trustee. A pensioneer trustee is an individual or company widely involved with occupational pension schemes and having dealings with the Pension Schemes Office who is prepared to undertake not to consent to an improper termination of the scheme. The pensioneer trustee is, in effect, a watchdog for the Inland Revenue, and is required to report any improper dealings involving the scheme.

Independent trustees

If an employer becomes insolvent, an independent trustee of the pension scheme must be appointed. An independent trustee, once appointed, cannot be removed until a new employer has taken the place of the old one. The independent trustee's fees are paid by the scheme. If the employer was the sole trustee, as often happens with small schemes, the independent trustee will take over. In other cases the independent trustee will act jointly with the other trustees.

The independent trustee must have no interest in the employer's or the scheme's assets and must not be connected with or an associate of the employer. In addition, the independent trustee must not have acted as an adviser to the employer or the other trustees in the previous three years.

Any fiduciary powers, eg about pension increases or disposal of surplus on a winding up of the scheme, whether given by the rules to the employer or the other trustees, are to be exercised *solely* by the independent trustee.

This means that it is not possible for liquidators or receivers, acting on behalf of the creditors, to exercise fiduciary or trust powers and divert surplus away from the members. This is a valuable protection for the rights of members of pension schemes when their company goes into liquidation or receivership.

There are other occasions, for example a threatened takeover of the employer, where it is often desirable to have independent trustees, who are not constrained by pressure from the old or new employer.

Disqualification

A trustee will be disqualified from being a trustee of any scheme if:
(1) He has been convicted of an offence involving deception or dishonesty.
(2) He has been made bankrupt.
(3) He has made an arrangement with his creditors.
(4) Where it is a corporate trustee, if any of the directors is disqualified from being a trustee.
(5) He is subject to a disqualification order as a company director.

Where someone has been prohibited by the Occupational Pensions Regulatory Authority (OPRA) from being a trustee or has been removed as a trustee by a court order on the ground of misconduct or mismanagement or is incapable because of a mental disorder, OPRA may disqualify him from being a trustee of any scheme. OPRA must keep a register of disqualified trustees and must disclose whether an individual is on the register.

Dismissal by the employer

An employee dismissed for carrying out or proposing to carry out functions as an employee trustee (not just a member-nominated trustee) will get special protection similar to that provided for trade union and health and safety representatives. Detrimental action short of dismissal will be subject to similar protection. The protection against unfair dismissal of an employee for these reasons applies regardless of his age or length of service.

Time off for trustees

Employee trustees (not just member-nominated trustees) must be allowed reasonable paid time off for trustee duties and training. But there is no requirement for mandatory training for trustees.

For an illustration of some of the problems that can arise with the appointment and removal of trustees, readers are referred to '*The Lawyer's Tales: The Seven Pillars of Wisdom*' and '*Put not your Trust in Princes*' which follow this chapter.

The Lawyer's Tale: The Seven Pillars of Wisdom

The shrill summons of Mike's telephone broke rudely in on his attempt to start the day's work. A succession of late nights had left him feeling frail. Last night's nurses party hadn't helped. It was David from Pan European Pension Services.

'Look, I've been trying to get you for ages. We've got a little problem with the Waters of Wells Pension Scheme. I need your help. Meet me at Sevenoaks station at 11 am tomorrow. In the meantime you'd best bone up on this *LRT* case I've been reading about. Have a word with Archie—he'll understand.'

Mike was not a little puzzled. Like so many people, David assumed everyone knew the background to what he was talking about, when patently they did not. Archie soon put him right.

'Waters of Wells is a very successful company near Tunbridge Wells bottling English spring water—The Royal Waters of Wells. It's run by Maud Belchamber, a sprightly 75-year-old, who happens to think I'm past it.'

Mike burst out laughing in spite of his sore head. 'We all know you're senile, Archie.'

Archie cut him short. 'Not so much of your lip, young man—just because you're 25. I happen to be 17 years younger than Maud. And I'm not past it. Maud eats young men like you and David. She gets excellent advice from me but she prefers it to be dispensed from younger lips. Good luck to the old harridan. I've no wish to meet her any more than she wishes to see me! But to work. What's David getting excited about now. He gets carried away with himself sometimes. I wish he'd tell us what it's all about instead of being mysterious about the *LRT* case. You'd better go and read it. The judgment's only 165 pages! You mustn't expect me to spoon feed you.'

Archie was in a sour mood that morning. To take a swipe at David and Mike—two of his favourites—was unheard of.

The next day was a glorious September morning. Mike's train broke through the tunnel under the North Downs and raced past oast houses and orchards through the Valley of Visions to Sevenoaks. David was sitting at the wheel of his open silver Porsche in the station yard. When Mike, in his Armani suit and shades, appeared, David gave a toot on the horn that made an old lady, waiting for her husband, jump into the air.

'Hi' said David as Mike got into the car. 'We'll just do a quick burn-up down the bypass to Tunbridge Wells. Maud always has her meetings at 11 am. We finish by 12 pm and then go off to the golf club for cocktails and lunch. I'd best tell you the problem. Last year Maud bought up one of her competitors in Sussex. The company had its own pension scheme, which actually has quite a large surplus. We immediately replaced the trustees with Waters of Wells Pension Trustees Ltd and then got a rude letter from the scheme's consultants requiring the company to resume contributions and saying my deed appointing the new trustee wasn't valid.'

While David was telling the story, Mike watched with horror as the speedometer needle went up to 100.

'I can't concentrate—you're going so fast. Archie warned me you were a demon driver.'

David grinned and slammed on the brakes. He was about to turn off the bypass anyway. 'Is that more to your liking? I haven't got all day to while away!'

Five minutes later a white faced Mike was deposited outside the Waters of Wells factory, and they were at their meeting.

Maud greeted David like a long lost friend. Her eyes sparkled as soon as she saw Mike. 'It's so nice to see you. David has told me wonderful things about you!'

Maud could, when she chose, pour out the charm like treacle. Even at 75, with her hair freshly mauve rinsed, she was a striking figure. On the other side of the table was the pensions consultant for the old scheme, Vincent and his client, Rainey, the erstwhile chairman of the scheme's trustees.

'I must protest, madam' Rainey started off. 'Vincent and I have been kept waiting here since 10 am. It's extremely discourteous of you.'

Maud's eyes flashed 'Hold your tongue, man. I have the factory to run. I can't be at everyone's beck and call, especially unimportant people like you. I was having my hair rinsed at 10. You've got to wait your turn in the queue. Stop whingeing and state your business.'

Vincent saw his chance 'There are two problems. First you can't replace the individual trustees of the scheme with a corporate trustee. The document drawn up by PEPS was invalid. They've obviously never heard of s 37(1)(c) of the Trustee Act 1925.' This was said with evident triumph. 'And just another little thing. Our scheme requires the company to pay contributions at twice the members' rate. That's

£250,000 you owe. Got a cheque book handy?'

This was dangerous talk. Maud went purple and brandished a ruler over the head of hapless Vincent. Her already not inconsiderable presence seemed to swell with her rage.

'Put him right, boys' she cried, 'and then put him out.' Subtlety was never Maud's strong point.

David looked at Mike who grinned. He was beginning to enjoy himself.

'Dave did it right. Mr Justice Knox in the *LRT Pension Fund* case decided that the trust deed and rules could override s 37(1)(*c*) of the Trustee Act. It all dates back to the Trustee Act 1893 and ...'

Suddenly he became aware of Maud's strong glare.

'Never explain' she interrupted. 'I can see you've been trained by that gormless old goat, Smithers. Don't ramble on like him. Stick to the point. David was right—right?'

'Right' grinned Mike.

'That's a relief' said David. 'After all, we've been doing it for years. It would have been a bit awkward if he'd decided it the other way. On the minimum contribution rule, don't you worry your head about that, Maud. We're going to merge the scheme with the Waters of Wells scheme so it won't matter.'

'Not so fast' said Vincent. 'I may not be a lawyer but the judge in the *LRT* case said you couldn't get rid of a minimum contribution rule when two pension schemes were merged by Act of Parliament. If you can't do it by an Act of Parliament, I'm hanged if I can see how you can get rid of it here. You can't just play fast and loose with the rules.'

'But don't your members want to join the Waters of Wells scheme? It's got much better benefits. We're proposing to give year for year past service—all on the Waters of Wells scale. You're not suggesting your members will give up that chance?' asked David in amazement.

'We want the arrears paid first. Plus you can't get rid of the rule through a merger. That's what the judge said' replied Vincent scornfully. 'Get your cheque book out.'

Before Maud blew her top, Mike rushed in 'That's not what the judge decided. I do wish consultants wouldn't give legal advice. No wonder they get it wrong! The *LRT* case was very unusual. It was a merger of the old Wages Fund and Staff Fund into a new scheme. It was effected by Act of Parliament. London Transport had no right to wind up the old schemes. That, coupled with the minimum contribution rule, created expectations, which although not legal rights, had to be protected. The judge would not therefore allow the new scheme to be on a balance of cost basis. But he stopped short of requiring London Transport to repay the £93 million it had wrongfully enjoyed as a contribution holiday. He sent the parties away to negotiate.'

This lengthy rigmarole had given Maud time to calm down and think. 'It seems to me, gentlemen' she said with icy sarcasm, 'you have a choice. You can keep your rotten old scheme and I'll write a cheque for £250,000. Luckily that's no problem to me—unlike your old company, Rainey, when you hadn't two brass farthings to rub together. But ...'

David quickly scented trouble. 'Maud' he cried, 'I think you want to say that even if you write the cheque, there's no certainty the members will ever benefit from it. Whereas if they join your scheme, they'll get immediate benefit improvements.'

Mike laughed out loud. 'It's all right, Maud. We'll tell you at lunch why you weren't going to say that they could whistle for any benefit improvements if they stayed in their old scheme. Like Maud said, gentlemen, we wouldn't want you to have the wrong impression.'

'It seems to me that you two—gentlemen, I think the word is— have no standing in this matter. Rainey's no longer a trustee. I got rid of him and the other trustees. Waters of Wells Pensions Ltd is the new trustee. Should it agree to merge the two schemes? I think the benefit improvements are a good deal for getting rid of a stupid minimum contribution rule, which makes no sense.

But, Maud' he continued looking at her with a winning smile, 'you know how careful you've got to be nowadays.'

'What have you in mind?' purred Maud. David always had her eating out of his hand.

'Well, I call it the seven pillars of wisdom. I suggest you give undertakings to the members of the old scheme, not formal legal obligations, you understand, but just general statements of intention:

   (a)   to maintain the scheme for at least five years;
   (b)   not to apply for an order to permit a refund of surplus to the company;
   (c)   to ensure that the trustee board contains representatives of the old scheme;
   (d)   to consider appointing an independent trustee;

(e) not to use the surplus in the old scheme to benefit the other members; and

(f) if the scheme is wound up within five years, to earmark the old scheme surplus for the transferring members.'

'I'll buy that' said Maud. 'No problem.'

'I don't want to be a wet blanket' interposed Mike, 'but you'll need to be careful about the drafting, plus I only counted six points—not seven.'

'Details, details' laughed David. 'Who ever heard of the six pillars of wisdom? And you'd better do the drafting so you get sued if you get it wrong!'

Ten minutes later, Rainey and Vincent having been sent packing, they were all at the bar of the golf club, drinking beakers of champagne.

'Did you see Vincent's cowboy boots' said David to Mike. 'I knew he'd no chance when I saw those boots' replied Mike.

'Boys, boys' said Maud with a smile 'By the way, how is old Smithers, Mike? He's happy in his eventide home, I trust.'

David nearly choked into his champagne 'I think they let him out every now and then. Would you like to see him, Maud?'

The Lawyer's Tale: O Put Not Your Trust in Princes

'It's all gone horribly wrong' said Paul to Mike in the Altruists Champagne Bar in Bow Lane one evening in early March. They were gearing themselves up for the evening ahead with the aid of a bottle of Bolly.

'What in particular?' asked Mike absently toying with a smoked salmon sandwich.

'I've got to go to the Magnificent Mutual down in Canary Wharf at 8 am tomorrow to see that odious pair, Philip and Colin Bell; plus I've got the dubious pleasure this time of Archie's company. I'm getting sick of bringing him up to speed, only to find later at meetings that he still hasn't got his head round the problem.'

'I don't know why we always have to go to clients' replied Mike. 'It would be so much easier if they came to us. After all no-one else at Megalaw goes out. I could have an extra hour in bed. You know I've got to meet you and Archie at Canary Wharf at 9.30 and then he and I are going on to bloody Braintree of all places to see his old pal Dick at the Man Made Fibres Corporation.' And so grumbling they turned their thoughts to an evening of discos and clubbing in the West End.

Even Paul had to admit that Docklands the next morning looked as if it had been polished with a giant duster. The light sparkled on the water and on the gleaming palaces of glass. It was hard to believe that all this opulence and glitter was a stone's throw from the grimy concrete ghettoes of Hackney to the north and Southwark to the south. The early spring morning seemed to have wrought an effervescent effect on Philip and Colin, if an effervescing actuary is not a contradiction in terms.

They were positively cordial with Archie; they even offered coffee.

'The problem, as you know, Archie' began Philip, 'is that we have 500 smallish group pension schemes with between, say 10 and 100 lives. And we've somehow got to cope with the new regulations on member trustees. We got our technical services people to look at them, but, to be honest, they're 27 pages long and drafted in dense prose. We're stuck. We've got to have a way of cracking the problem that is cheap and cheerful and doesn't involve loads of extra work.'

'We work on fixed fees by and large,' butted in Colin, 'not like you fat cats with exorbitant charge out rates.'

'Well,' started Archie brightly, 'let's just talk ourselves through the new rules. First of all each scheme must have at least one third of its trustees selected by the members ...'

'Give over, Archie' said Colin a tad sharply. 'You're not on conference autopilot now. We know the rules as well as you. Like Philip said, we've got 500 bog standard schemes. What we want is one bog standard answer in a cheap and cheerful package.'

Paul was, a little unwisely, enjoying Archie's discomfiture, when he caught Colin's rolling eyes.

'Come on Paul, you're not just here to carry the goat's bags. He's not capable of giving us the answer.'

Quick as a flash Paul burst in 'It's all quite simple really (I wonder where I got that expression from). The regulations have now given us the details of the prescribed appropriate rules. These are the rules of last resort, where the trustees and the members cannot agree about selection procedures; but there is nothing to stop them from being used at the beginning if the trustees want to. In the words of the DSS "they are designed to be quick to implement, easy to operate and avoid unnecessary cost."'

'That's a bit more like it, lad' nodded Colin approvingly. 'Go on'.

'The great beauty of the prescribed rules is that only the active members are involved; no bothering about tacky old pensioners or deferreds' continued Paul with a sideways grin at Archie.

'The actual rules are very simple:

(a) the trustees must give written notice to the *active* members inviting nominations;

(b) anyone may be nominated but non-members must be approved in writing by the employer;

(c) nominations must be made by an active member and seconded by an active member;

(d) nominations must be made by written notice to the trustees and with the consent of the nominee;

(e) if the number of nominees does not exceed the vacancies, they will become member-nominated trustees;

(f) if the number exceeds the vacancies, there must be a ballot of the *active* members;

(g) if the arrangements provide for the filling of a vacancy caused by insufficient nominations, further nominations may be made and members may be selected; and

(h) if the arrangements provide for the vacancy to remain when there are insufficient nominations, nominations may not be made without the trustees' consent.'

'That sounds ideal' said Philip. 'Our schemes don't have many pensioners or deferreds. On the whole we buy them out whenever we can. Why don't you knock us up a quick set of rules that we can bung off to all our schemes. But how is a ballot conducted?'

'OK' said Paul, 'I'll do that. The regulations leave the arrangements for a ballot to be decided by those who conduct it. There are no requirements for independent scrutineers or even secrecy. Ballots will be decided by a simple majority of those voting.'

'What do you reckon, Philip?' asked Colin without waiting for an answer. 'I reckon that our notices, expensively drafted by young Paul, will go in the trash can; after all that's what happened in Ireland. I don't believe we'll ever have to bother with a ballot. We'll be lucky if we even get any nominations at all. Then it's back to normal for the next six years before we need start it all over again.'

'Ireland' said Archie, feeling he must make his presence felt, 'is different; their rules place the onus on the members to trigger the appointment of member trustees.'

'Hey, knock it off' cut in Colin with a great cackle. 'Your lad's given us the answer. Now get off back to the City before you rack up our bill even more!'

Outside in the warm spring sunshine they found Mike ensconced in the nearest coffee bar.

'By the standards of the Magnificent Mutual that was a fairly civilised meeting' said Archie with a rather forced smile. 'We'd best get on to Braintree, Mike. Thanks, Paul, we'll see you back at the ranch.'

An hour later they arrived at the Man Made Fibres Corporation's offices, a striking building in Stalinist style with a frieze depicting heroic workers, which was a little out of keeping with the virtually automated production lines inside.

Here they were met by Archie's old friend from Oxford, Dick, the company secretary and Gloria, the glamorous pensions manager, her hair gelled and bleached in the latest Essex style. She knew Mike well as they both taught on Pensions Elementals. Having kissed Mike and Archie warmly she outlined the problem.

'As you know we've got an entrenched independent trustee—the Great and the Good Trust Corporation. I think we have you, Archie, to blame—I mean thank—for that. Now s 16(7) of the Act says that the functions of the member-nominated trustees must not differ from those of any other trustee. So, do our member trustees acquire the special powers of the Great and the Good by a sort of statutory osmosis or, heaven forbid, do their special powers disappear in a statutory black hole? We've always had member trustees; in fact we have 50:50 with the Great and the Good holding the balance.'

'But your member trustees are not selected by the members, are they?' asked Mike.

'Well no,' said Dick, 'the personnel department put forward the names of those they consider to represent the membership as a whole. If we had elections, you'd never know who you'd get. That wouldn't do at all.'

'And' went on Gloria, 'we want to alter the composition of the member trustee places to include one special slot reserved for a pensioner trustee. After all we've got more pensioners than active members now.'

'And how do you propose to choose your pensioner trustee—with a puff of smoke from the factory chimney?' asked Mike sarcastically.

'Mike' said Archie angrily. 'That's too much. If you want to go on as you are, but with one of the active member trustees being replaced by a pensioner, you'll have to go down the employer's opt out route. You, Dick, wearing your company secretary hat—not chairman of trustees—will have to put forward proposals to all the active and pensioner members plus such of the deferreds as the trustees think should be involved under the statutory consultation procedure. As long as your proposals are not rejected by 10 per cent, or 10,000 if less, of the membership, all will be well.'

'As our arrangements have been tried and trusted for years, I think it would be very unlikely they would be thrown out' replied Dick.

'What saddens me' said Archie on the way back to London, 'is my old friend, Dick. When we were at Old College in the 60s, we were flower children. We went to San Francisco for the long vacation and even occasionally smoked pot. Why can't he trust his members to choose their trustees? Why should he know best? In the words of the Psalmist:

"O put not your trust in princes nor in any child of man; for there is no help in them."'

'The Psalmist, was it? I should have thought someone else would echo that' replied Mike with a laugh.

Chapter 3

State Pensions, Occupational and Personal Pensions

State pensions

The old age pension—flat rate

The State pension scheme consists of two parts—the basic flat rate State retirement pension and the earnings related supplement—the State Earnings Related Pension Scheme (SERPS). The basic flat rate State retirement pension (the old age pension) is (as at April 1997) £62.50 per week for a single person and £99.80 per week for a married couple. It is dependent on having made enough National Insurance contributions and is, so far at any rate, not means tested. It is payable at age 65 for a man and age 60 for a woman. The Pensions Act will equalise State pension ages for men and women progressively over ten years from 6 April 2010.

The State Earnings Related Pension Scheme

Unless an employee becomes a member of an occupational pension scheme which is contracted-out of SERPS, he or she will pay full rate National Insurance contributions and receive an additional earnings related pension based on earnings between the lower earnings limit —£62 per week (as at April 1997) and the upper earnings limit— £465 per week (as at April 1997). The SERPS pension is based on a percentage of revalued average lifetime earnings. The SERPS pension is also currently payable at age 65 for men and 60 for women.

Earnings above the upper earnings limit are not pensionable under SERPS. An employee can also contract-out of SERPS by becoming a member of an appropriate personal pension scheme but in that case he or she will still pay full rate National Insurance contributions.

State pensions not funded

Both the flat rate and the earnings related pension, when they come to be paid, are revalued in line with prices. They operate on a pay as you go system—that is, out of current government revenue. They are not funded out of contributions invested separately and set aside.

Contracting-out

It is possible to contract-out of SERPS by joining a scheme which promises equivalent benefits or by paying minimum contributions to an employer's scheme or a personal pension. A scheme which is contracted-out of SERPS by paying equivalent benefits is very different from a scheme which is contracted-out on the basis of paying minimum contributions. This aspect is considered below.

Occupational pensions

Money purchase schemes

Occupational pension schemes are sponsored by an employer who has to contribute to the scheme. They are either defined contribution (or money purchase) schemes or defined benefit (or salary related) schemes. Money purchase schemes are simple and produce for each member a pot of money when he or she retires which is the product of the employee's and employer's contributions plus their investment return. This pot of money is then used partly to provide a tax-free lump sum for the member and, as to the rest, a pension for the member, or his spouse and dependants, as he or she chooses.

Salary related schemes

A salary related scheme does not depend on the amount of the contributions or the investment return. It guarantees the members a pension related to their salaries when they retire. Members do not, therefore, have to worry about inflation during their working lives or about stock market conditions.

Salary related contracting-out

A scheme which contracts-out of SERPS on a salary related basis has to satisfy a benchmark scheme benefits test. The main requirements are:

(a)   a pension for the member for life starting at age 65;

(b)   the annual rate of pension is to be 1/80th of average qualifying earnings in the last three tax years for each year of contracted-out service from April 1997, not exceeding $^{40}/_{80}$ths;

(c)   a pension payable on the member's death to the member's spouse for life equal to 50 per cent of the member's pension; and

(d)   pensions in payment accrued since 6 April 1997 will have to be indexed in line with the Retail Prices Index with a maximum of 5 per cent. For pensions accrued before 6 April 1997 the percentage figure is 3 per cent, with any balance up to the Retail Prices Index being paid by the Department of Social Security. For pensions accrued since 6 April 1997 the DSS safety net has been removed.

A member's qualifying earnings are 90 per cent of the difference between the lower and upper earnings limits.

A scheme will satisfy the contracting-out requirements if the pensions provided are broadly equivalent to or better than the legal requirements. The scheme actuary has to certify that the broad equivalence requirements are met. The test must be satisfied on an overall basis for the members as a whole. But the actuary will not be able to give his certificate if the pensions to be provided for more than 10 per cent of the members are not broadly equivalent.

Before 6 April 1997 salary related contracting-out was on the basis of guaranteed minimum pensions. The scheme had to guarantee benefits equivalent to the SERPS benefits foregone by providing guaranteed minimum pensions.

Money purchase contracting-out

A money purchase scheme which is contracted-out of SERPS does not have to provide equivalent or guaranteed benefits. Here contracting-out of SERPS is on the basis of minimum contributions—the difference between full rate National Insurance contributions and reduced rate National Insurance contributions on earnings between the lower and upper earnings limits. Because the member is contracted-out of SERPS, the member and the employer do not have to pay for SERPS benefits, hence the difference between the two rates of National Insurance contributions. The only requirement here is that the minimum contributions must be invested on a money purchase basis to provide a pension for the member and his or her spouse. What that pension will be cannot be known in advance and depends on the amount of the contributions and the investment return, and annuity rates when the member retires. It is not guaranteed.

Members of schemes contracted-out on a money purchase basis (including personal pension schemes) also benefit from age related rebates from April 1997. These will differ across the age range from 3.1 per cent (3.4 per cent for personal pensions) for the youngest rising to a maximum of 9 per cent for the oldest.

Protected Rights

Contracting-out on the basis of minimum contributions produces protected rights. Protected rights are money purchase benefits and they represent what can be bought with the proceeds of the minimum contributions and the age related rebate.

Protected rights must be used to buy an annuity for the member's life. Protected rights which accrued before 6 April 1997 must be used to buy a unistatus annuity, one determined without regard to the member's marital status. But members who are unmarried at retirement will be able to buy either a single or joint life annuity with their post-6 April 1997 protected rights. Married members will still have to buy a joint life annuity which provides for a 50 per cent spouse's pension.

Annuities derived from pre-6 April 1997 protected rights must be indexed in line with the Retail Prices Index with a maximum of 3 per cent a year (or a fixed rate of 3 per cent each year). Annuities derived from post-6 April 1997 protected rights must be indexed in line with the Retail Prices Index with a maximum of 5 per cent.

Personal pensions

Personal pensions are simply a method of providing for old age, on an individual, rather than a collective, basis. They are attractive to a government which dislikes collectivism. They were invented in 1956 for the self-employed and those who had no pension scheme open to them. In 1988 they were extended in two ways. Employers were for the first time allowed to contribute and it became possible to contract-out of SERPS on the basis of minimum contributions through a personal pension. They are money purchase schemes. Sometimes an employer will set up a group personal pension scheme. Basically this is not an employer's scheme at all but just a series of individual personal pensions with the advantage of better terms from the provider because a group is involved. Sometimes the employer will only agree to pay contributions to a group personal pension scheme.

For an illustration of the differences between an employer sponsored pension scheme and a personal pension scheme, see *'The Lawyer's Tale: The Parting of the Ways'*, which follows this chapter.

The Lawyer's Tale: The Parting of the Ways

Pan European Pension Services, or PEPS for short, was an international employee benefits consultancy that used Docs Galore, the niche pensions boutique founded by Archie Smithers and his friend David, to provide documentation and other services. The managing director of PEPS was Charles Evans, an old friend of Archie's. They used to have lunch together regularly to bounce ideas off each other.

At one of these lunches they were discussing the latest news before settling down to eat. Archie sensed, however, that Charles' attention was not as riveted on the subject as no doubt it should have been; his eyes were beginning to glaze over.

Charles rather abruptly suggested they sit down and then, quickly before Archie could start again, said 'You know we've been planning to bring our docs work back in-house.'

'Yes, yes' replied Archie testily. 'We discussed all that last time. I'm quite relaxed about it. But you've had some trouble getting someone to do the work.'

'Well,' said Charles, 'we haven't succeeded in getting who we want. In fact,' he continued quickly as if to avoid any further interruption, 'we want the best docs specialist money can buy.'

Archie could not resist preening himself. Whether or not Charles noticed is not certain but he went on 'We want your colleague, David—how do you feel about it?'

It was not often that Archie was lost for words. Eventually he said 'I'm not a slave trader. If you want David, you'd better talk to him, not me, but if it's what he wants, I won't stand in his way. It's a strange coincidence. Our work has succumbed to the latest wave of pensions litigation. David isn't all that keen on that. I'll talk to him when I get back.'

Back at the ranch, Archie did as he promised. 'I'd be sad to leave Docs Galore, Archie' David said after some thought. 'But you're right—I'd like to go back to my roots, if you can call docs that. I have to admit I get cheesed off with all these lawyers arguing about costs and requiring copper bottomed guarantees before they'll even look at the file. If the terms are right, I'd be prepared to go. I'll have a chat with Charles.'

And so Archie went on to talk to the others at Docs Galore, Martin, Matt, Nige and Bel. Archie knew that the law firm they sub-contracted their litigation to—Megalaw—had been putting out feelers for ages. He knew the managing partner quite well. The others were all for selling out to Megalaw. 'Then we'll all become partners in one of the top City law firms—that's better than Docs Galore anyday' said Nige with a quick eye to the main chance.

And so it looked as if everyone but Archie was happy to separate. Archie sadly accepted the position. He left it to David and the others to sort out the terms.

David had negotiated an excellent deal for his move to PEPS. Megalaw had come up trumps with their terms. Indeed they also agreed to buy the shares in Docs Galore for £1m. David and the others stood in a semi-circle round Archie's desk looking like they were waiting for their prizes on speech day.

'Well,' said Archie, 'I have to admit you've all secured good terms, but what about our pensions?'

Docs Galore had its own small self-administered pension scheme of which Archie was inordinately proud.

David butted in 'We haven't forgotten, Archie. I'll take a transfer to the PEPS scheme; the rest of you will, I guess, transfer to personal pensions.'

'And what about the earnings cap' asked Archie. 'You're all yuppies, or at any rate were when yuppies were fashionable. Don't you care about your pensions being capped?'

David was a little nettled and replied 'Steady on, Archie. I've negotiated a better car—a Jaguar XJS—as compensation for being capped. You've still got an old s 226 contract with the Magnificent Mutual and the others joined the Docs Galore scheme after 1 June 1989; so they're already capped.'

'And why do you think I want to give up our own self-administered scheme and go back to letting the Magnificent Mutual look after my money—or what's left of it after their charges and expenses have been paid?' asked Archie petulantly. 'By the way, while you're thinking about that, I can tell you, David, how to keep your Jag and not worry about the cap. If we all sold our shares in Docs Galore to PEPS, it could become the new principal employer. In other words PEPS would buy you and the scheme, David. No new scheme—no cap.'

'But' said David, 'PEPS doesn't want Docs Galore; they want me. It's Megalaw that has agreed to buy Docs Galore. They want the business closed and transferred to Megalaw to found their shiny new employee benefits department.'

'David' replied Archie a little sarcastically. 'I don't know how you'll manage when I'm not there to guide you.'

'Don't you worry your head about that' cut in David, 'PEPS are going to use Megalaw for legal services. I'll still have the benefit of your advice.'

Archie smiled and continued 'If PEPS bought the shares and then sold the business—the assets and goodwill—to Megalaw, it would then all work out.'

'Details, details' cried Nige and Bel in unison. 'We'll work all that out in the draft sale agreement. We know how you love your old SSAS but the new self-invested personal pensions are just as good. You've no doubt been preoccupied recently but you ought to keep up with new products.'

This was more than Archie could stand. 'There are very important differences between a SSAS like our scheme and a SIPP. I'm going to bore you with them.

(1) With a personal pension the charges will usually be a fixed percentage of the fund. With a SSAS the charges will be fixed and so the bigger the SSAS fund, the cheaper it is to set up and run. In case you've forgotten there's over £800,000 in the Docs Galore scheme.

(2) SIPPs are personal pensions and so capped, but I accept that I might be able to get the Magnificent Mutual to do a deal on self-investment for my retirement annuity contract.

(3) With a SSAS we can invest up to 25 per cent of the fund in shares in a private company—Docs Galore or whatever. With an SIPP shares have to be quoted securities.

(4) So long as the contributions are not excessive in relation to the benefits to be provided, there's no limit on company contributions to a SSAS. With a personal pension there are fixed limits. You can stuff a lot more under the mattress with a SSAS.'

Archie sensed that he was losing his audience.

'Stuff the pension, Archie, I want my Jag' said David. 'I've got life to look forward to.'

'And we want to be partners in Megalaw' chorused Martin, Matt, Nige and Bel. 'It's the largest law firm in the world.'

Archie continued dryly:

'(1) Loans to a member are prohibited in the case both of a SSAS and a personal pension. Loans to the employer within limits are permitted for a SSAS; but with a SIPP the security would have to be quoted, ruling out, for example, a loan to Docs Galore.

(2) Apart from lump sums, there are no benefit limits with personal pensions. A SSAS is of course subject to the normal Revenue limits. You could therefore—at any rate in theory—do better with a personal pension, but I guess the security of a targeted final salary benefit is the better bet.

(3) On the other hand there's no carry forward or carry back of contributions with a SSAS. You get your relief in the year the contributions are paid. And the tax treatment of lump sums under a personal pension is more favourable than under an occupational scheme.

To sum up, a SSAS is more suitable for the proprietor of an incorpo-rated family business. He has greater control and freedom to invest in the company than with a SIPP. But an executive, who is not a major shareholder or who is self-employed, wouldn't really need to worry about control or self-investment. He might be attracted by the freedom of investment and the freedom from his company given by a SIPP. You do at any rate avoid any transfer problems when you change jobs.'

Nige coughed delicately. 'If you're finished, Archie, can I just give you this note. It's about the Megalaw Friendly Society. I don't need to tell you that you could, if you wished, take a transfer from the Docs Galore Scheme to the Megalaw Friendly Society. That would give you beloved freedom to control your investments. So it looks like we're all satisfied.'

'I'll leave you all to thrash out the small print with Megalaw and with PEPS then' said Archie.

The following week Archie had a case in the High Court. The learned gentlemen in horsehair took their turn at droning out the evidence to the judge. At the end of a tedious day the order was final-ly made. Archie heaved a sigh of relief. It was done with one day to spare before he set off for a business trip to the West Coast of America.

The meetings and presentations in San Francisco, Los Angeles and San Diego went well, and Archie and his wife Bella ended up for a week's vacation on the Pacific coast at La Jolla in southern Califor-nia. As they returned to the hotel one evening, the bell person handed Archie a fax from London. It was from David saying that terms had now been finally agreed with PEPS and Megalaw—David would be leaving Docs Galore in three months time.

Archie's face crumpled. He quickly said he would like to take a walk along the beach while Bella changed. After an hour's solitary pacing amidst the joggers by the thundering surf, Archie returned. Bella quickly poured him a large gin to drink on their balcony.

'What's the matter, Archie?' she asked. 'David wanted to go to PEPS; you and the rest are going to Megalaw. You seemed quite happy about it all before we left.'

'I'm all right now' said Archie. 'It's just that David and I founded Docs Galore; it was our company. We were a winning team. Now we're all going to work for strangers. Let's talk about something else. They have some superb Gundlach Bunschu Chardonnay on the wine list. We might need more than one bottle tonight.'

'Archie' interjected Bella, 'we'll drink to new beginnings—not maunder about the past!'

Chapter 4

Taxation and Revenue Limits

Taxation

Exempt approved schemes

If an occupational pension scheme is approved by the Inland Revenue, it is then called 'exempt approved'. An exempt approved scheme has the following tax advantages:

(a) contributions by members are allowed for tax at their highest tax rate;
(b) contributions by employers are similarly tax deductible;
(c) employees are not taxed on the value of their employers' contributions as benefits in kind;
(d) the investment return of the scheme is largely exempt from income and capital gains tax;
(e) pensions are taxed as earned income;
(f) part of the member's pension can be commuted for a tax-free lump sum; and
(g) lump sum death in service and death in retirement benefits can be paid free from inheritance tax.

Approved pension schemes are subject to other forms of taxation such as tax on their trading income and VAT.

Revenue limits

Occupational pension schemes approved by the Inland Revenue are subject to various benefit limits and a limit on the amount of a member's contributions.

Contributions

A member's contributions cannot exceed 15 per cent of his or her taxable pay in any tax year. Taxable pay for pension scheme purposes was capped from April 1989. The cap however only affects pension schemes set up on or after 14 March 1989 and members of schemes in existence on 14 March 1989 who join the scheme on or after 1 June 1989. The cap, which started off at £60,000, will normally rise in line with the Retail Prices Index. The figure for the tax year starting 6 April 1997 will be £84,000. There is no limit as such on the amount of the employer's contributions, but they must be reasonable in amount and not excessive in relation to the benefits to be provided.

Final remuneration

The limits on benefits are defined by reference to a member's final remuneration. This is defined as either:
  (a) remuneration for any one of the five years preceding normal retirement date. Remuneration means basic pay plus fluctuating emoluments, eg bonus or commission averaged over three or more years; or
  (b) the average of total remuneration for any three or more consecutive years ending not earlier than ten years before normal retirement date.

Dynamised final remuneration

These figures can be adjusted for inflation when final remuneration is the remuneration of a year other than the 12 months ending with the member's normal retirement date. For members who retire on or after 17 March 1987 the definition of final remuneration has been changed in three ways:
  (a) excluding gains from share options and golden handshakes;
  (b) higher paid employees earning £100,000 a year or more must use the second definition of final remuneration; and
  (c) 20 per cent directors must also use the second definition of final remuneration.
A 20 per cent director is a person who, within ten years of retirement, has been a director and either on his or her own or with associates has owned or been able to control 20 per cent or more of the company's ordinary shares.

Limits on pension

The normal pension limit is $^1/_{60}$th of final remuneration for each year of service with a maximum of 40. Thus 40 years' service produces a pension of $^{40}/_{60}$ of final remuneration (ie $^2/_3$). The Revenue, however, allows a quicker build up to a pension for those members who have completed 20 years' service. In such cases a member is allowed a pension of $^1/_{30}$ of final remuneration for each year of service with a maximum of 20 years (ie $^2/_3$). But when the quicker build up of pension is taken advantage of, benefits from previous schemes or personal pensions are taken into account in the calculation. More generous calculation rules apply to members who joined their scheme before 17 March 1987. Such members can get a full pension after only 10 years' service.

Limits on lump sum benefits

Part of the member's pension may be commuted for a lump sum not exceeding 3/80 of final remuneration for each year of service with a limit of 40. There is an increased scale for lump sums which permits commutation of $1^1/_2$ times final remuneration after 20 years' service, but only if a $^2/_3$ pension can be provided for the same period of service. There is an overall limit of £150,000 for lump sum benefits but this only applies to members who joined their scheme on or after 17 March 1987 and before 1 June 1989. This limit does not reduce total pension benefits. For members who joined their scheme before 17 March 1987 the maximum lump sum is $1^1/_2$ times final remuneration after 20 years' service.

For members who joined their scheme on or after 1 June 1989 the lump sum benefit is of course restricted by the earnings cap which limits pensionable pay. Such members can also use a formula of $2^1/_4$ times the amount of pension before commutation if it produces a larger figure.

Lastly, it is not possible to commute any part of the pension benefits secured by additional voluntary contribution arrangements entered into after 7 April 1987.

Limits on death benefits

A lump sum benefit on death in service of up to four times remuneration at the date of death can be paid plus a sum equal to a return of the member's contributions with interest. If the member dies within five years after retirement, a lump sum equal to the balance of five years' instalments may be paid.

Pension benefits on death

A spouse's pension on death in service of up to $2/3$ of the member's maximum approvable prospective pension is allowed. A spouse's pension on death in retirement of up to $2/3$ of the member's maximum approvable pension is allowed. Similar pensions can be paid to other dependants, eg children, so long as the total of all such benefits does not exceed the member's maximum approvable pension. Children's pensions must cease on attaining the age of 18 or, if later, on ceasing full-time educational or vocational training.

Limits on benefits for early leavers

For pension schemes set up on or after 14 March 1989 and members of schemes in existence on that date who join the scheme on or after 1 June 1989, the benefit limit is a deferred pension of $1/30$ of final remuneration for each year of service subject to a maximum of $2/3$ final remuneration, taking into account benefits from previous schemes or personal pensions.

The maximum deferred lump sum benefit is $2\frac{1}{4}$ times the amount of pension before commutation.

For other early leavers benefit limits are either:

(a) $1/60$th of final remuneration for each year of service (with a maximum of 40 years), or, if it is more favourable,

(b) the amount produced by the formula:

$$\frac{N \times P}{NS}$$

Where:

N equals actual years of service;

NS equals potential years of service to normal retirement date;

P equals the maximum approvable pension based on service to normal retirement date, taking into account benefits from previous schemes or personal pensions.

Lump sum benefits are similarly calculated by reference to the $3/80$ths formula.

Increases to pensions in payment

Pensions in payment may be increased in line with the Retail Prices Index. Other acceptable ways of increasing pensions are:

(a) fixed increases of 3 per cent compound, whether or not price inflation reaches that level; or

(b) providing for regular reviews of pensions in payment and for increases not exceeding the rise in the Retail Prices Index at the employer's or trustees' discretion; or

(c) a combination of the two methods above; or

(d) increases reflecting the rise in the Retail Prices Index not exceeding a stated maximum percentage.

A scheme which uses one of these methods for increasing pensions in payment does not have to use the same one for increasing deferred pensions during the period of deferment.

For an illustration of the way in which Inland Revenue limits operate, see *'The Lawyer's Tale: Disengaging Docs'*, which follows this chapter.

The Lawyer's Tale: Disengaging Docs

The new brooms at the Magnificent Mutual Life Assurance Society were determined to make the company more profitable. Everyone had to earn their crust—even unimportant people like the docs department.

They had sent in time and motion study experts to evaluate the Magnificent Mutual's 'peripheral' activities. What was a little unfortunate was that the time and motion expert had visited the docs department when Archie Smithers—in charge of the department—was on holiday and young David, his assistant, was playing in a local cricket week and could only spare a couple of hours each morning for his work. Despite that, it all got done—that was the trouble!

The experts concluded that the department should be closed and the docs work sub-contracted. Philip, the pensions actuary, accepted the recommendation. However, he was well disposed to Archie and David and by way of compromise he invited them to take part in a beauty parade to tender for the docs work.

When Archie got back from his holiday, David confronted him with the bad news:

'Me and you've been made redundant, Archie. It's shocking for someone of your age. You'll never get another job. It's OK for me. I can get one with a 50 per cent pay hike without a doubt.'

Archie took the news philosophically. 'I've always wanted to retire early and run a little hotel in the Cotswolds' he said. It was different however when he got home that evening and told his wife, Bella, the news.

'It's disgusting' she said. 'They didn't even wait to tell you in person when you got back. They got David to do their dirty work for them. You've never been appreciated at the Magnificent Mutual. For goodness sake, dust yourself down and go out and get a decent job.'

'It's easier said than done' repeated Archie. 'People don't want to know you after the age of 35. But I've got two ideas. The first is to take early retirement, sell up and buy a hotel in the Cotswolds. You and I would make a great success of that. It would be fun' he said with shining eyes.

'You can forget that for starters' said Bella. 'I live for my painting. I'm not going to help you drink the profits of some crummy dump in the country. What's your second idea?'

'My second idea' said Archie, 'is to set up a little business providing documentation services for insurance companies and the like. Philip said David and I could tender for the Magnificent Mutual's work. I'm sure I could get some more. I'll have to make a few phone calls.'

'Well that's a bit better than your first idea' Bella replied. 'But I don't want you under my feet all day, demanding cups of coffee. I've got my own life to live.'

Comforted by his wife's enthusiasm Archie put his thinking cap on and took to the telephone. The following morning he went to see Philip and asked him what the Magnificent Mutual had in mind by way of severance terms.

'After all, I've worked for the company for 30 years and David has for seven' Archie explained.

'Well' said Philip, 'we don't want to be ungenerous. We're going to put the docs work out to tender. You and David are invited to take part in a beauty parade but we are going to ask Ebenezer & Frump, the company's solicitors and one other firm to compete. The winner will get a three year contract for all our docs work. You would, of course, be on the inside track, Archie.'

'Thank you for nothing' bristled Archie. 'After all, Ebenezer & Frump don't know anything about pensions. You're going to have to get someone to do the work. Who better than me and David?'

'Don't worry Archie' said Philip. 'We'll pay a fair whack for the job and you can always take an early retirement pension. Plus you can do a little bit of other work on the side!'

The beauty parade was held. Although Archie did not realise it at the time, the result was a foregone conclusion. Naturally he was pleased to be wanted once again, but he knew he was now in a position to drive a hard bargain with Philip. And so he set out his terms.

'David and I' Archie explained, 'want to set up our own company— Docs Galore—to provide documentation services for the Magnificent Mutual and anyone else who wants to use us. At my age, naturally I'm worried about my pension and I don't want to be caught out by the earnings cap.'

'There is no need for you to worry about that' said Philip patronisingly. 'You're not an actuary you know!'

Archie ignored this and continued 'We have decided to set up our own pension scheme, but since we're being made redundant, we expect decent severance pay plus a full past service reserve transfer value to our new scheme. We're not going to be fobbed off with cash equivalents.'

'Stop fussing about details' said Philip, 'it's most unlike you, Archie. I told you we'd be generous. You can both have a year's pay as compensation and of course you can have a full transfer payment.'

'Well,' said Archie somewhat mollified, 'this is what we have in mind:

(a) the Magnificent Mutual will establish a new subsidiary company 'Docs Galore' with a £100 share capital;

(b) our contracts of employment will be transferred to it;

(c) a new pension scheme will be set up for Docs Galore but in the interval Docs Galore will have to participate in the Magnificent Mutual scheme;

(d) David and I will be given an option to acquire the share capital of Docs Galore for £100 on six months' notice;

(e) Magnificent Mutual will enter into an agreement with Docs Galore to provide documentation services for three years.'

'It's all a bit heavy, this, isn't it' said Philip in rather exasperated tones.

'Just let me finish' said Archie,

'(f) when we have set up the Docs Galore scheme and we've bought the shares, Docs Galore can withdraw from the Magnificent Mutual scheme; and

(g) finally the Magnificent Mutual trustees will pay a full past service reserve transfer value—based on our pay when we leave the Magnificent Mutual scheme—to the new scheme.

That's all—nothing very complicated—even an actuary can understand that! I'll have to get David's agreement to the details and no doubt you will want to run through all this with Ebenezer & Frump' he finished.

Ebenezer & Frump gave the plan their blessing. The truth was that they hadn't the slightest idea what it was all about.

David, however, took a lot more persuading.

'I don't want to leave you in the lurch, Archie' he said, 'but I don't know that I want all this. I must have my money at the end of each month to pay the mortgage. I'd be better off with another job. I know you're more than half way to death but I'm not. Why don't you do all this by yourself?'

'Well,' said Archie, 'they want us both for the docs contract. Otherwise there'd be no cover. What's more Docs Galore is going to double our salaries.'

'But Docs Galore is us' said David perplexed. 'It's no good giving yourself a raise. You're just living in a fool's paradise.'

'Not so' smiled Archie. 'First we get a year's pay tax free. Second we get a contract for three years from the Magnificent Mutual which will guarantee our present pay index-linked. Third we can do what other work we can get. I've been making a few enquiries. We could double our work load without any trouble. That's why we can double our pay. Now do you see why I was fussing about the earnings cap. What's more, if it doesn't work out, I'll be the loser—you can always get another job.'

'OK' said David, 'I'll give it a whirl but I must have time off for cricket and rugby. Just tell me again how it's going to work.'

'Well,' said Archie, 'once we've set up the new company and the pension scheme, we can exercise our option to buy the shares from the Magnificent Mutual. That means that Docs Galore will no longer be a subsidiary of the Magnificent Mutual and will have to leave their pension scheme. At that point, we will be masters of our own destiny and can double our pay.'

David still looked a bit doubtful and so Archie went on:

'What makes it seem complicated is the need to achieve three different aims:

(a) the first is to avoid the early leaver syndrome and get a full past service reserve transfer payment instead of cash equivalents;

(b) the second is to establish a new pension scheme which won't be treated by the Revenue as a new scheme and so escapes the new limits; and

(c) the third is that if we double our pay before we leave the Magnificent Mutual scheme, we will double the transfer payment.'

'OK—details, details' said David beginning to tire of the conversation. I can see that if we get past service reserve, we do a lot better than cash equivalents. I like the idea of doubling our pay. I also twig that if we do that at the right time, we'll double our transfer payment. Won't old Philip be hopping mad when he finds out? I'd love to be a fly on the wall when someone tells him the good news.'

'That only leaves the other aim' said Archie, 'of making sure that our scheme won't be treated as a new scheme. I have looked into this and checked out the Transitional Provisions Regulations. The Revenue won't apply the new restrictions in the Finance Act 1989 or the Finance (No 2) Act 1987, come to that, when benefits under the old basis cease to accrue under a scheme for a member who joins another scheme established by an associated employer. What is vital is that when the Docs Galore scheme is set up, Docs Galore Ltd is owned by the Magnificent Mutual so as to fall within the terms of the Regulations. It won't then count as a new scheme and the subsequent change of ownership of the shares won't alter the position. We then exercise our option to buy the shares, acquire the business and give ourselves a pay rise.'

'But I'm not earning £84,000 a year.' said David.

'Not yet you're not' continued Archie. 'But I will be after we've doubled our pay. In any case we were both members of the Magnificent Mutual scheme before 17 March 1987. I don't want any cap on my tax free lump sum. It would be crazy to throw away advantages like that.'

'OK, I agree' said David 'It seems a pretty smart scheme you've dreamed up Archie. Not bad for someone more than half way to death.'

'That's better than being half dead, which is what you often seem like on a Monday morning, David' replied Archie cheerfully.

'What about moving on to a more exciting topic like company cars. We'll both be directors of Docs Galore. We'll obviously have to do a lot of travelling. What kind of car takes your fancy?'

'That's easy' replied David, quick as a flash, his interest immediately aroused. 'I'll have a nice new shiny red Porsche.'

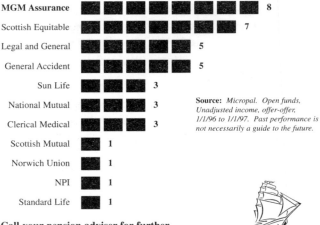

Chapter 5

Investment

The investment rules

Trustees must act in accordance with the terms of the investment rules of their scheme; they must also act with due prudence. The first test is whether the proposed investment is authorised. Nowadays pension scheme trust deeds and rules confer wide powers of investment on trustees. It is still necessary to check, however, that they are authorised to enter into, for example, subunderwriting contracts or traded options. If the scheme rules are up to date, they probably will be authorised. It could be that an old fashioned scheme limits the amount which can be invested in equities. Such schemes do exist. It is a point to be watched and may need to be checked by an expert.

Statutory investment powers

Trustees have the same powers of investment as beneficial owners, subject to any restrictions imposed by the scheme rules. 'Restrictions imposed by the scheme' relates to types of investment eg a total ban on employer-related investments. Any requirement for the employer to approve the exercise of the trustees' investment powers is banned.

Investments do not include non-income producing assets such as futures so investment rules will have to confer suitable powers. Furthermore beneficial owners cannot invest in certain unit trusts which are confined to exempt approved pension schemes. Again suitable powers will have to be conferred. Trustees' powers of investment may be delegated to anyone authorised, or treated as being authorised, under the Financial Services Act. If so, the trustees will not be responsible for the fund manager's acts or defaults if they are reasonably satisfied that he has the appropriate knowledge and experience and that he is carrying out his work competently and complying with the rules about choosing investments—see below. Trustees can also delegate their investment powers to two or more of their number or to a fund manager who is not authorised but they will then remain liable for their acts or defaults. This liability can be excluded, where the delegation is to a fund manager who is not authorised under the Financial Services Act, but not when the delegation is to some of the trustees, so long as the trustees are satisfied that the manager has the appropriate knowledge and experience and is carrying out his work competently and complying with the statutory rules on investments. If the delegation is to an unauthorised manager, the delegation can only be in relation to decisions about investments which would not count as UK 'investment business' under the Financial Services Act such as cash, property or investments overseas.

The prudent man

If the trustees can, under the rules, make the proposed investment, should they? The law says that the trustees must look after trustee investments as if they were looking after them for someone else. One may take risks on one's own behalf, but must be more careful with other people's money. The trustees have to act with due prudence.

The best interests of the beneficiaries

Trustees must put aside their own personal interests and views. They must put the best interests of their beneficiaries first, and normally the best interests of the beneficiaries are their financial interests. These points are illustrated by the case of *Cowan v Scargill* in 1984—the National Union of Mineworkers case. The mineworkers' pension scheme had a five-year investment plan which was up for review. The investment managers were suggesting that more money should be invested overseas and in oil and gas stocks. The scheme had five union trustees and five management trustees and no provisions for breaking a deadlock. The union trustees opposed the investment managers' proposals because they thought the money should be invested in this country, not overseas, and in the coal industry, not in competing industries. The judge did not uphold their views. The

mineworkers' scheme had a good proportion of members who had retired and were pensioners, plus many members who had left the industry but kept an entitlement to a preserved pension in the
scheme—pensioners and deferred pensioners. It was not in their best
financial interests to invest money in the coal industry if a better return could be obtained elsewhere. And so the judge decided in favour
of the management trustees, who agreed with the investment managers' report.

Expert advice

Trustees must obtain and take heed of proper expert investment advice. The obligation is to take heed of it, not necessarily to follow it.
Trustees must be wary of rubber stamping the advice of their experts.

Diversifying investments

Trustees must have regard to the need for diversification of investments. They should not put all their eggs in one basket. If they do
this and are successful, they will be acclaimed. If they fail, they will
face the risk of being sued for breach of trust.

Investments must be suitable

Trustees must hold investments which are, in themselves, suitable.
For example, an investment in a brothel or a casino would not strike
one at first sight as an entirely suitable investment for trustees
whose duties include looking after widows and orphans. Not only
must the investments be suitable in themselves, they must also be
suitable having regard to the scheme's liabilities. An example of this
would be an investment in property when a number of members' re-
tirements are coming up on the horizon. If in a small scheme a
number of members are due to retire shortly, there will be a need for
cash to pay the tax-free lump sums and, perhaps, purchase annuities
for them. Putting all the scheme's spare cash into an office block
would hardly facilitate this. Property is notoriously difficult to

realise quickly. Putting the money on deposit would be more suitable having regard to the scheme's liabilities.

In addition trustees must bear in mind the scheme's mix of active members to pensioners. This may well have an effect on the ratio of equities to fixed interest investments.

Statement of investment principles

The trustees must maintain a written statement of investment principles. The statement must cover the trustees' policy for complying with the minimum funding requirement, and:
  (a) the kinds of investments to be held;
  (b) the balance between different kinds of investment;
  (c) risk;
  (d) expected return; and
  (e) realisation.
Before preparing the statement the trustees must consider the advice of a suitable expert and consult the employer.

Wholly insured schemes are not required to prepare such a statement.

Trustees retaining any investment must decide at what intervals they should get written expert advice about whether it is still satisfactory. The trustees or their fund manager must exercise their powers of investment with a view to giving effect to the statement of investment principles.

Self-investment

A worry for trustees arises when the employer suggests self-investment. Self-investment occurs when the trustees buy shares in the employer or buy property for occupation by the employer. Any such transaction must be carried out at arm's length, with the benefit of independent professional advice and on ordinary commercial terms. Nevertheless, self-investment places trustees in a conflict of interest, where their duties and loyalties can be divided. The National Association of Pension Funds has therefore recommended complete avoidance of self-investment by pension scheme trustees. Trustees should check the investment rule, if self-investment is proposed, to see if there are any restrictions on their powers. There could well be.

The Pensions Act gives power to regulate self-investment or investment in 'employer-related assets'. Regulations made under the Act have been issued which limit employer-related investments to 5 per cent of the assets of the scheme.

The Act imposes criminal penalties for non-compliance on trustees or fund managers who agreed to the investment. Others who fail to take all reasonable steps to secure compliance with the rules will be liable to a civil penalty. Any employer-related investments in excess of the permitted level (ie zero for loans and 5 per cent for other investments) are to be excluded in testing for compliance with the minimum funding requirement. But during the transitional period ending on 6 April 2007 all legally held employer-related investments (whether or not in excess of the 5 per cent limit) eg existing investments in property or unlisted securities, may be included for this purpose.

Loans by the trustees to the employer are completely forbidden. In addition any guarantees or security given by the trustees in respect of liabilities incurred by the employer will be treated as loans to the employer. Any lending arrangements made by the trustees where repayment is dependent on the employer count as loans. And so any attempt to avoid the rules by providing financial assistance to the employer through intermediaries will be caught.

Certain existing employer-related investments can be retained. Existing loans (other than listed debt securities eg debentures) can be retained until 5 April 2002. But if repayment cannot under the terms of the loan, be required by that date, the loan can be retained until the earliest date on which repayment can be enforced. Any other existing employer-related investment legally held in excess of the 5 per cent limit, eg unlisted securities or property, can be retained indefinitely. However, these exemptions will cease to apply as soon as an investment becomes listed on a recognised stock exchange.

The regulations do not apply to schemes which:

(a) have less than 12 members who are all trustees of the scheme; and

(b) have a rule that any decision to invest in employer-related investments has to be agreed in writing by all the members.

'The Lawyer's Tale: Self Sacrificing', which follows this chapter, illustrates the problems.

The Lawyer's Tale: Self Sacrificing

Maud Belchamber, 12 months after her husband Cecil's death, began to enjoy herself for the first time in years. Cecil had been a selfish, bad-tempered invalid. He was the proprietor of a business called Waters of Wells, based in Tunbridge Wells, which bottled water from the springs in the area. On Cecil's death Maud took over the business and it flourished as never before. True, the problems of one of her competitors across the Channel plus a hot summer could not have come at a better time. So great a boost did this give that it caused problems at the bank; she exceeded the company's overdraft limit.

Unlike Waters of Wells, the Caring Bank was doing badly. Her bank manager, Rainey, was under pressure from head office to reduce customers' debit balances. Being a man of neither sense nor sensibility, he promptly called in the overdraft. 'If the overdraft is not repaid by the end of the month, I will sell your business over your head' he said. Considering how he had in previous years encouraged Maud and Cecil to borrow from the bank, this treatment was a little rich. His one piece of advice came *via* head office.

'You've got a pension scheme with a surplus that's sufficient to repay the bank. If you don't want to lose your business, you'd better get money out of the pension scheme. The law now lets trustees invest 5 per cent of their assets in the shares of the sponsoring employer.'

In desperation Maud turned to the pensions superintendent at the Magnificent Mutual who looked after the Waters of Wells Pension Scheme. This was Douglas Livingstone, a bright young man with an unruly shock of hair smartly dressed in a dark grey chalk stripe suit. Sensing trouble Doug decided to take with him to see Maud his friend David, who worked at Docs Galore, the specialist pensions boutique used by the Magnificent Mutual.

And so the following day they set off in David's red Porsche to Tunbridge Wells. Waters of Wells occupied a modern factory on an industrial estate out by the bypass. Maud had a penchant for handsome young men and Doug and David were old favourites.

She started by opening a bottle of champagne and pouring out three glasses 'It's only 11 am' she said, 'but one of my late husband's better habits was to drink a pint of champagne each day at 11 am for the sake of his health. So here goes. We're in hock to the bank to the tune of about £1million and I've got to pay it off by the end of the month.'

She explained Rainey's suggestion that the pension scheme bought shares in the company, and asked Doug how much money there was in the scheme.

'Well,' said Doug, '£20 million but that doesn't mean the trustees should buy shares in the company.'

'I don't understand' cried Maud, 'Rainey said the trustees could buy shares.'

'My friend Doug always was incoherent' said David, 'so I'd better explain. Rainey is not right in saying that the law now allows trustees to spend 5 per cent of the scheme's assets on buying shares in the company. It says that's the most they can do. But it doesn't say they should do it in the first place. Trustees should not normally do this kind of thing. As the pension scheme already owns the factory, I guess there's no security the company can offer. That's why the bank are running scared.'

'Oh dear,' cried Maud, 'whatever shall we do?' and opened another bottle of champagne.

David's tongue was beginning to loosen, 'The trustees have to consider the interests of the members of the scheme—not the company. It cannot be in the members' interests to make this investment. It's just not a prudent investment for trustees.'

'But what about their jobs?' interrupted Doug who was getting irritated that his friend was hogging the limelight.

'They don't want to lose their jobs if the company goes down the tube, do they?' he asked sarcastically.

'No' said David, 'I know there are cases like *Evans v London Co-operative Society* which ruled that in some cases, where companies had problems in raising capital, they could tap the pension scheme. Since all the members were employees of the company, and dependent on it for their wellbeing, the trustees could take this into account. But, of course, your scheme has got pensioners and deferred pensioners as well as active members, Maud.'

'Once they've retired, don't they care about the company any more?' asked Maud.

'Yes, of course' replied David, 'but they're no longer dependent on it. In the *Mineworkers Pension Scheme* case Sir Robert Megarry made it clear that under a trust for the provision of financial benefits, like a pension scheme, the paramount duty of the trustees is to provide the greatest financial benefits for the present and future beneficiaries. And so, in my view, the investment in the company's shares is out.'

Maud looked very upset and Doug interrupted 'If the monologue has come to an end and I'm allowed a word in edgeways, may I make a suggestion. After all, we've come here to solve Maud's problems, or have you forgotten that?'

David was about to reply when Doug waved him to keep quiet. 'The Waters of Wells Scheme has got a big surplus, you know; about £5 million. Since that's money not required to provide the benefits, why can't the trustees use part of it to make the investment? That way the members are no worse off.'

'If only you'd let me finish' cried David, 'I'd come up with a solution. Your argument won't hold water because under the winding up rule—which would operate if the company went bust—the trustees have an unfettered discretion to pay the surplus to the members. So the members would lose out.

But—and now I am coming to the point—there is a solution. If the company agrees to the trustees giving benefit improvements out of the surplus, then I think they could make the investment.'

By this time it was getting on for lunch, and Maud suggested they adjourn to the golf club. Soon they were settled in comfortable chairs by the bar with pint-sized gins and tonics in their hands.

'What about these benefit improvements?' Maud asked. 'What sort—how much?'

'Oh, I think Doug could be left to sort out the details' said David patronisingly. 'But if you want an investment of £1 million, you ought to spend a corresponding amount on benefit improvements. As the surplus is £5 million, you've got plenty of fat.

The trustees are not really investing at all. They're doing a deal with the company. For every pound spent, a pound is allocated to benefit improvements. That way everyone's happy. If it goes wrong, the trustees can still look the members in the face and say—look what improvements we got.'

'Capital' said Maud 'Let's have another gin before we eat. I've ordered fillet steak. Plus a round of golf afterwards. I hope that's all right.'

'Fine' said Doug. 'but before we start enjoying ourselves I've got a slight spanner to throw in the works.

I'm sorry I didn't explain this to you on the way down, Dave, but you've overlooked the self-investment regulations. No doubt you're too busy jet setting around the world to bother with details. But you did know, didn't you, that the pension scheme owns the factory which the company leases back. If you'd troubled to look at the last trustees' report, you'd have seen it was worth £5 million.

These regulations, which seem to have escaped your notice, limit self-investment to 5 per cent of the scheme's assets.'

David tried unsuccessfully to stem his friend's flood.

'I know' continued Doug, raising his voice to drown the interruption, 'that the property investment was already in existence before the regs came in. And there's no time limit for bringing property investment down to 5 per cent. But you can't invest another 5 per cent on top, or am I wrong?'

'You know you're not. You wouldn't have asked the question otherwise' replied David. 'But I did read the regs while I was away in Jasper, Alberta. You complained I was being negative. Like you said, Doug, let's find solutions, not problems.

It's all quite simple really. I wonder you hadn't thought of it before. I suggest the trustees sell the factory to the Magnificent Mutual. It'd be a good investment for their Property Fund. That gets rid of the self-investment problem and leaves the trustees a free hand to invest £1 million in the company.'

'Boys, boys' said Maud with evident approval. 'Let's start lunch. I've ordered a couple of bottles of Australian Cabernet—Shiraz. I hope you like Ozzie wine. I'm looking forward to ringing up old Rainey and giving him and the Caring Bank the push.'

Doug and David were old sparring partners and enjoyed a good argument—as well as a good lunch. On the way back to London several hours later, revived by their round of golf and just about fit to drive, David asked 'By the way I forgot to ask. Who are the trustees? Oughtn't they to be separately advised?'

'That's no problem' replied Doug. 'The company is the sole trustee of the scheme. That's the way Maud wanted it. And that's the way Philip, the pensions actuary, thinks pension schemes should be run.'

'Oh' said David, 'try telling that to the NAPF. They don't like companies being sole trustee of the pension scheme.'

'What makes you think Philip will buy your idea of the Magnificent Mutual purchasing Maud's factory. You're a bit free with other people's money aren't you? said Doug.

'And another thing, that investment in the company's shares will be very expensive. The company will have to pay dividends and agree to pound for pound benefit improvements. Philip won't like that.'

'Well,' said David, 'I don't work for Philip any more. Of course he'll say I'm spending other people's money. Plus I realise the investment is expensive. But it's better than the Caring Bank, isn't it. At least the benefit goes back to the members, including Maud. What else could you have done?'

Chapter 6

The Financial Services Act 1986

The Financial Services Act affects pension scheme trustees in a number of ways.

Investment management

The need for authorisation

The Act regulates investment management and requires investment managers to be authorised or exempt from authorisation. Trustees of pension schemes are regarded as being in the business of managing investments and thus will require to be authorised unless they delegate all investment management or all day-to-day investment management to someone who is authorised or exempt. Most trustees will not want to become authorised. It requires an application to the Investment Management Regulatory Organisation (IMRO) for which fees have to be paid each year. Few trustees have felt this to be necessary. In practice most trustees do delegate all investment management or day-to-day investment management to someone who is authorised, such as a merchant bank or an insurance company.

Day-to-day investment management

Not many trustees will want to delegate *all* investment management. What then does delegating 'day-to-day' investment management mean? There is no definition in the Act but the Securities and Investments Board—the body responsible for implementing the Act—has given guidance. Day-to-day decisions do not include strategic decisions such as portfolio weighting; for example, how much money is invested overseas (in other words the big decisions).

Decisions the trustees can take

Trustees can require to be consulted in certain circumstances, for example:

(a) in a takeover;
(b) where the investment manager has a conflict of interest;
(c) about certain sensitive decisions like buying shares in a competitor; and
(d) when policy considerations are involved—for example, should the trustees buy shares in tobacco companies?

Frequent interventions by trustees

It is a question of degree so that frequent interventions by the trustees outside the regular investment review meetings would probably amount to day-to-day investment management. The initial decision by the trustees to invest in, say, a managed fund policy would be regarded as strategic. If the trustees want to exercise their rights to switch between funds, it all depends on how often the trustees want to do this and how much detail they get involved in. If they switch no more than three or four times a year, that is regarded as being a strategic decision. Decisions on how much of the fund goes into equities, property, etc are also regarded as strategic; but if the trustees get involved in picking particular funds or unit trusts, the decisions could, especially if they are taken frequently, be regarded as day-to-day investment management and so require authorisation.

Advice on investments

Trustees are often asked to advise a member about joining or leaving the scheme, about the various options open to an early leaver and about paying additional contributions. If the trustees are engaged in the business of advising on investments, they will need to be authorised by one of the recognised regulatory bodies. There are two aspects to this.

The business of investment advice

If the trustees are paid, for example by receiving commission, then they will be regarded as being in the business of giving investment advice. If they do not get paid but give advice frequently and systematically, they will still be regarded as being in business. But if they do not get paid and only give advice on an irregular and unsystematic basis, they will not need to be authorised.

What is an investment?

Investments exclude property and deposit accounts with a bank or building society and a member's interests under an occupational pension scheme. Rights under a personal pension scheme, unless it is deposit based, will count as investments. It follows from this that trustees can, without fear of transgressing the Act, advise a member on the merits of the occupational scheme as contrasted with personal pensions. But they must not go from general to specific advice about personal pensions. In other words they must not get dragged into advising about particular personal pension products. Trustees can inform early leavers about the options open to them—a preserved pension, a transfer to a new scheme or to a personal pension. But they must not recommend particular buy out policies or personal pensions. They can talk about the differences between the in-house voluntary contribution arrangements (rights under an occupational scheme) and free standing additional voluntary contribution schemes (FSAVCs) which will usually be investments. But, again, they must not advise on the merits of particular FSAVCs.

Arranging deals in investments

If the trustees are in the business of arranging deals in investments, they will need authorisation. The question of what is meant by being 'in business' has already been covered under 'Advice on Investments'. Trustees will be regarded as arranging deals in investments if, for example, they make arrangements with an insurance company offering a special deal on buy out policies and get paid in commission or fees for doing this. If they do not get paid, they will not normally be regarded as being in business unless they make such arrangements regularly and systematically. Trustees who want to help their members in this way would be safer if they made a special arrangement, not directly with the provider but with an independent intermediary—for example, an insurance broker.

Best advice

There is another aspect of the Financial Services Act 1986 which will have an effect on trustees. Investment sales representatives will have to comply with the rules of their regulatory body. In particular, they will have to give best advice and to know their client. This means knowing the client's financial needs and circumstances, including the availability of an occupational scheme. And so the sales representative should get hold of the scheme booklet and learn the main features of the scheme. Otherwise he or she cannot know the client and give best advice. The result is that, in theory at any rate, a member of an occupational scheme should not be able to be seduced into leaving it and taking out a personal pension. The same should also be true for someone who could join but has not yet done so. The current furore about the mis-selling of personal pensions to members of good pension schemes and the resulting demands for reinstatement illustrates graphically the problems which have occurred. Often the trustees will learn of the sales representative's approaches. There is no reason why they should not 'sell' their scheme; it is not an investment. As long as they stick to comparing occupational schemes and personal schemes, and pointing out the advantages of the company scheme, they need not fear the Financial Services Act. They must not, however, comment or advise on the particular personal pension product.

A great deal of nonsense is talked about the effect of the Financial Services Act on pension scheme trustees. It does not stop them from doing their job of looking after their members or of giving them advice about the choices open to them. The only thing they must not do is give advice about a particular investment product.

For an illustration of the way the Financial Services Act works in practice, readers are referred to *'The Lawyer's Tale: A Question of Rank'* which follows this chapter.

The Lawyer's Tale: A Question of Rank

Monty Murgatroyd, the Chief General Manager of the Magnificent Mutual Life Assurance Society, was in an irascible mood. The new business figures were poor and the staff were getting lax. At the summer staff dance a visitor, surveying the crowded floor, had asked him how many people worked for the company. 'Only one or two,' he had replied testily, 'the others just come to the office to draw their pay and rest up for their free-time activities.'

And so he had instituted a crackdown; the superintendents were berated for their excessive expense accounts and daily client visits were banned.

Not that Murgatroyd was against visiting clients. On the contrary, it was more necessary than ever to visit clients regularly and give presentations about the effects of the new pensions regime.

'But let the young ones have a chance' he continued. 'Let's have some fresh blood on the scene. Some of you are looking decidedly jaded. A few months confined to your desks, deprived of high cholesterol lunches, will do you a power of good.'

An exception to the rule was Larry Robinson, the new business manager. Soon after the ban Larry was out visiting a company with Sarah Potts, the pensions administrator who actually ran the scheme, and young David who helped Archie Smithers run the documents department.

They were visiting Colonel Braithwaite, who was the managing director of United Widgets.

As an old military man, the Colonel ran his company like a regiment. He knew Sarah and she was just introducing David when Larry joined them. Unfortunately the Colonel took Larry for the chauffeur, perhaps because of his vast cigar.

The Colonel bristled ominously 'Put out that cigar and wait outside. You obviously don't know that smoking is not permitted in my presence. In any event, drivers wait in their vehicles until they are wanted.'

Larry backed out scarlet with rage but was afraid to take on an important client like Colonel Braithwaite. Sarah managed to control her giggles and she and David were introduced to the other two trustees. Miss Mather, the Colonel's confidential secretary who in fact ran the company, and Ron Taylor, the company's accountant who was absolutely terrified of his employer.

'Before we start' began the Colonel, 'I read an article in the *Financial Times* about some Act which says I can't invest my money as I want to. If this journalist johnny is right, I have got to go cap in hand to some investment manager before I can invest the pension fund's cash.'

Unlike Larry, David was not frightened by the Colonel.

'There is a difference between investing your own money and that of the pension fund,' he said.

'It's all the same to me,' interrupted the Colonel. 'It's all mine.'

Sensibly David let this pass, and continued 'The Financial Services Act regulates investment management and requires registration of investment managers. It will be a criminal offence for trustees to be responsible for investment unless they register with the Investment Management Regulatory Organisation—IMRO. That will mean filling in a long and complicated form and proving that you are a fit and proper person to invest other people's money. What's more you will have to pay a hefty annual fee to IMRO plus a contribution to their compensation fund.'

'Goodness gracious me,' shouted the Colonel, 'where do you get all this bureaucratic gobbledygook from? Are you sure you've got it right? I remember Archie Smithers lecturing me at great length about the trustees' investment duties.'

'Times have changed Colonel,' said David bravely. 'Archie was of course right, but the effect of the Act is, curiously, to deprive trustees of one of their main duties—investment—unless they go through the hoop of registering with IMRO. But pension fund trustees who are not responsible for day-to-day investment management will not need to register—provided they delegate investment management to someone who is either registered or exempt.

'So it all turns on what is meant by "day-to-day investment management". Luckily the Securities and Investments Board has produced a guide for trustees. While it does not have any legal effect, it does give much useful advice on this point.'

'Well, well,' said the Colonel admiringly, 'you'd better tell us all a bit more about this piece of government interference.'

'Day-to-day investment management is not defined in the Act,' continued David smiling, 'but the SIB memorandum and speeches by government Ministers have shed some light.

'There are some areas where trustees can have their say without being in charge of day-to-day investment management:

(1) Portfolio weighting—the balance between income and capital—what proportion you invest overseas, you can decide all that sort of thing without falling foul of the Act.
(2) Strategic decisions—this overlaps portfolio weighting, but is about how much you put into equities, how much into gilts— that sort of thing.
(3) Decisions not to invest in certain areas; for example, casinos or tobacco shares.'

At this point Miss Mather burst in 'Oh good, we can stop the brokers investing in those dreadful companies that experiment on animals.'

Not to be outdone Ron Taylor piped up 'We'll be able to decide not to invest in casinos.'

'Stop blithering, you two,' said the Colonel. 'Let's get on with it. It will soon be noon and my system needs its first gin injection then.'

'I'll try to be quick,' said David. 'You can also reserve the right to decide about sensitive matters like takeovers—not just of the company but others in the industry. You might want to help or hinder the takeover of a competitor. That will not count as day-to-day investment.'

'So apart from these cases,' said the Colonel, 'my investment adviser rules OK? It's certainly not OK by me—I give the orders to the brokers. I pay the advisers—not the other way round. They do what I tell them. And since that's that, we'll just have five minutes to learn all about personal pensions.'

'Well, sir' said David, 'perhaps Sarah could have her innings now and tell you about personal pensions and buy out policies.'

'Capital,' said the Colonel, 'I must say I like dealing with you two better than that Mediterranean lounge lizard you brought with you.'

'Right,' said Sarah. 'First of all, trustees can advise about the merits of their own company scheme as opposed to a personal pension. As long as you don't advise on the merits of particular personal pensions and just confine yourself to general advice, then you won't be caught by the Act. Likewise with buy out policies. You can advise employees about the options open to them when they leave—deferred pension, transfer or a buy out policy—but not about the merits of rival insurance company products.'

'Well, that's your department, Miss Mather' said the Colonel. 'You sort out all the troublemakers. If they want a personal pension rather than the company scheme, more fools them. I wouldn't try and stop them. If they want to leave a good job here and try their luck elsewhere, then as far as I am concerned they are defectors and I wouldn't waste words on them—let alone advice.'

Sarah smiled sweetly and blew away the Colonel's wrath. 'Perhaps I should just finish,' she said, 'by explaining that a member's rights under an occupational scheme are not 'investments' as defined in the Act, whereas a member's rights under a personal pension are classified as 'investments' unless the underlying investment is cash; for instance, a cash deposit arrangement with a bank or building society. That is because the Act does not regulate deposit accounts with banks and societies.'

'Well, that is all very interesting, I am sure,' said the Colonel. 'But the bar beckons. You will of course stay for lunch. Your chauffeur chappy can take himself down to the local for a sandwich.'

Later that afternoon, after an excellent lunch, followed by a frosty drive back to the office with the furious Larry, Sarah and David met up with Archie Smithers.

'I say,' he said, 'you two went down well with the Colonel. He's been on the telephone to say how marvellous you both were. I must admit I was surprised about his cavalier attitude to employees who opt for a personal pension. But I am not sure we pensions people don't over-egg the pudding sometimes. There will be plenty of employers like the Colonel who will simply say that if you don't know a good thing when you see it, that's up to you. Don't forget they will save money with such people.'

'In any event members should not be seduced into leaving a good company scheme for a personal pension without the trustees being forewarned and having a chance to sell their scheme. Insurance salesmen will have to comply with the Conduct of Business Rules and will be under a duty to give best advice for their client's needs. In other words, they would need to know the main features of their client's occupational scheme before they could compare it with a personal pension. I don't really think that a lot of people will opt out of a good company scheme, at any rate after all this mis-selling scandal. The insurance companies just won't take on the business. But equally we must take trouble to advertise virtues of our scheme and not leave all the running to the personal pensions salesmen. But enough of all that; otherwise I will begin to rival the Colonel for verbosity.'

PROFESSIONAL TRUSTEESHIP

Are you looking for a Professional Trustee who

- Demonstrates Independence

- Is Regulated by a Statutory Body

- Carries Professional Indemnity Insurance

- Has Industry-Wide Pension Experience

If so contact:

PAN Trustee Services Limited

which is committed to be the UK's
leading supplier of Independent Trustee Services

To find out more call Ann Hearn or Andrew Cheeseman
On: 01737 222402 fax: 01737 222403
or write to
PAN Trustees Services Limited at:

77-81 Bell Street
Reigate
Surrey
RH2 7AN

committed to Independent Trustee Services
Registered Number: 3005366

Chapter 7

Responsibilities of Trustees

To get to know the scheme

A new trustee must first of all familiarise himself or herself with the rules of the scheme, the assets and the members. The trustee will need to study the booklet, and read the trust deed and rules. He or she should get a list and valuation of the scheme's investments and details of the members. For this purpose, members means not only active members but pensioners and deferred pensioners. Deferred pensioners are members who have left the scheme but not taken a transfer of their accrued rights to a new scheme or a personal pension. They thus have an entitlement to a preserved pension from the scheme when they retire. The new trustee should also study the latest actuarial valuation and the trustees' last annual report. He or she will face an onerous task; one that should not be undertaken lightly.

Conflicts of interest

The trustee may face conflicts of interest. He or she will probably be an employee of the company and may be one of its directors. He or she could be a member of a trade union or be a union official. The trustee will probably be a member of the scheme. There will then be conflicting loyalties between his or her duties to the union, or to the company, and to the scheme. Trustees have to learn to split themselves in two and separate their roles. When wearing the trustee's hat, the individual must address only the interests of the members. He or she must not act in the interests of the company. The interests of a trade union are not necessarily the same as those of the scheme members and, as such, those interests must be put aside. A trustee's duty is not normally to negotiate benefit improvements for the members but to administer the pension scheme in accordance with the rules. Accordingly he or she must see that the scheme is operated as provided in the trust deed and rules.

Main duties

The principal duties of a pension scheme trustee are summarised below.

To hold the assets of the scheme for the benefit of the members

For example, the trustees should carefully check the credentials of someone claiming a benefit. Is the person claiming to be the member's spouse, and so entitled to a spouse's pension, really the legal spouse? Birth and marriage certificates have to be checked to establish the relationship.

To act impartially towards all the beneficiaries

This means that not only have the interests of active members (people still in employment) to be considered, but also those of pensioners (those who have retired), and deferred pensioners (who have left the employer with an entitlement to a preserved pension from the scheme and who have not taken a transfer payment). There is a danger that the interests of deferred pensioners in particular will get overlooked. The employer is not interested in them; after all, they have left his or her employment. The trustees cannot take that attitude.

To carry out their duties with reasonable care and good faith

They must not be careless or act otherwise than in the best interests of all the members.

To obtain and consider proper expert advice in areas where the trustees themselves are not experts

Typical examples of this duty relate to actuarial matters, investment decisions and questions requiring legal advice. Where the trustees are making a transfer payment, they must obtain the advice of their actuary on its amount. Investment is considered to be a specialist field best left to the expert. Trustees should not therefore make investment decisions without taking advice from an expert. Where legal questions arise, the trustees should consult their lawyer. While trustees are obliged to obtain and consider expert advice, they should not merely rubber stamp it; that would be as bad as not taking the advice in the first place. Experts have as great a capacity to be wrong as anyone else. Clearly there are dangers in ignoring the advice of experts, especially if they prove to be right after all. It is not possible to lay down hard and fast rules, but a degree of discretion has to be exercised.

To see that money owed to the scheme is paid

The problem here is unpaid contributions, usually from the employer. Employee contributions are deducted from pay by the employer and handed over with the company contributions to the trustees at regular intervals. That, at any rate, is how life should be. It sometimes happens, however, that an employer gets into financial difficulties and, in effect, borrows the employee contributions for the purposes of the business. Ultimately, if all goes well, both employee and company contributions are passed over to the trustees for investment. If all goes badly, this does not happen, the employer becomes insolvent and the contributions are lost. If the employer becomes insolvent there are certain limited rights of recourse against the Government Redundancy Fund and the trustees will be preferential creditors. But this is not as good as having got the money in and invested.

There are specific time limits for reporting non-payment of contributions to OPRA and the members. These are dealt with in more detail in Chapter 13.

Where the employer deducts contributions from pay and fails to pay them to the trustees within 19 days of the end of the month in which the deduction is made, without reasonable excuse, the employer is guilty of an offence.

Where an employer pays benefits instead of the trustees, any benefit not paid to a member within two working days of receipt by the employer must be paid into a separate bank account.

To record the transactions and proceedings of the scheme

This means that the trustees should keep proper accounts of the income and outgoings of the scheme and have them audited by a professionally qualified auditor. The accounts and the auditor's statement must accompany the trustees' annual report. Trustees must also keep minutes of their meetings and record the decisions taken by them.

Bank accounts

The trustees must maintain a separate bank account for the scheme for money received by them. The requirement does not, therefore, affect trustees if money is not received by them, as happens in many insured schemes where all money is paid direct to an insurance company. Nor does the requirement apply to money held on behalf of the trustees in a separate account.

Books and records

Books and records must be kept showing:
- (a) contributions received;
- (b) the date on which a member joined the scheme;
- (c) payments of pensions and benefits;
- (d) payments made on behalf of the trustees to anyone, including professional advisers, with the name and address of the payee and the reason for payment;
- (e) any movement of assets from the trustees to anyone, including professional advisers, with the name and address of the transferee and the reason for the transfer;
- (f) the receipt or payment of money or assets in respect of transfers in or out of the scheme, including:
  - (i) the member's name;
  - (ii) the terms of the transfer;
  - (iii) the name of the transferring or receiving scheme;
  - (iv) the date of transfer; and
  - (v) the date of receipt or payment of the money or assets;
- (g) payments made to a member leaving the scheme, other than on a transfer, including:

  (i)   the member's name;
  (ii) the date of leaving;
  (iii) the member's entitlement;
  (iv) the method of calculating entitlements; and
  (v)   how the entitlement was discharged;
(h) payments made to the employer;
(i) other payments to, and withdrawals from, the scheme
    including the name and address of the payee or payer.

Minutes

Written records of trustees' meetings (including meetings of any of
their number) must be kept stating:
  (a) the date, time and place of the meeting;
  (b) the names of all the trustees invited to the meeting;
  (c) the names of the trustees who attended and those who did
       not;
  (d) the names of any professional advisers or any other person
       who attended the meeting;
  (e) the decisions made; and
  (f) whether, since the last meeting, there has been any occasion
       where a decision has been made by the trustees, and, if so, the
       time, place and date of the decision and the names of the
       trustees who took part in it.
The trustees' books and records must be kept for at least six years
from the end of the relevant scheme year.

To appoint advisers

A scheme auditor and actuary and an authorised fund manager must
be appointed by the trustees in the case of most schemes. But an auditor is not required for small self-administered schemes or earmarked insured schemes where all members are trustees and all
trustee decisions are unanimous.

An actuary is not needed for money purchase schemes.

A fund manager is not needed for small self-administered schemes
or wholly insured schemes.

Anyone who is:
  (a) a member of the scheme;
  (b) employed by the trustees;
  (c) an employer in relation to the scheme; or

(d) ineligible to audit the employer's accounts;
cannot be appointed as the scheme auditor.

Appointment and removal of professional advisers

Appointments of professional advisers must be in writing and state:
(a) the effective date of the appointment;
(b) to whom the adviser should report; and
(c) from whom the adviser is to take instructions.
The appointed adviser must acknowledge the notice of appointment within one month and must confirm that he will notify the trustees of any conflicts of interest as soon as he becomes aware of them.

An adviser may resign at any time by giving written notice to the trustees. In the case of the auditor or actuary the resignation notice must state any circumstances connected with the resignation which significantly affect the scheme or that there are no such circumstances.

Trustees can remove a professional adviser by giving him written notice. Where the auditor or actuary is removed by the trustees, he must give the trustees a statement of any circumstances connected with his removal which significantly affect the scheme or say that there are no such circumstances. The trustees must appoint a new auditor or actuary within three months of the removal, resignation or death of the old one. The new auditor or actuary and the remaining actuary or auditor (as appropriate) must be given a copy of the old auditor's or actuary's resignation or removal statement.

Duty to disclose information

The employer and the employer's auditor or actuary must disclose on request to the trustees such information as is reasonably required for the performance of their duties or those of their advisers.

The employer must automatically, within one month, disclose to the trustees any event relating to the employer which there is reasonable cause to believe will be of material significance in the exercise by the trustees or their advisers of any of their functions.

Where the employer provides for the administration of the scheme, it must disclose to the trustees the terms on which the services are provided and information about the administrator.

The trustees must disclose to their advisers such information and make available such books and records as are reasonably required for the performance of their duties.

A trustee who relies on certain kinds of adviser not appointed by the trustees may be removed or suspended by OPRA or be liable to penalties. The advisers in question are:

(a) auditors;
(b) actuaries;
(c) custodians;
(d) fund managers; and
(e) legal advisers.

For an illustration of trustees' duties see *'The Lawyer's Tale: Trouble at T'Mill'* and *'Problems come in Bulk'* which follow this chapter.

The Lawyer's Tale: Trouble at T'Mill

A lovely summer day at the beginning of July saw young David in his new silver Porsche driving his friends Colin Bell, the actuary, and Doug Livingstone to a trustees meeting of the Waters of Wells Pension Scheme.

'You had a red car last time I saw you, Dave' said Colin accusingly. 'Yes, I know—that was the Jag. But it got dirty and I fancied a change. Besides it had a bit of a "boy racer" image. I persuaded the company that a new Porsche would fit the bill better!'

'There's no justice in this world' cried Colin in disbelief. 'I'm just a poor actuary; I couldn't afford a Porsche.'

'Well, you'd better be a better actuary; then you'd have a better car.' replied David.

'Stop squabbling you two' said Doug from the back. 'Save your energy for the meeting.'

Waters of Wells was a company producing English spring water in a factory on the outskirts of Royal Tunbridge Wells. That enabled them to call their water 'Royal Wells Water'. It went from strength to strength, helped no doubt by the scandals that racked their rivals across the Channel. The owner of the company was Maud Belchamber, a formidable woman of large proportions and even larger personality. Maud had a weakness for handsome young men and Doug and Colin, but especially David, were old friends of hers. Pension scheme meetings were held with a regularity and a surfeit of professional advice that sometimes seemed a little over the top given the modest size of the scheme. However it had assets of £20 million and upwards of 100 members.

Soon after arriving at Waters of Wells the trustees meeting began. Apart from Maud, the other trustees were Ron Smith, the company secretary and Peter Huxtable, the foreman at the main bottling plant. It was set to be a routine meeting but for the last item on the agenda. Doug took the trustees through it carefully. One of the members had just retired. He was the old company secretary, Rainey, brother of the local bank manager in Tunbridge Wells. There was rather a serious discrepancy between the pension as shown on the benefit statement which Doug had sent him on his retirement, £7,000 a year, and the pension shown by the benefit statements issued a few years back of £12,000 a year.

'Well I'd be very upset if that happened to me.' said Maud. 'How on earth did you come to make such a dreadful mistake, Doug?'

'It's nothing to do with me or the Magnificent Mutual' cut in Doug quickly. 'It's all the fault of the previous administrators before we took over. Rainey started off in the old Works Scheme which he joined in 1957. That was discontinued back in 1975 when we amalgamated the Works and Staff Schemes. The terms of the amalgamation were that all he was entitled to was a deferred pension from the Works Scheme plus a pension from the new scheme based on service from 1975. Result £7,000 a year.'

'Well, what went wrong then?' asked Ron Smith.

'The old administrators forgot about the deferred pension and backdated his service counting for benefits in the new scheme to 1957. Result £12,000 a year. They issued annual benefit statements on this basis.

When we took over a couple of years ago, we spotted the mistake and issued correct benefit statements. As far as we're concerned, it was all put right then. It's no good him whingeing now.'

'He's the brother of our bank manager, the whingeing Rainey, so of course whingeing runs in the family.' said Maud. 'But it doesn't seem right to me. He came to see me last week. I can't stand his brother but our Rainey is not too bad. He said he'd planned his retirement on the basis of a pension of £12,000; he would have paid AVCs if he'd realised the truth. You know what it's like—you never look at your benefit statements after you've seen the first one.'

'Whatever shall we do?' asked Huxtable, the other trustee.

'It's tough' said Colin. 'You can't play fast and loose with pensions. He'll have to get what the rules provide.'

'We've all heard that about AVCs before' said Doug. 'It's easy to say; hindsight comes cheaper than shelling out to pay AVCs.'

'What do you think David?' asked Maud. 'You know how I value your judgment!'

'Fetch a bucket, quick.' said Colin in an aside to Doug. Luckily Maud didn't hear.

David went puce and said 'I agree with you, Maud. You can't just fob him off with £7,000 when he's got benefit statements and expectations of something completely different. Plus it was not unreasonable for him to think his service started in 1957. I don't think you can stand by the correct figure of £7,000. It doesn't seem right to me.'

'Eh' cried Colin accusingly, 'the trouble with you, Dave, is that you think money grows on trees, especially other people's money. You spend money just like a politician. You can't solve problems with a cheque book.'

'Well I would.' replied Dave, rather rattled. 'There's a big surplus in the scheme; what are you worrying about. I thought the trustees duty was to look after the members.'

'Boys, boys' interrupted Maud, 'this isn't getting us anywhere. What do Ron and Peter think?' It wasn't often that Maud consulted her co-trustees and it didn't do her any good this time.

Peter agreed with Maud and David that the higher pension should be paid. Ron Smith sided with Colin and Doug. The fact that there was no love lost between him and his predecessor was beside the point!

Maud went a rather dangerous shade of purple and said quickly: 'David, I want this settled. I've booked a table for lunch at the golf club. We've never had a disagreement before and I don't want to spoil the day with my young men quarrelling with each other.'

David smiled peacefully at his colleagues and said 'Don't worry, Maud. I'll sort it out for you. Colin and Doug are just jealous of my new Porsche. Doug got his seventies style hair cut ruffled on the journey down. What I propose is that we all pay a visit to my old boss Archie Smithers at Megalaw. He'll tell us what to do.'

'OK' said Maud, 'but count me out; you know I can't stand the old goat.'

'I agree' said Colin. 'He ought to have been put down years ago. It would have been a kindness.'

'I'll fix an appointment for the three of us to see him tomorrow morning' continued David, 'and we'll report back to you afterwards.'

And so the following morning David, Doug and Colin met Archie at the offices of Megalaw in their new building at Canary Wharf with spectacular views of the City and West End.

'I don't know how you can concentrate with a view like this' said David.

'You find that difficult at the best of times, don't you, Archie. I hear you lose consciousness in the afternoon' interjected Colin.

'Gentlemen, why don't we reserve your little jokes till lunchtime. I've got to be in the West End at 3 pm so I've booked a table for the four of us at the Riverside restaurant at the Savoy. That should suit your jet set life style, David. Why don't you tell me the problem. We can catch up on the gossip later.'

And so David, with promptings from Colin and Doug, told the

story of Rainey's pension. Colin and Doug said they had advised the trustees that they could only administer the scheme in accordance with the rules. The mistake in the old benefit statements had been corrected years ago. If Rainey wasn't satisfied, he could always sue the former administrators for negligence in issuing incorrect statements. The trustees could not be bound by the wrong benefit statements.

David explained that both he and Maud felt that the trustees, whatever the reasons, had issued statements on which Rainey had relied. You couldn't just reduce his pension from £12,000 to £7,000 when, if he'd realised the awful truth, he would have topped his pension up by paying AVCs.

There was a pause and the three of them looked expectantly at Archie, who had shut his eyes in thought.

'Has he gone then?' asked Colin.

'Not yet' said Doug, 'I think he's trying to think!'

'Gentlemen' interrupted Archie, 'if I may have your attention for a moment. I know how limited your attention span is, so I'll make it brief. It's all quite simple. I don't know why none of you thought of it before.

I think the trustees can't go back on the old statements. Quite clearly from what you told me, Rainey relied on the promise and ordered his life accordingly. I know that gives him a greater entitlement than the rules but, as David said, there's a surplus in the scheme. Rainey relied on the statements and to pay him a pension of only £7,000 would mean that he suffered loss. He had no reason to dispute the 1957 date as the date of commencement of service. Technically it was wrong, but not so obviously wrong that he should have realised it and brought it to the trustees attention.'

'Good' said David beaming, 'so me and Maud were right and Col and Doug were wrong.'

'Not so fast' continued Archie.

'I think the trustees should pay him a pension according to the rules of £7,000 but it should be increased to whatever level would have been secured if he had paid maximum AVCs throughout the relevant period.'

'But he didn't, you old clothhead.' shouted Doug.

'You really should restrain yourself Doug and wait for the good news.' replied Archie with a smile. He continued 'Payment of the augmented pension would be conditional on Rainey paying the trustees an amount equal to the total of AVCs he would have paid during that period. He could pay this by deduction from his pension over a suitable period. In other words what the trustees in effect have to compensate him for is the loss of investment return on his notional AVCs. I take it that there's no problem with the pension exceeding Revenue limits.'

There was a silence, broken by David, 'That's a true judgement of Solomon, Archie. I know the trustees will buy that. I didn't know you had it in you, I must admit.'

Colin and Doug nodded their heads approvingly.

'Right, that's sorted out' said Doug. 'What are we waiting for? We'd best get to the Savoy for lunch. You're paying, Archie, but as you've come up with an answer for once, you can stick it on the bill. Miscellaneous travelling and incidental expenses covers a multitude of sins.'

The Lawyer's Tale: Problems Come in Bulk

The helicopter, as if by magic, lifted itself off the helipad on top of one of the City of London's skyscrapers and gathered speed towards its destination in the Midlands. On board were John Watson of the Magnificent Mutual Life Assurance Society, his colleague, the pensions actuary, Colin Bell and David from Docs Galore, the specialist pensions boutique used by the Magnificent Mutual. John Watson was the pensions superintendent responsible for the Automated Widgets Pension Scheme.

The Managing Director of Automated Widgets, Colonel Braithwaite, had rung John the previous day; he explained that they were having a spot of trouble over a couple of bulk transfers and summoned John to a trustees meeting at one of the Automated Widgets factories in Sutton Coldfield. In view of the Colonel's ferocious reputation for getting his own way, John thought he had better be fully briefed and so took with him not just Colin but also young David.

None of them had been in a chopper before and they were not a little nervous. David declared that the mere sight of Colin in a striking black and white check suit with matching two-tone shoes was enough to put anyone off.

'It'd serve you right' said David, 'if me and John were sick all over your disco suit.'

Luckily the journey passed without mishap and two hours later they were at the trustees meeting.

Apart from the Colonel, the other trustees were Simon Jones, the company secretary who had the happy knack of getting the Colonel to believe that all his suggestions originated from the Colonel himself. The other trustee was Major Frump, the retired senior partner of Ebenezer & Frump, the company's solicitors. The Colonel had read about the importance of having independent trustees and had hit on the idea of appointing Frump when they met at the golf club. Frump was an idle, opinionated, addlepated humbug. His virtue in the Colonel's eyes was that he would cause no trouble.

The Colonel started by saying that they had just completed the sale of three non-core businesses employing about 250 people apiece.

'Years ago' the Colonel said, 'these merchant bank johnnies were all into diversification—it was the flavour of the month. Now they want me to concentrate on our core business—widget making—and not divert management time elsewhere. I wish they'd make their minds up, but I suppose they've got to earn their vast fees.

Well, our first sale was of the fast food business to one of the American giants. They'd got a good final salary scheme and said they would give year for year past service so we agreed to pay a past service reserve transfer.

The second business was our car leasing company; that went to a French company anxious to set up in the UK. Since it was a new venture, they hadn't got a pension scheme; but their consultants set up a money purchase scheme with targeted final salary benefits. As part of the deal we agreed a past service reserve transfer to them.

The third business was a double glazing company. The buyers are sharp operators. They don't know anything about pensions and don't want to know. But Huxtable, the manager of the business, wants to set up a group personal pension scheme and has demanded a transfer on the same basis as the other two.'

Simon, the company secretary, took up the story. 'We were only planning to give cash equivalents in this case. Huxtable is a trouble maker; that's one reason we were keen to get rid of the business. But he's threatened us with the Ombudsman if we don't treat all the transfers alike. So we thought we'd better get some expert advice.'

At this stage Frump, never at a loss for words, asked if he could introduce his partner, Nigel Morton. 'After all, it's trust law we have to know about as trustees. You need a lawyer to tell you that—not a crowd of number crunchers' he concluded glaring balefully at the trio from the Magnificent Mutual.

Nigel was a prematurely bald young man, with a bow tie and outsize moon spectacles.

'As Major Frump, says, we are dealing with trust law here; pensions is just a branch of trust law; we're not talking about how to add up the figures. Once I've given you my legal ruling, then no doubt you lot' he said glancing dismissively at John and his colleagues, 'will apply it to the facts of each case.'

'Capital, capital' cried Frump. 'Like Nigel says, it's principles we're concerned with—the clerks can sort out the details later.'

'Well, Mr Morton' said John Watson in glacial tones, 'perhaps you'd like to tell us our job.'

'Certainly. The first duty of trustees is to act fairly towards all classes of their beneficiaries, holding the scales of justice, and weighing them carefully in each hand.'

'Eh, lad' said Colin in broad Lancastrian tones, 'do descend for a moment to the level of us poor clerks and give us a bit more practical advice.'

Stung by Colin's sarcasm, Nigel continued 'If only you'd let me finish, I would have told you that you have to treat each transfer alike. In other words, although I don't quite understand the jargon, Huxtable is right. The double glazing people have got to be treated in the same way as the others. That's my ruling as a trust lawyer; you must now go back and apply it.'

'Poppycock and twaddle. I've never heard such rubbish in my life' interjected the Colonel; he was never one to suffer fools or those of opposing views gladly.

'David, I won't let Huxtable get away with this. No scheme—no transfer; am I right or am I wrong?' thundered the Colonel.

'You are, of course, right' replied David. 'The first duty of trustees is not to sit on Mount Olympus and mouth platitudes and dispense justice. I'm afraid it's a bit more down to earth and boring. It's to familiarise themselves with the trust deed and rules and administer the scheme in accordance with them.'

The Colonel noticeably brightened and Colin and John began to grin.

'I'm going to be boring. When you sold the fast food business, Colonel, you sold a subsidiary company. That brought into play what us clerks call "the partial winding up rule". Your partial winding up rule requires the trustees to transfer "the appropriate portion of the fund as decided by the trustees after obtaining actuarial advice". Hence my friend in the disco suit, Colin, quite properly in my view, advised the trustees that a past service reserve basis was appropriate for calculating the bulk transfer.

But the car leasing and double glazing businesses are operating divisions—not subsidiaries. The partial winding up rule doesn't therefore bite. The members are leaving the scheme and are entitled only to withdrawal benefits, or if our learned friend will bear with me, cash equivalents.'

'Dave, you did know, didn't you' said John Watson, 'that we're giving past service reserve for the car leasing division. It's in the sale agreement.'

'Relax' smiled David, 'I do know what day it is. The buyers have got an occupational scheme; maybe it's money purchase but it's got final salary target benefits. The company is entitled to say to the trustees that it's reasonable to augment the benefits here. After all, there's more than enough fat in the scheme. The trustees can't augment benefits unilaterally, but they can if it's a good idea and the company wants it.'

'So that leaves the double glazing business' said Frump. 'How are you going to explain that away?'

'It's all quite simple, really' replied David with a smile. 'They haven't got a pension scheme at all. The trustees don't have the power to pay more than cash equivalents. The company in the circumstances is not prepared to intervene.'

'But that's outrageous' cried Nigel. 'I've just bought a book in two volumes on pension law. I didn't realise it was quite so complicated. No doubt that's why the book is so expensive. I'd better go back and look into it further' he whinged.

John Watson thought it was time to pour oil on troubled waters.

'The point is, like Dave said, selling a business is a commercial operation; pensions is just part of it. What you should have is a bulk transfer rule which applies to sales of assets as well as subsidiaries and requires the trustees to pay cash equivalents—the legal requirement—or more, if the company requires, up to a share of the fund. After all, for tax or industrial relations reasons, the company may want to dispose of surplus. So that's what the rules should say.'

'Well, clever clogs' shouted Frump in a fury, 'since the Magnificent Mutual are responsible for the rules, why don't you practice what you preach?'

John and David grinned. David quietly said 'We do; if, Colonel, you looked at rule 16.4 in the draft of the new rules we sent you last year, you'd see we did just that. You referred the draft to your solicitors. Since then we've had a long silence.'

Redfaced and in a fury Nigel replied:

'That's not fair: I only got this book last week. I haven't got round to your draft yet.'

'Save your breath and get back to debt collecting or conveyancing or whatever you're fit for and leave pensions to the experts' said Colin in triumphant support of his friend.

'Excuse me' said the quiet company secretary, Simon, 'but aren't we in danger of generating more heat than light? We do have a large surplus. Should we be giving a health warning to would be transferees about losing out on discretionary pension increases from our surplus if they transfer?'

'You stupid fool' cried Frump now thoroughly rattled. 'That's giving financial advice. You'll land us all in gaol!'

'Not so' replied John imperturbably. 'If you had taken the trouble to study Schedule 1 of the Financial Services Act, you'd know that rights under an occupational pension scheme don't count as investments. There's nothing to stop you giving a health warning if you want to. But should you? What do you think, Dave?'

'I think, Colonel, that if we may, we should discuss that with my colleague Archie Smithers, before we express a view. It's a difficult question. My initial reaction is that trustees can do this if they want, but don't need to feel obliged to give financial advice. By the way, Archie apologised for not being here today, but he is rather tied up at the moment.'

'All I can say' replied the Colonel, 'is heaven help us if that old goat is going to advise us. He doesn't even know what day of the week it is—not unlike our friend Frump and his lawyer. Let's have a large brandy to fortify you for the ride back to town.'

On their return to London, David was comforted that the old goat, Archie, agreed with his initial reaction.

Chapter 8

Trustees' Discretionary Powers

Why trustees have discretions

If every eventuality were written down in the rules, the rules would be even longer and more complicated than they are now. And so trustees are given discretions to deal with certain matters not covered by the rules or only covered in general terms. Some discretionary powers require a decision in principle, for example, should the scheme accept transfer payments from another scheme. Once that decision has been made, there is no need to consider each case. Other powers require an individual decision in each case, for example, to whom should the trustees pay the discretionary lump sum death benefit payable on death in service. Here the trustees must make proper enquiries before exercising their discretion. Let us examine these discretionary powers in more detail, starting first with decisions in principle.

Decisions in principle

Transfer payments

Transfer payments have to be made on the member's request to other pension schemes approved by the Inland Revenue or to a buy out policy or a personal pension when a member leaves the scheme with two or more years' qualifying service. Even here, however, although the transfer payment has to be calculated in accordance with the Transfer Value Regulations, the trustees have to take certain decisions. Should their actuary take discretionary pension increases into account when doing the calculation? If the trustees do not tell the actuary to ignore these, they will have to be taken into account. And so the trustees must reach a decision and inform the actuary. It would clearly be a misuse of their powers if they varied the decision from case to case. They must reach a decision in principle which can be applied to all cases. Although trustees must permit transfers out of the scheme, they cannot be compelled to accept transfer payments in. Usually they do so and they should make a policy decision about this. They should also settle in principle what benefits they will give in return—added years of pensionable service or an additional amount of pension or money purchase benefits. This is an area where actuarial advice will be needed. Having made their decision, the pensions manager or the actuary should be able to apply it in each individual case without having to refer back to the trustees. It should be borne in mind that the method of calculation of transfers out has to be consistent with transfers in.

Late entry

Should the trustees permit someone who has left the scheme, or who has not joined it when he or she was first eligible to do so, to join or rejoin later? Sometimes the rules regulate this and permit one or two second chances. But often the matter is left to the trustees' discretion. This is an area where they should probably reach a policy decision. If only future service rights are to be granted, they may well feel that, as long as a satisfactory medical report has been obtained, they should permit late entry. If the employer wants the trustees to grant back service, then an individual decision will have to be made. Medical evidence is needed, if only to satisfy the scheme's insurers, before the late entrant can be covered for death in service benefits. Accordingly, late entry may require both a decision in principle, with an individual decision in a particular case if there are questions about the medical evidence or of granting past service rights.

Commutation

Usually scheme rules give the member the right to take a tax-free lump sum on retirement. Part of the pension will have to be given up to provide for the lump sum. Often the rules give the trustees a discretion both to permit this and to fix the amount of the lump sum. If this is the case, the trustees should not make individual decisions. They should settle the commutation factors in conjunction with their actuary and decide that commutation on that basis will be open to all members. It would clearly be inequitable to allow commutation in some cases, but not in others.

Early retirement

Scheme rules sometimes give the member the right to retire on or after age 50 or even earlier on grounds of ill-health. Sometimes this option requires the consent of the employer or of the trustees. This again is an area where individual decisions would be seen as being unfair. If the early retirement pension is reduced to take account of early payment, a cost factor will not be involved. There are, of course, employment considerations, which is why the employer may want to be consulted and to give consent. That aside, there is no reason why the trustees should not reach a policy decision about such cases. It is usual, except in the case of ill-health retirement or early retirement caused by redundancy, for an actuarial reduction to be made to a pension starting to be paid early—because it is likely to be paid for a longer time than a pension starting to be paid at normal retirement date. If an actuarial reduction is not applied, that will impose a cost burden on the scheme. If this has not been taken into account by the actuary in recommending the rate of contributions, the trustees should not permit early retirement unless they are satisfied that money is available to meet the cost.

Pension increases

Often the trustees are given power at their discretion to increase pensions in payment. It would normally be a breach of trust to give some members, but not others, a pension increase. That is not to say that trustees cannot distinguish between different classes of members. For example, members who retired in the 1970s might be given an additional increase to compensate for the hyper inflation of that decade. The trustees should not, however, make individual decisions in this area. The rules will often require the trustees to obtain the employer's consent before giving an increase. This is because there is a cost factor involved. The extra money has to be found from extra contributions or out of any surplus in the scheme. Whether or not the rules require the employer's consent, the trustees should, because of the financial implications, consult the employer and also the actuary.

The Pensions Act introduces requirements for pensions, once they come into payment, to be indexed. Pensions in payment will in future have to be revalued in line with the Retail Prices Index up to a maximum of 5 per cent—limited price indexation or LPI.

Both final salary and money purchase schemes must award LPI to pensions in payment so far as they are earned by service after 6 April 1997. The first increase must take effect not later than the first anniversary of the date on which the pension is first paid and subsequent increases must take effect at intervals of not more than 12 months. The LPI requirement does not apply to free-standing additional voluntary contribution schemes or to pensions derived from in-house AVCs. Nor does it apply to personal pensions except so far as they are used to contract-out of SERPS.

In addition, before a refund of surplus can be made to the employer, the scheme must provide LPI for pensions in payment based on all service, not just service after 6 April 1997.

Individual decisions

Individual decisions are required in the following areas.

Death benefits

Lump sum benefits—usually a multiple of the member's pay—are nearly always held on discretionary trusts for the member's relatives or dependants. They are not usually payable as of right to the member's spouse or to a nominated beneficiary. This method of payment is used to avoid inheritance tax. The member is given the right to nominate his or her chosen beneficiary to receive the lump sum benefit. But this does not bind the trustees, although they should give it serious weight when deciding how to exercise their discretion. The Inland Revenue requires the trustees to make their decision within two years of the member's death, failing which the money has to be paid to the member's estate. This is an area where knowledge of the member's family and financial circumstances is essential before a sensible decision can be reached. In most cases the member's nomination form will be followed. But what if there isn't one or it is out of

date? What if the member's nomination is unreasonable, for example, if he or she nominates the cats' home and is survived by a spouse
and children. There are no hard and fast rules. Trustees must act
honestly and reasonably and set aside their own political, religious
or moral views or prejudices. They must not discriminate on these
grounds. But so long as they reach their decision fairly, having made
proper enquiries, on the basis of knowledge of the member's family
and other circumstances, their decision will not be disturbed by the
courts or the Pensions Ombudsman. It is sensible not to give or
record reasons for their decisions, although the decision itself must
be recorded in the trustees' minutes. For some illustrations of the
problems that can arise, readers are referred to '*The Lawyer's Tale:
Bangle Bill*' which follows this chapter.

Augmentation

Trustees are often given power to increase or augment the benefits
payable to a member or beneficiary. Usually the employer's consent
is required because of the financial implications, ie increasing benefits costs money, someone has to pay. And so, as with pension increases, whether or not the rules require the trustees to obtain the
employer's consent, they would be wise to consult both the employer
and the actuary. In any event, it is usually the company that triggers
a request for augmentation. They may want, for example, to provide
for the retirement on full pension of certain senior executives at age
60 or 62, when the normal retirement date is 65. If there is sufficient
money in the scheme, or if the employer agrees to pay the additional
contributions recommended by the actuary, should the trustees
agree to the employer's request? This is an area which frequently
causes great problems to trustees. The favoured members are usually senior, better paid, employees. Why should they be given better
benefits than the rest of the members? The answer is that so long as
there is no disadvantage to the other members, there is no reason
why not, and indeed every reason why the trustees should agree. It
must be remembered that the employer did not have to establish the
pension scheme in the first place, that he or she can usually reduce,
suspend or terminate contributions and that the employer may, depending on the rules, be able to trigger a winding-up of the scheme.
It is therefore in the interests of the members as a whole not to lose
the employer's goodwill. Trustees should normally, therefore,

exercise their powers of augmentation on the employer's request, so long as the other members are not disadvantaged.

Rule changes

Most pension schemes give the employer and the trustees power jointly to change the rules. This power must be exercised by the trustees in the interests of all the beneficiaries—current members, early leavers and pensioners. No one class should be left out of consideration. The trustees must be even-handed. This does not mean that all members must share equally in any benefit improvements, merely that the trustees must give consideration to the different classes of members and ensure that their interests are taken into account. For example, if it is decided that a given amount of money should be allocated to benefit improvements, the trustees should ask the actuary to cost out a number of different options. They may wish to guarantee a certain level of pension increases, or to increase the rate at which they grant discretionary increases. They may wish to improve the death in service benefits or improve the rate at which pensions accrue. They may well take a different view about deferred pensioners—those who have left the employer's service. They may feel that some greater measure of revaluation should be applied than the statutory minimum, or they may feel, having regard to their length of service, that that is enough. Their interests must be thought about, however, that does not mean that the trustees must give them benefit improvements, or benefit improvements of equivalent value. But they must not be overlooked.

This is another area where no hard and fast lines can be laid down. It is a matter for the trustees' discretion and as long as they act fairly, their decision will not be overturned by a court or the Ombudsman. Often the impetus for benefit improvements comes from the employer. As long as the trustees are satisfied, having taken actuarial advice, that the money needed to pay for the improvements is either available or will be forthcoming, they should usually agree. If in doubt, the trustees should obtain advice from their experts.

Readers are referred to 'The Lawyer's Tale: The Quick and the Dead', which follows the next chapter, for an illustration of some of the problems that can arise in the exercise of trustees' discretionary powers.

The Lawyer's Tale: Bangle Bill

The third Viscount Bedfont was Chairman of the court of Governors of the Magnificent Mutual Life Assurance Society and also Chairman of the trustees of its Staff Pension Scheme. He was a tall, patrician figure, originally an actuary by training and with all the lofty arrogance sometimes displayed by members of that learned profession. He had summoned their consultant, David, and his friend, the scheme's lawyer, Mike, to see him in his penthouse offices high up in Docklands. Thoughtfully he had arranged for his chauffeur to pick them up from the City in his racing green Bentley. This gave David the opportunity to bring Mike up to speed.

'I don't suppose you ever knew Bangle Bill. He was a pensions administrator who worked for the Magnificent Mutual?' he started off.

'No I didn't' replied Mike. 'Why "Bangle Bill" and why "worked"; what happened?'

'Bangle' continued David, 'drowned on holiday in India 18 months ago. When I first knew him, he wore a white suit and his left arm was covered with gold bangles from wrist to shoulder; he had a silver cross beneath his tie and a pair of earrings. Not what you expect in a staid old life office. When Monty Murgatroyd spotted him, he was banished to the Accounts Department. Last year he went off to Southern India and joined the travellers at Kovalam. Unfortunately he got swept out to sea and drowned.'

'And so' murmured Mike.

'Well, the trustees decided to pay the lump sum death benefit to his live-in lover. He left a nomination form in favour of his mother but it was signed yonks ago. Bill's mother kicked up a stink and went off to the Ombudsman's office. His Lordship has had a letter from the Ombudsman's office and he doesn't like it one bit. By the way, watch it with Charlie boy, as I call him. He likes to stand on his dignity!'

Minutes later they were ushered into Lord Bedfont's palatial office. He rose and graciously extended his hands.

'Welcome, I'm Charles Bedfont. Do sit yourselves down. We're having a spot of bother with the Ombudsman.'

Being Lord Bedfont, he of course used the Scandinavian pronunciation, omitting the 'o' in Ombudsman with a curious guttural strangling noise. Mike looked down at the floor and avoided David's eyes.

'One of his lackeys' his Lordship continued, 'has sent me a most impertinent letter asking me to explain:

(a)   which of the trustees took part in the decision about Bill's benefit;

(b)   the grounds on which they reached that decision;

(c)   whether they took account of Bill's family circumstances; and

(d)   what enquiries were made?

Of course I immediately telephoned my brother, who is the presiding judge at the Old Bailey. He confirmed my view that the decision about who poor Bill's benefit should be paid to was for the trustees. Indeed he said that no court, let alone an Ombudsman, had the right to interfere with our decision. My brother thought that the trustees' lawyer should write to the Ombudsman's office to explain the law to him.'

He smiled silkily at Mike. 'Well, your Lordship, it's not quite as simple as that' said Mike.

Lord Bedfont bridled 'Are you venturing to disagree with my learned brother?' he asked staring down his aquiline nose at poor Mike. David was beginning to enjoy himself but thought he ought to help his friend.

'The trustees decided to ignore Bill's nomination form because he'd signed it years ago when he joined the scheme. He had lived with his partner on a stable basis for the preceding five years. His mother had refused to have anything to do with him. Indeed there had been no contact until she found out that he'd died.'

'Quite so' purred Lord Bedfont. 'David understands the position perfectly. Kindly write the letter my brother suggested.'

'But, Lord Bedfont' Mike struggled going scarlet in the face, 'the Ombudsman can make you answer those questions. With due respect to your brother, I don't suppose he has ever read Pt X of the Pension Schemes Act 1993. The Ombudsman has jurisdiction over pension scheme trustees where there are disputes of fact or law or complaints of injustice arising from maladministration. He can require the production of documents and the giving of evidence, just like your brother. In fact he's got more powers than your brother because you can't appeal against the Ombudsman except on a point of law.'

'Who is this supremo who is even mightier than my brother?' cut in Lord Bedfont in icy tones.

'Well' gushed David, 'he was invented to provide a quick, inexpensive and informal means of settling complaints and disputes about occupational pensions where members find themselves in conflict with trustees who have large resources and may sometimes (rightly or wrongly) be thought to be more attentive to the views of the employer than those of the employees.'

Mike hurried on 'In a recent case Mr Justice Walker said:
"The relevant statutory provisions are often lengthy and obscure and the same is unfortunately true of many trust deeds and rules. Countless ill-drafted amending deeds … are out there somewhere like rusty unexploded land mines. The Pensions Ombudsman's task in delivering rapid, unlegalistic justice, without cutting too many legal corners, is a dauntingly difficult one."

By the way, was he having a go at you, David, and your old boss, Archie Smithers when he talked about the "countless ill-drafted deeds"? Sounded like a direct hit to me!'

'Hmph' said his Lordship. 'Pray continue.'

'Well' said Mike, 'why did you pay the benefits to Bill's partner and override the nomination form?'

'I know the family' snapped Lord Bedfont. 'In fact I introduced Bill to Murgatroyd and recommended that he be taken on. His mother is a cantankerous old crow who has got more money than she needs. She didn't approve of Bill's lifestyle and, as David said, she made no attempt to get in touch until he died. Bill and his partner set up house together over five years ago. They bought a flat in Docklands which neither could have afforded by themselves. They both had jobs of course but their joint income supported their apartment and an otherwise unaffordable lifestyle. So we concluded that Bill's partner was his 'dependant' under the rules. As I said, the rules gave that power to us, not to anyone else. You are not suggesting, or are you, that my brother and I are wrong?'

'Of course not' blushed Mike 'but in the words of another judge, Mr Justice Carnwath:
"Trustees are subject to review by the court, not as a Court of Appeal but with a limited role.

(1)   The trustees must ask themselves the correct questions.
(2)   They must direct themselves properly in law. In particular they must adopt a correct construction of the Pension Fund Rules. And
(3)   They must not arrive at a perverse decision, ie a decision at which no reasonable body of trustees could arrive. They must take into account all relevant but no irrelevant factors."

'This lecture is becoming tedious' his Lordship growled. 'What is your point?'

'My point' replied Mike, 'is that I'm not sure that Bill's partner was a dependant. If so, since the partner was not a relative or a nominated beneficiary, the trustees misdirected themselves and would be guilty of maladministration.'

Sensing the looming storm clouds he rushed on:

'The person in question

"must be dependent in the proper sense of that term and it is
not sufficient if he was merely deriving benefit from the
earnings of the deceased; he must be to some extent dependent
upon him for the ordinary necessaries of life having regard to
his class and position in life."

Didn't Bill and his partner give up their financial independence as a matter of choice, but not of necessity? Had you any evidence that Bill's partner was not able to manage independently if required to do so?'

'This is too much' exploded his Lordship. 'It is not unknown for married women, even today, to give up their full-time jobs on or shortly after marriage. Does that mean that their dependency is then self-induced? I can't believe that my brother or his learned brethren would decide in this way. In any event it's irrelevant. What is your point?'

'Well' crooned Mike, 'the Ombudsman ruled in a similar case that the trustees had not made proper enquiries, had misinterpreted the test of dependency in the rules and were guilty of maladministration. And he whacked them £500 each for compensation for distress and inconvenience.

His ruling about maladministration was upheld by the High Court, although you'll be glad to know that the compensation order was not. The rules provided that a trustee was not to be personally liable in the absence of dishonesty. There was nothing to justify imposing a personal liability on a trustee contrary to the clear intention of the rules.'

'Are you quite sure you've finished?' asked Lord Bedfont sarcastically. 'You've either gone mad or you're not aware of the facts. You seem to think that Bill's partner was another man; that's not the case—she is a woman and they got married at Limehouse Registry Office before they went to India. They then had some kind of religious ceremony shortly before the dreadful accident. The trustees were quite within their rights to decide as they did. As she was a 'relative', whether or not she was a dependant was totally irrelevant.'

With that he rose to his feet and summoned a flunkey.

'Rainey, show these gentlemen out and direct them to the station'.

Looking at Mike he concluded 'When you get back to your office, reflect on what you have learned today and don't assume that other people are as stupid as you. Kindly fax me a draft letter to the Ombudsperson as I asked you to do in the first place.'

'Phew' said a subdued Mike to David outside. 'That was a scorcher. Why didn't you tell me all this?'

'Because I didn't know. The partner in fact was originally a man, a transvestite, who underwent a sex change. I suppose that meant they could get married. We'd best go to the nearest pub to recover! I don't know which I would sooner face—the Ombudsman or Lord Bedfont in a rage!'

The Lawyer's Tale: The Quick and the Dead

'Me and Martin are off to the Countess's tomorrow for a Waters of Wells meeting' said Mike sliding through Archie's door.

'Me and Martin indeed! You'd think an expensive education at Oxford would at least teach you to speak the Queen's English. Martin and I ... if you please' spluttered Archie petulantly. 'And why, pray, are you taking a whole day for this jaunt, and why Martin?'

Martin was in charge of employment law at Megalaw, in his mid 30s, tall and with floppy prematurely grey hair.

'I need Martin because one of the problems we'll be dealing with is a member who has been presumed dead. It's a bit off beam so I thought I'd take Martin with me' replied Mike.

'Plus David as well, I suppose' said Archie sarcastically. David was the consultant to the Waters of Wells Pension Scheme.

'Yes, of course. Is something bugging you, Archie? You seem a bit more cross-grained than usual. You must need a break; after all you haven't had one for a month now.'

Before Archie could riposte his telephone rang and pre-empted further discussion.

The next morning Rainey, the chauffeur picked up Mike, then David and Martin in the Countess's coroneted Rolls. The Countess had been, until her recent elevation on the death of her uncle, plain Maud Belchamber, proprietor of the Waters of Wells, a profitable business based on bottling spring water outside Tunbridge Wells. Soon they were deposited at Sheffield Castle, the Countess's seat in the garden of England.

It was a fairy tale moated medieval castle and on this gorgeous May morning the park and lakes and gardens were at their best. The first of the coaches was piling into the car park disgorging visitors who had come to admire the rhododendrons and azaleas and the bluebell woods.

Maud made her usual dramatic entrance. 'Darlings' she crooned, 'how wonderful to see you and who is this splendid hunk of a man?' Resplendent in a new lime green ensemble and green bouffant hairstyle, Maud immediately lit on Martin. 'Let's begin' she continued, clapping her hands. 'Gorgio, bring us coffee' she said to the young waiter who appeared as if by magic. 'Don't worry, in spite of his name Gorgio is not one of our snail eating friends. I got him on a business training scheme so the taxpayer pays half his wages. But I'm rambling, in fact like your friend, Archie Smithers. Where was I?'

David started 'You've got a couple of problems with your members. Lily Smith went missing seven years ago and has been presumed dead. Her husband is claiming the lump sum benefit plus a spouse's pension and pensions for the two kids. Plus Tom Robinson has been diagnosed as in the final stages of cancer and has only two months to live.'

'Thank you, David' said Maud taking the chair. You would never have guessed she was 75. Indeed she spent thousands of pounds each year on preserving that illusion.

'Of course it's a lot of nonsense about Lily. She's no more dead than I am. Now if it were your old boss, Archie, I could have imagined it; after all he's been brain dead for years. The gossip is that Lily, tired of her husband, and they can be very tiresome, eloped with a young man from the bottling plant to start a new life in Tasmania. She was the foreperson in charge of the bottling plant. My dears, the orgies of initiation—quite shame-making.'

'But Maud' interrupted Mike, 'we've got an order from the court presuming her dead. The trustees have got to pay the death in service benefits; they've got no choice.'

Maud's eyes flashed imperiously: 'Young man, I don't care for un-palatable advice. That's why I sacked Smithers. What if Lily turns up again? You'll be paying her a pension next.'

'I wonder' said Martin 'if it's quite as simple as that, Mike. You pension lawyers aren't really proper lawyers, are you? You say, Maud, that seven years ago Lily upped and offed taking with her one of her colleagues and she's never been heard of since. What did you do about her pay and her personnel records?'

'We made enquiries, found she'd gone walkies, so we stopped her pay. I've got her file here. As you can see, it's marked "Terminated"!'

'Great' said Martin with a smile. 'I don't think you need pay any benefits at all. Her contract of employment was frustrated by her un-explained absence—say after six months; and so, in Maud's words, it terminated. She has not therefore died in service but in deferment. There's no lump sum benefit on death in deferment.'

'But,' cried Mike, 'you don't understand. The Waters of Wells Scheme is contracted-out. At the least, Lily's husband would get a spouse's GMP.'

It was not Mike's day. David gently reminded him that widower's GMPs were only payable in respect of contracted-out service after

6 April 1988—when Lily disappeared. There was no post-1988 contracted-out service.

'But surely you've got to give the husband and kids something' said Mike feeling somewhat nettled.

'I haven't got to do anything at all, young man' said Maud magisterially. 'But as chair of the trustees and as M.D. of the company I will direct payment of children's pensions to Lily's two boys and give them a lump sum of £10,000 each. Lily's husband is better off without her; in any event he's got a good job and has remarried. That's what he got the court order for.'

'Perhaps we'd best get on to Tom Robinson now that we've dealt with Lily' said David, always the diplomat. 'I've got the medical report. It's tragic. Tom is only 30, and has been given at best six months to live. He was a member of the local rugby club as well as a leading light in the cricket team. Why has this got to happen to him?'

'Quite so' said Maud with real sympathy. 'So we'll give him an ill-health early retirement pension. I think you said that could be commuted for cash, didn't you, David?'

'Yes' replied David looking a trifle embarrassed, 'but I'm afraid there's a problem with the rules. They give the trustees power to commute the pension where the member is "in exceptional circumstances of serious ill-health".'

'You can hardly deny that Tom satisfies that' said Maud quietly.

'No' said David looking even more troubled. 'The medical report makes that very plain. But the trustees have got to assume that the member is in normal health for the purposes of calculating the lump sum. You know that under the rules projected service to normal retirement date is used for an ill-health pension. Tom has got five years' service; that plus 35 years' projected service will cost about £300,000. It's all because we have to assume that Tom was in normal health' he concluded rather miserably.

'Mike' said Maud rather sternly. 'Who's responsible for this mistake?'

'It's certainly not me; I didn't draft your rules.'

'I know, I know' rushed in David. 'It was Archie. But I've been checking up. It's a perfectly normal provision, at any rate in insurance company rules. If you don't make that assumption, there's not much point in commutation. Tom would only get the capital value of six months' pension. I assume that's not what you intend. I agree some rules leave it all down to the actuary, but how on earth is he to do the calculation?'

Martin had, while all this was going on, been looking at the rules. Turning on his charm he rushed in:

'What's all the fuss about? The rule is quite correctly drafted. If you retire early, but not because of ill-health, you get your accrued pension with a reduction for early retirement. There's no reduction for ill-health. What the rule is saying is that for the purposes of commutation you treat the pensioner as not suffering from ill-health, but as a normal early retiree with the usual reduction factor. Mike, what day of the week is it? No wonder you look bombed-out half the time. Don't worry Maud, tell the actuary to calculate the lump sum as the capital value of a normal early retirement pension. It seems quite obvious to anyone who's not a pension lawyer!'

Maud was positively purring 'Pity' she said with a laugh. 'I'd like to have stuffed a writ for negligence down old Smither's throat. But seriously is commutation the best for Tom? How can you tell anyone that he's in "exceptional circumstances of serious ill-health". It's not going to do him a lot of good, is it?'

'As ever, you are, of course, absolutely right' David gushed in his relief at Martin's words of wisdom. 'What good employers, like Waters of Wells, often do is to retain the member in service until he dies. After all, a few months' pay is no big deal. Then you can pay the lump sum death benefit. That does seem a more humane way of going about things.'

Maud, with her customary good humour restored, snapped her fingers for Gorgio. 'Champagne and canapes immediately, Gorgio. And tell Rainey to polish the Royce and take us to the clubhouse for lunch. We'll have a foursome of golf afterwards.

While we're drinking, explain to me all about this dreadful Pensions Act, which is going to take away all my powers and leave me quite naked. You did send me, Mike, a splendid plain English guide to it. I read the introduction but then it got lost. Tell me all about it.'

'Our guide was in fact written by Archie. You are, if I may say so, a teeny bit harsh on Archie, Maud' replied Mike blushing. 'He's been a good boss to both me and you, Dave.'

'Very supportive' cut in David quickly.

'And no doubt you've been very good to him' replied Maud. 'But boys, let's not spoil a lovely day. Your loyalty to the old goat, however misplaced, does you credit. But get on with the Act.'

'Well' replied Mike, 'the Act does change the balance of power from the employer to the trustees in a number of areas:

- (a) deciding on the matters to be shown in the contributions schedule, thus giving the trustees power to settle the employer's contribution rate;
- (b) preparing the statement of investment principles after "consulting" as opposed to considering the interests of, the employer;
- (c) having to have one third member-nominated trustees;
- (d) appointing advisers who will be solely responsible to the trustees;
- (e) power to refund surplus to the employer being placed in the hands of the trustees who must be satisfied that it is in the members' interests; and
- (f) requiring trustees' consent to repayment of surplus to the employer on winding up.'

'Crypto-communists, bourgeois hyenas, counter-revolutionary communist running dogs' muttered Maud, well into her second bottle of champagne. 'I don't know what the government's coming to.'

Chapter 9

Disclosure

The Disclosure Regulations

The Disclosure of Information Regulations require trustees of occupational pension schemes to disclose certain information about the scheme to the members and other people within certain time limits. The regulations do not apply to schemes with one member or to schemes which provide only death benefits. The information that has to be disclosed will seem a little daunting but it will be more digestible if it is broken down under a number of different headings.

Types of information to be disclosed

A brief outline of the requirements may be helpful. There are five basic types of information.

(1) *The constitution of the scheme*

Here the information only has to be made available—not given automatically.

(2) *Basic scheme information*

Here the information has to be given automatically.

(3) *Information for individuals*

Here the information has to be given automatically on a triggering event; for example, when a benefit becomes payable, or on a member's death, or when a member leaves. Otherwise it only has to be made available on request.

(4) *Scheme winding up*

Here the information has to be given when winding up commences, at yearly intervals after that and when the assets have been realised.

(5) *Trustees' report, accounts, auditor's report, actuarial valuation and statement and other documents*

Here, rather surprisingly, the information only has to be made available—not supplied automatically.

Money purchase schemes

In the case of money purchase schemes, annual benefit statements must be given automatically. An option statement about the member's protected rights has to be given automatically, normally at State pension age. If a contracted-out money purchase scheme ceases to be contracted-out, the members must be told automatically; and they must also be given certain information automatically about their protected rights.

The constitution of the scheme

What information has to be disclosed?

Copies of all trust deeds, rules and deeds of amendment, including the names and addresses of all participating employers.

Who is entitled to the information?

(1) Members and prospective members (people entitled to join in the future).
(2) Spouses of members and prospective members.
(3) Beneficiaries under the scheme (other than members).
(4) Recognised trade unions.

Information only has to be disclosed if it is relevant to the rights of the members concerned.

How is the information to be given?

By allowing those entitled to inspect copies free of charge within a reasonable time at a reasonable place. Copy documents must be supplied, if asked for, on payment of the actual expenses incurred in copying, posting and packing.

When is the information to be given?

The information must be disclosed within two months of the request.

Basic information about the scheme

What information has to be disclosed?
  (1) Who is eligible to join, the conditions of eligibility, whether those who are eligible to join are admitted only by application or automatically unless the person chooses not to be admitted and whether admission is subject to the employer's consent.
  (2) The period of notice, if any, which a member must give to opt out of the scheme while remaining in service and whether, and if so on what terms, an employee may rejoin the scheme.
  (3) How members' and the employers' contributions are calculated and what the AVC arrangements are.
  (4) Whether the scheme is tax approved or, if not, whether an application for this is before the Inland Revenue.
  (5) Whether any employments are contracted-out and, if so, on what basis.
  (6) The scheme's normal pension age.
  (7) What the benefits are and how they are calculated, the conditions on which they are paid and whether they are discretionary with details of the definition of pensionable earnings and the accrual rate.
  (8) What the arrangements are for pension increases.
  (9) What the arrangements are for early leavers, including estimates of cash equivalents, guaranteed cash equivalents, refunds of contributions and deferred pensions and transfers.
  (10) How transfer values are calculated and, if applicable, a statement that discretionary benefits are not taken into account in calculating transfer values.
  (11) Whether, and if so, on what basis, the trustees accept transfers in to the scheme.
  (12) A statement that the annual report is available upon request.
  (13) Whether information about the scheme has been given to the Registrar of Pension Schemes.
  (14) Details about the internal dispute resolution procedure, OPAS, the Ombudsman and OPRA.
  (15) The name and address for enquiries.

Who is entitled to the information?

  (1) Members and prospective members.

(2) Spouses of members and prospective members.

(3) Beneficiaries under the scheme (other than members).

(4) Recognised trade unions.

Information only has to be disclosed if it is relevant to the rights of the members concerned.

How is the information to be given?

Information should be given in writing. Members and beneficiaries have to be notified of any material change whenever it is practicable before it takes effect; and otherwise within three months of the change.

When is the information to be given?

The information must be given automatically to all prospective members, if practicable, before they join the scheme and if not within two months of joining. To the extent that any of this information has not previously been given to a person who was a member of the scheme on 5 April 1997, it must be given by 5 April 1998.

This information must also be given on request within two months of the request to members, prospective members, their spouses and beneficiaries and recognised trade unions.

Information for individuals—what has to be disclosed?

Benefit statements

These should include the amount of benefit, the conditions on which it is payable, the provisions for increase and death benefits.

This information must be given automatically when a benefit becomes payable or within one month afterwards. In cases of early retirement the time limit is two months. When the amount of a benefit is about to be altered, the beneficiary must be told before or within one month afterwards. Otherwise members of salary related schemes have to ask the trustees for a benefit statement if they want one, and the trustees must comply within two months. But a member cannot do this more than once a year. Even though not a legal requirement, the trustees of many salary related schemes automatically give members a benefit statement every year. Money purchase schemes must give each member an annual benefit statement automatically once a year.

Statements about death benefits and options

The following must be disclosed:
  (a) the rights and options available on the death of a member or beneficiary; and
  (b) the provisions (or a statement that there are none) under which survivors' benefits may or will be increased, and whether such increases are discretionary.

The information must be given automatically when a member or beneficiary dies, within two months after the notification of death, to anyone over 18 who has rights under the scheme, so long as the trustees know his or her address. The information must also be given on request within two months to a personal representative or someone authorised to act on behalf of the person entitled to the rights. The trustees do not have to accede to such a request more than once every three years.

Early leaver statements

The following information must be provided:
  (1) The rights and options available to an early leaver. This information must be given within two months of the member's request, but the trustees do not have to accede to such a request more than once a year. In addition, the information must be given automatically within two months after the trustees are told that his or her service is to end.
  (2) Whether any transfer value is or would be available; and if so:
    (a) an estimate of its amount;
    (b) the rights to which it relates;
    (c) whether any part is attributable to additional benefits awarded at the trustees' discretion; and
    (d) if the estimated amount is less than the statutory norm, this must be explained plus the estimated date for giving the full amount, and the member must be told of his or her right to get further estimates.

This information must be given within three months after the member's request, but the trustees do not have to accede to such a request more than once a year.

(3)   Whether a contribution refund is or would be available, and in what circumstances, with an estimate of the amount and an explanation of the method of calculation.

This information must be given within two months after the member's request, but the trustees do not have to accede to such a request more than once a year.

(4)   A statement of entitlement to a cash equivalent, with information about whether discretionary benefits are taken into account, any reduction that will be applied, the amount of the guaranteed cash equivalent and how to apply for it, information about the right to further statements of entitlement and details of any cash equivalent for money purchase benefits.

This information must be given to deferred members of salary related schemes within ten working days of the guarantee date set out in the statement.

In cases where cash equivalents do not take account of discretionary benefits, an active or deferred member must be given, within one month of his request, a copy of the actuary's report on the funding implications.

Statements about transfer credits

A member must be told if the scheme will accept a transfer payment from another scheme and, if so, the amount of the transfer credit. The information must be given within two months of the request but the trustees do not have to accede to such a request more than once a year.

When any information is given to individuals, they have to be told that further information is available, giving the address for enquiries.

Statements about bulk transfers

Where it is proposed that a bulk transfer of members' rights to another occupational pension scheme takes place without the members' consent, information about the transfer must be given one month before the transfer takes place.

Winding up the scheme

When trustees start to wind up a scheme, they must automatically and within one month inform all members and beneficiaries explaining the reasons for winding up and informing active members whether death in service benefits will continue to be payable and at least one of the trustees must be independent in cases where the employer is insolvent.

In addition, on winding up and at yearly intervals until winding up is completed, information about the action being taken to establish liabilities and recover assets will have to be provided and when it is anticipated that final details will be known. Where trustees have enough information they will have to tell members about any likely reduction in benefits.

After the assets have been realised and after they have been applied under the winding up rule, they must automatically and within three months:

(a) inform every member and beneficiary of the amount of benefit payable;

(b) if a benefit is payable periodically, the conditions on which the payment will be continued, and the provisions (if any) under which the amount payable will be altered;

(c) inform every member of the amount of his or her own benefits and of his or her survivors' benefits payable from normal pension age or later death. This requirement does not apply to money purchase benefits;

(d) inform every member and beneficiary whether, and, if so, by how much, the benefits are reduced because of insufficient resources;

(e) who will be liable to pay the benefits after winding up; and

(f) the address for enquiries about entitlement to benefits after the scheme is wound up.

Money purchase schemes

The regulations have imposed certain additional requirements for money purchase schemes.

Annual benefit statements

A member of a money purchase scheme must receive an annual benefit statement, whether or not he or she asks for it. This statement must show:

    (a) the amount of contributions credited to the member in the previous scheme year, and, if the scheme is contracted-out, how much was attributable to the contracting-out rebate and how much to any incentive payments made by the Department of Social Security and details of age-related debates;

    (b) the value of the member's protected rights and the value of the member's rights (other than protected rights); and

    (c) if the value of the member's transfer value rights payable on leaving the scheme is less than the value of the member's total rights under the scheme, the difference must be shown. This relates, for example, to an insurance policy surrender penalty.

Option statements

A member must be told of the options for his or her accrued rights under the scheme six months before normal pension age or the agreed retirement date.

The duty of disclosure does not apply in certain cases:

    (a) to any person whose benefits have been extinguished;

    (b) to any member or prospective member if the trustees have not been told about him or her; or

    (c) to a recognised trade union if the trustees have not been told about it.

Penalties

There is a specific penalty for breaches without reasonable excuse of the disclosure requirements ranging from low (maximum fine of £200 for individuals and £1,000 for companies) to medium (maximum fine of £1,000 for individuals and £10,000 for companies). The medium penalties will be payable for failing to supply:

    (a) basic scheme information; and

   (b)   information required to be made available to individual members.

Other breaches attract low penalties.

'*The Lawyer's Tale: Open Government*', which follows this chapter, explains the changes to the Disclosure Regulations.

The Lawyer's Tale: Open Government

Normally after lunch on Sunday Sir Hector Grandison, the Chief Executive of Anglo-Metals plc, went off to the conservatory to 'catch up' with the papers he didn't have time to read during the week. Chief among these was the *Weekend FT* which kept Sir Hector in touch, in a relaxed way, with the latest financial news.

Miles away from Sir Hector in his conservatory in Godalming was his PA, Bellwinch, nervously contemplating a lonely Sunday afternoon in Muswell Hill. It was a beautiful day, the tulips were out, the sun was shining and he would have loved to walk his dog on Primrose Hill. But he knew of old that Sir Hector liked to be in touch and that the peace and relaxation which Sir Hector was enjoying over the *FT* often led to what he was pleased to call his 'brainwaves'. Not content to let his ideas mature until the cold reality of Monday morning, he was wont to phone Bellwinch several times on Sundays and on occasion to demand his presence in far away Surrey.

Sir Hector, like all senior executives, although constantly bewailing the cost of the company pension scheme, was not overly keen to let his shareholders learn of the true cost of his pension, especially as his bonus—all pensionable—seemed to go up each year without any correlation to the level of the company's profits. Disclosure was not his favourite word.

The *Financial Times* that weekend had published a series of articles by so-called experts on various aspects of the new regulations coming out thick and fast under the Pensions Act. When he read that pension schemes with discretionary entry were to be opened up to public gaze, he exploded and reached for the phone.

'Bellwinch,' he began without ceremony, 'read page B6 of the *FT* and assemble our pension experts to meet me at 6 pm today to discuss this latest bombshell. I'll explain in greater detail when we meet.'

Bellwinch knew better than to argue with his master. The chances of locating their pensions consultant, David or the scheme's lawyer, Mike, on a Sunday afternoon were remote. Needless to say they were both out doing sensible things, like playing golf in David's case, and in Mike's being proud father with his new baby in Greenwich Park. Colin Bell, the scheme's actuary, had gone to Brussels on Eurostar for a gastronomic weekend. Luckily Sir Hector forgot the subject in the excitement of other items in the paper. All in all Bellwinch escaped with three more calls and no further mention of the dreaded subject of disclosure.

On Monday morning Bellwinch quickly convened a meeting of the three experts at the Anglo-Metals offices in Colindale so that they could be on hand to address Sir Hector if required. And so at 3 pm he asked Colin to explain the workings of the Anglo-Metals Supplementary Scheme.

'Well' started Colin, 'the Supplementary Scheme is a top up scheme which:

(a) has an accrual rate of 30ths;
(b) treats all PAYE earnings and benefits in kind as pensionable;
(c) provides index-linked pensions; and
(d) has a 2/3rds spouse's pension.

Entry is restricted to those invited by the Board, which in practice means Sir Hector. Plus, needless to say, it's non-contributory. Do you want me to look up the company contribution?'

'No no' said Bellwinch, blanching nervously. 'That won't be necessary.' The mere suggestion set his indigestion pains going like red hot needles in his stomach.

'Well, what's the problem?' asked Mike sitting back in all innocence. 'It's presumably restricted to senior executives or whatever. The benefits are not relevant to anyone else. If you want me to be boring, the Disclosure Regulations say that:

"where different information is applicable to different members, prospective members and beneficiaries, nothing ... shall be construed as requiring the trustees to disclose information in relation to a member that is not relevant to his rights under the scheme."'

'So' butted in Colin 'you needn't tell the poor and huddled masses outside on the factory floor about Sir Hector's and your ill-gotten gains.'

Bellwinch flinched with indigestion and disgust.

David, as ever the charmer, poured oil on troubled waters.

'It's not that simple, Mike. In theory the scheme is open to all—by invitation; it's certainly not restricted by categories of employment. For example, Sir Hector's chauffeur and personal secretary are both members but Mr Bellwinch is not.'

'That is so' agreed Bellwinch. 'But that's because, in my case, I'm a 'Johnny come lately' in Sir Hector's eyes. I've only been his PA for 10 years. Whereas Percy, his chauffeur, was his batman throughout the war and Miss Blenkinsop started as his secretary in 1946.'

'I see the problem now' said Mike thoughtfully. 'The new regulations require automatic disclosure as part of the basic information about the scheme about whether "persons who are eligible to be members of the scheme are admitted to it subject to the consent of their employer". It used to require disclosure only about whether admission was automatic or optional. It's now been expanded to cover discretionary entry.'

'Yes, yes' interrupted Colin 'but you've only got to give basic scheme information 'as of course' (even an actuary can parrot the regulations) to members within 13 weeks of joining.'

Mike looked at Colin with his cat-like smile: 'If you're going to quote the law, actuary man, you'd better get it right. Now you will have to give the basic information

"as of course, where practicable, to every prospective member and where it has not been practicable to do so, such information has to be given within two months of joining the scheme."

A prospective member, by the way, means:

"any person who, under the terms of his contract of service and the scheme rules ... may be admitted subject to the consent of his employer."

You'd best check the contracts of employment to see what they say about pension schemes but from what you say, Mr Bellwinch, it looks like everybody working for Anglo-Metals is a prospective member. And its hard to see why it would not be practicable to give everybody information about the Supplementary Scheme.'

'But this is terrible' groaned Bellwinch. 'Sir Hector will hit the roof.'

'Well, what did the expert in the *FT* advise?' asked David with a soothing smile.

'He didn't, that's the point. They never do, do they? They're too busy racking up fees. The article just said the point should not be overlooked. Don't forget that Sir Hector likes advisers who provide solutions, not difficulties' Bellwinch concluded menacingly.

'Well' replied David, with another of his disarming smiles, 'It's all quite simple really. You just change the eligibility rule to employees of a specified category who are invited to join by the Board.'

'And how are you going to define the specified category, you grinning jackass; that's the rub' cried Colin.

'Oh, that's quite simple too' said David. 'Something on the lines of:

"Entry shall be restricted to senior employees who are invited by the Board to join the scheme. For this purpose a senior employee is an employee who is classified as such by the Chief Executive of the Principal Employer by reference to seniority of service or seniority of status and the decision of the Chief Executive shall be conclusive and binding"'

At this point Sir Hector strode into the room. Bellwinch reminded him of the problem. Instead of explaining that he couldn't get hold of their advisers on Sunday, he improvised boldly and said that notwithstanding the urgency of the problem, Sir Hector had forbidden unnecessary meetings with professional advisers except during normal working hours. He had found by long experience that if he attributed his own decisions to Sir Hector, they were rarely disavowed.

Bellwinch let David, an old favourite of Sir Hector's, do the talking.

'Capital, capital, put it in hand immediately. While you're all here, are there any other nasties in the new rules that these socialist johnnies are festooning us in?' asked Sir Hector.

Colin, David and Mike all looked at their feet, not expecting this. Luckily Mike had brought the regulations with him. Fishing them out of his briefcase and improvising wildly, he started 'Apart from the new item about discretionary entry, you'll have to give as part of basic scheme information the following new details:

  (a) AVC arrangements (right up your street, Colin);
  (b) the definition of pensionable earnings;
  (c) the accrual rate;
  (d) a statement that the annual report is available on request;
  (e) how transfer values are calculated;
  (f) the internal dispute resolution procedure; and
  (g) the jurisdiction of OPRA.

But you won't have to give details of discretionary pension increases in the past 10 years any longer. That at least is a relief. And don't forget that this time round trustees who don't comply with the new rules are liable to what the DSS quaintly classify as 'medium' penalties—£1,000 for individuals and £10,000 for a company. You wouldn't want that would you, Sir Hector?'

However it was too late. Sir Hector's attention span was on to pastures new. Between intervals during a conference call to New York, he was ordering Bellwinch to get his Concorde tickets for tomorrow, while waving farewell to the advisers.

When they emerged into the spring sunshine outside, all three collapsed with laughter by way of reaction to the strain of Sir Hector.

'By the way who was the so-called expert who wrote the *FT* article?' asked Mike.

'Need you ask?' said David. 'It was Archie Smithers, your boss, Mike.'

'But he's gaga now. They oughtn't to let him loose stirring up trouble like this' said Colin with profound disbelief.

'Well, it keeps him out of our hair and look at all the fees he's generated for us today. Besides if he gave the answers in his articles, that would never do, now would it?' replied Mike.

'But what's this I hear about your new job, Colin? I hear you're going to become a client instead of an adviser. Is that right?'

'How did you know?' asked Colin in surprise. 'It's still secret, but so long as you keep it under your hat, yes, I'm going to be the new Pensions Director at the People's Bank. I've still got a few loose ends to sort out but by the end of the month I'll no longer be a consulting actuary. I'll be a client instead!'

'Ooh' murmured Mike, 'you'll need a new pension lawyer and a nice friendly pensions consultant, won't you?'

'Down, Fido, down' grinned Colin. 'My first job is to get to grips with the Bank's overseas pension arrangements. It's got businesses in the States, Hong Kong and South Africa. For starters, I'm off to Chicago and New York for a month and then to Cape Town. I'll look out for you in the First Class Lounge. When I get back I'll be doing a review of the UK advisers. You don't need me to remind you that professional advisers should be appointed by the trustees, not by the Director of Pensions.'

'But you'll put a word in for us, won't you?' asked Mike.

'Too right, I will. I'll tell them that no one in their right minds would appoint you two. You know what my speaker's profile says— "Pet hates; cats, children and especially pension lawyers." Luckily the authors of the Pensions Act seem to agree that pension lawyers, unlike the actuary and auditor, are an unnecessary luxury.'

Chapter 10

Accounts and Trustees' Reports

Audited accounts

Audited accounts must be prepared for each scheme year within seven months of the end of the scheme year which ends after 6 April 1997. An auditor must be qualified and cannot be:
    (a)   a member of the scheme;
    (b)   employed by the trustees;
    (c)   an employer in relation to the scheme; or
    (d)   ineligible to audit the employer's accounts.

What the accounts must contain

    (1)   An account of the financial additions to, and withdrawals from, the fund during the scheme year.
    (2)   A statement of the assets at market value (or the trustees' estimate where the market value is not easily come by) and the liabilities of the scheme (other than liabilities to pay benefits after the end of the scheme year). If the value of any assets is estimated, the reason why must be given. The asset statement must show the distribution of investments between each of the following categories:
        (a)   insurance policies;
        (b)   public sector fixed interest investments;
        (c)   other fixed interest investments;
        (d)   index-linked securities;
        (e)   equities;
        (f)   property;

(g) property unit trusts;
(h) other unit trusts;
(i) property managed funds;
(j) other managed funds;
(k) loans;
(l) cash deposits; and
(m) other investments.

Each category must show UK and overseas investments separately and must state, in the case of unit trusts and managed funds, whether the managers are UK registered or not.

(3) A reconciliation of the income and expenditure account with the statement of assets and liabilities.
(4) In the case of non-sterling assets or liabilities, the sterling equivalent with the basis of conversion.
(5) Details of any investment comprising more than 5 per cent of the scheme's assets.
(6) Details of the scheme's assets invested in employer-related investments, and where that exceeds 5 per cent, the steps being taken to reduce it to 5 per cent.
(7) For every amount shown in the accounts, a statement of the corresponding amount for the previous year.
(8) The total of purchases and sales of investments in the scheme year.
(9) A statement about whether the accounts have been prepared in accordance with the current Statement of Recommended Practice Pension Scheme Accounts with details of any significant departures.

True and fair view

The accounts must also show a true and fair view of the financial transactions of the scheme and of the disposition of the assets and liabilities. Liabilities to pay benefits after the end of the scheme year do not have to be included. The accounts must also contain the auditor's report.

The auditor's report

The auditor's report must say:
(1) whether or not the statutory requirements are satisfied;

(2) whether or not contributions have been paid in accordance with the schedule of contributions or payment schedule; and

(3) if either or both of these statements are negative or qualified, the reasons why.

Trustees who fail to obtain audited accounts without a reasonable excuse will be guilty of a criminal offence and liable to fines of up to £5,000.

Actuarial valuation and statement

What they must contain

The trustees have to obtain an actuarial valuation of the scheme's assets in relation to its liabilities. This must:

(a) enable the expected future course of the contribution rates and funding level to be understood;

(b) state whether it has been prepared in accordance with current professional guidelines; and

(c) indicate whether there are any significant departures from these guidelines.

An actuarial valuation is not required for public sector schemes, unfunded schemes, money purchase schemes and overseas schemes.

Time limits

The first valuation has to be made within three years from the scheme's start date.

Subsequent valuations must not be later than three years from the previous one.

Valuations must be obtained within one year of the effective date of the valuation and must be available for inspection within two months of a request.

The actuarial statement

Each valuation must be accompanied by a statement describing:

(a) the effective date of valuation;

(b) the security of accrued rights—whether the assets fully cover the liabilities;

(c) if less than 100 per cent, the measures to be taken to bring these to 100 per cent and the expected date of achievement;

(d) the security of prospective rights—whether the scheme resources are likely to meet in full liabilities as they fall due; and

(e) a summary of the methods and assumptions used.

The trustees' report

The annual trustees' report has to contain:

(1) The latest audited accounts and auditor's statement.

(2) Details of whether the accounts have been prepared and audited in accordance with legal requirements.

(3) If the auditor's statement is negative or qualified, the reason why and when it is likely to be resolved.

(4) The latest actuarial statement including the actuary's MFR statement, if required.

(5) The names of the trustees or directors of the trustee company.

(6) The provisions for appointing and removing trustees.

(7) The names of the actuaries, auditors, solicitors, banks, custodians and other persons retained by the trustees with details of any changes since the previous year.

(8) The address for enquiries about the scheme or benefits.

(9) The number of members and beneficiaries at any one date during the year.

(10) The percentage increases made during the year to pensions and deferred pensions, with a statement about whether the increases were discretionary, and, if so, to what extent. If there have been different increases for different individuals or groups, the maximum, minimum and average percentage increases must be given.

(11) A statement about whether any transfer values paid during the year were calculated in the prescribed way, whether they were less than the statutory norm, and, if so, why, and when full values are likely to be available.

(12) Whether discretionary benefits are included in the calculation of transfer values and, if so, the method of assessing their value.

(13) If the auditor's statement shows any discrepancy about contributions, the reasons must be given and when it is likely

to be resolved.

(14) If any such discrepancy was left unresolved in a previous year, how it is likely to be resolved.

(15) A review by the trustees of the financial development of the scheme during the year and its financial prospects.

(16) Who has managed the investments and the extent of any delegation of investment management.

(17) Whether the trustees have prepared a statement of investment principles and, if so, that a copy is available on request.

(18) The trustees' policy on custodianship.

(19) An investment report containing:
  (a) a statement about whether the investments are in line with the statement of investment principles and, if not, why not and when it will be put right;
  (b) a review of investment performance during the year and also for a longer period of between three to five years.

(20) The scheme's auditor's or actuary's resignation statement. Where an auditor or actuary resigns or is removed, he or she must state whether there are any circumstances connected with his or her resignation or removal significantly affecting members' interests, or that he or she knows of no such circumstances.

(21) The percentage of the scheme's resources invested in employer-related investments, and if that exceeds 5 per cent, the percentage of the scheme's resources which are lawfully retained employer-related investments, and if any of the scheme's resources are invested in contravention of the self-investment regulations, the steps being taken to secure compliance.

The trustees' report must be prepared within seven months of the end of the scheme year.

Availability of audited accounts, actuarial valuations, statements, trustees' reports etc

Who is entitled to the information?

The following are entitled to the information:

(a) members and prospective members (people entitled to join in the future) and their spouses;
(b) beneficiaries; and
(c) recognised trade unions with members in the scheme.

How is the information to be given?

The information is given by allowing those entitled on request to inspect copies free of charge within a reasonable time at a reasonable place. Copies of the latest document must be supplied, if requested, within two months. The trustees can make a charge not exceeding the cost of copying, post and packing, except in the case of their report which must be provided free of charge. When any of these documents are supplied, there must be a written statement that further information about the scheme is available, giving the address for enquiries.

The documents which the trustees must make available are the latest actuarial and MFR valuations, the schedule of contributions or payment schedule and the latest statement of investment principles, as well as the trustees' report, audited accounts and auditor's statement.

Readers are referred to 'The Lawyer's Tale: The Duty to Tell', which follows this chapter, for an illustration of how certain disclosure problems can be resolved.

The Lawyer's Tale: The Duty To Tell

Maurice Meredith, a fussy little man with a bow tie, was the company secretary at Anglo-Consolidated Investments in the City. It was a smallish investment management house with about 30 employees and a good final salary pension scheme. He had spent an enjoyable Saturday morning reading the *Financial Times* as was his routine. He explained to his wife that it was a necessary part of his work and that he must never be disturbed unless, of course, the chairman rang. Mrs Meredith guessed the truth—that it was all an elaborate charade designed to avoid his having to go shopping with her.

This particular Saturday Meredith got a shock. He had read an article on the disclosure regulations. They would force pension trustees to reveal all sorts of things that in a well regulated company remained hidden from public gaze. The author was saying that copies of all the trust deeds and rules had to be given on request to members and that if a scheme provided different benefits for different classes of employees, that would now be brought out into the open. Alternatively there would have to be a separate scheme set up for the members with different benefits. It was this that had given him such a shock.

Anglo-Consolidated's pension scheme was with the Magnificent Mutual and was one of the jewels in its crown. There were not all that many members but they were all highly paid, and the total contributions each year were astronomical. There was the usual benefit structure that one would expect from a good scheme, but in the case of one or two members, better benefits had been promised. The favoured few, namely the chairman and a couple of directors, got an accrual rate of 30ths instead of 60ths, four times (instead of twice) salary lump sum death benefits and two-thirds, instead of one-half widow's pensions. Recently Meredith had been elevated to the category of senior executive. He knew how strongly the chairman felt about the confidentiality of the arrangements and how upset he would be if they came out.

Meredith's pleasant Saturday routine therefore received a very unpleasant jolt. He immediately telephoned the chairman, Sir Lancelot Chrimes. Sir Lancelot had a very simplistic view of life, which probably explained why he had made so much money in the City. He listened tolerantly to Meredith's prediction of trouble and said 'Look here, Meredith, you and I don't waste our time on worries like that. There is always a way round these problems. Get on to the lawyers on Monday and tell them to come up with a solution.'

Meredith sighed. Anglo-Consolidated's lawyers, Sue, Grabbit and Run, were a small City firm. They were good commercial lawyers but knew nothing about pensions. This was one of the attractions of the Magnificent Mutual so far as Meredith was concerned. Pensions were their business. John Watson, the pensions superintendent, who looked after the Anglo-Consolidated scheme, was calm, competent and capable. In his care the scheme ran like clockwork. Meredith knew from bitter experience, as did Watson, what a meal the lawyers had made of the draft trust deed and rules which the Magnificent Mutual had produced for the scheme. Meredith would rather have consulted John Watson about the problem. But when Sir Lancelot spoke, he expected his orders to be carried out.

Meredith duly rang the lawyers on Monday morning and explained the problem. The partner admitted that he was not *au fait* with the regulations but would look into the matter. Meredith correctly surmised that he had never even heard of them; he often thought they got far better value from their subscription to the *Financial Times* than from the vast fees they paid to their lawyers.

A week later Sir Lancelot asked for a progress report. Nothing had happened reported Meredith. He was promptly told to chase the lawyers. Emboldened by this Meredith asked if he might consult John Watson about the problem. After all, pensions were his business.

'Capital idea,' said Sir Lancelot. 'Why didn't you do it before? We get their advice for nothing. You can't expect me to have to tell you everything. I have the responsibility for running the company—details are for you, Meredith.'

This was a typical stroke of Sir Lancelot's genius for latching on to other people's ideas and promptly claiming them as his own. So Meredith phoned John Watson and asked him to come and see him to advise on how to get out of the difficulty.

John of course knew all about the disclosure regulations. Archibald Smithers, the Magnificent Mutual's in-house lawyer, had provided the superintendents with a comprehensive briefing on the subject. Smithers had recently taken a grip on himself after his recent shortcomings, bought a new suit, got his hair cut and received old Murgatroyd's permission to hire an assistant.

The assistant was a clean-cut fresh faced young man called David. He had gently and tactfully reorganised Smithers, taking over much of his documentation work, thus leaving him free to get up to date and give the advisory service to the superintendents which he had so signally neglected.

John sought out Smithers to consult him about the problem. He found him with Larry Robinson, the Magnificent Mutual's brash new business manager. Even the born-again Smithers looked dowdy and down at heel compared with Larry with his animal vitality bursting forth in his fashionable light grey suit and black suede shoes. This was all part of Larry's new youthful go-go image. Luckily, Larry was just leaving and so John was relieved that he would not have to pour oil on the usually stormy waters of the relationship between the two men.

Smithers immediately asked John how these additional benefits in the Anglo-Consolidated scheme were granted—was it by individual letters or were they spelt out in the booklet and in the rules.

'Oh no,' said John, 'there are so few involved that we just prepare individual benefit letters for signature by the trustees.'

'That's all right then' said Smithers. 'It's only booklets, trust deeds and rules that have to be available to all members, their spouses, other beneficiaries and trade unions. Not individual letters like these, because they don't affect the members generally. You won't, therefore, have the hassle of setting up a new scheme for the senior executives.'

'What a relief that will be for Meredith,' said John. 'While I'm here, can you bone me up on any other features of the regulations that I should be telling him about.'

'Certainly,' said Smithers, 'but wouldn't you like me to come along with you to the meeting?'

'No, no,' said John a little too quickly. 'That won't be necessary.'

Why was there such a reluctance, thought Smithers huffily, to let docs people, as they were called in the industry, come out of their closets? He didn't after all have two heads. Docs people were expected to be neither seen nor heard—one worse than small children. Oh well, Smithers sighed, here goes.

'We have already discussed the requirement to disclose the constitution of the scheme, the trust deeds and rules and any amending deeds. The law also requires basic information about the scheme to be given automatically to members, beneficiaries and trade unions. This is more or less the old Revenue requirement of communicating the essential features of a scheme and is usually done through a scheme booklet. However beneficiaries, such as spouses, and trade unions now have a legal right to the information.

'Probably the commonest item of information not normally in a booklet is the requirement to state whether there is power to increase pensions and whether it is discretionary.'

'Some employers are not going to like that, Archie' said John.

'Well, there it is' said Archie. 'That is what the regulations say.' They then went through the requirements about individual benefit statements and the trustees' report and its accompanying audited accounts and auditor's and actuarial statements.

A few days later John Watson presented himself at the offices of the Anglo-Consolidated. He sat down with Meredith and gave him the good news about the senior executives' benefits. For good measure he relayed the advice given to him by Smithers about the other requirements.

He explained that the trustees' annual report had got to contain:

(a) the names of the trustees and the rules for appointing and removing them;

(b) names of the actuaries, auditors, solicitors, custodians and bankers (there was a nice free plug for the professionals, thought Meredith);

(c) the numbers of members; and

(d) the percentage increases made to pensions and deferred pensions, whether they were discretionary; and if there had been different increases for different individuals or groups, the maximum, minimum and average increases must be given.

At that point, Meredith, whose eyes had been beginning to glaze over, sat up and said 'We will have to watch that one carefully when Sir Lancelot retires ...'.

'You won't get out of that quite so easily as you have with your senior executives' letters,' said John. 'Some schemes will either have to change their ways or publish what they have done.'

Meredith blanched but recognised that that problem was not for this year.

John concluded: 'The report will also have to include:

(a) a financial review of the year;

(b) details of the investment managers; and

(c) an investment report including performance.'

'That could be embarrassing if we don't perform well,' said Meredith.

The Magnificent Mutual had been forced to delegate investment management to the Anglo-Consolidated as the price for getting the scheme.

'Curiously enough,' said John, 'although Parliament requires all this information to be published for members, it only has to be available. In other words it does not have to be sent out to the members. But the trustees do have to include a statement in the scheme booklet that the annual report is available on request.'

During this recital the office clock had ticked on to the magic hour of 12.30 pm. 'If you've finished,' said Meredith courteously, 'will you be good enough to meet Sir Lancelot for a pre-lunch drink and then have lunch with me in the directors' dining room? I am sure Sir Lancelot will be delighted to hear your advice.'

A few minutes later John had in his hand one of the traditional City pint-sized gin and tonics and was telling the good news to the chairman. 'Capital, capital' he said. 'Horses for courses, Meredith. No use going to Sue, Grabbit and Run about a thing like this. Lawyers don't know about pensions. Told you to consult young Watson in the first place.'

Meredith knew his chairman well enough to take this for the compliment it was meant to be. But honest John Watson began to go red.

'I have taken the advice of our own lawyer about this. He is an expert in the field. Indeed he is a member of the Association of Pension Lawyers. Pensions law is very specialised and it would be unwise to consult a lawyer who didn't have an intimate knowledge of the subject.'

'Quite right. As I said, horses for courses. You don't go to a butcher to cut out your appendix. Your candour does you credit, young man. And now, if you will excuse me, I must be off to lunch with our brokers. Look after our visitor well, Meredith.'

The moral, John mused later that day, was that Smithers was right. Trustees and employers would have to have more of an eye on the audience. They would have to be careful about discretionary benefits. But if all this expensively produced information just ended up in the bin, like so many company reports, what was the point of it all? John instinctively grasped this. His conclusion was that while yet another load of bumph was going to have to be produced by the hard-pressed pension administrators, it was unlikely that the members would be much better off as a result.

Chapter 11

Equal Treatment

The background

Article 119 of the Treaty of Rome requires each Member State to ensure that men and women should receive equal pay for equal work. Pay means

'the ordinary basic or minimum wage or salary and any other consideration, whether in cash or kind, which the worker receives, directly or indirectly, in respect of his employment with his employer'.

If pension benefits from company pension schemes count as 'pay' within Art 119, then schemes which have different pension ages for men and women will be in breach. Since 1940 the UK has had different State pension ages for men and women—65 and 60 respectively. Occupational pension schemes have tended to follow suit and dovetail their benefits in line with the State scheme to avoid duplication.

After a number of years of uncertainty, the European Court of Justice in *Barber v Guardian Royal Exchange* on 17 May 1990, laid down in clear and unambiguous terms for the first time that pension benefits from occupational (but not State) schemes counted as pay.

It took a further ten cases, culminating in the *Coloroll* case, before the European Court of Justice clarified most (but not all) of the problems arising out of the *Barber* judgment.

The Pensions Act equalises State pension age for men and women at age 65 progressively over ten years from 2010.

The impact of the *Barber* case

The implications of this historic decision are far reaching. Pension schemes which had been funded on the assumption that men will be entitled to pensions later than women faced a big bill to guarantee that all members had the same pension rights. The financial effects were potentially so serious that the court made a rare exception from its normal practice and said that its decision would not be retrospective.

The decision applies throughout the European Community but does not affect the State pension scheme or personal pension schemes.

The Pensions Act and the Equal Treatment Regulations give effect to the detailed requirements of European law as laid down by the European Court of Justice.

Equal treatment rule

All occupational schemes will be treated as if they have an equal treatment rule relating to the terms for eligibility and treatment of members. Where a member is employed on similar work to or work of equal value as a member of the other sex, any of the terms treating such a member less favourably will be treated as modified to remove the inequality. The equal treatment rule will not apply if the trustees (not the employer) can prove that the difference is due to a factor which is not sex-related, but is a material difference between the man's case and the woman's case. The equal treatment rule so far as it relates to treatment of members, as opposed to eligibility, applies only to pensionable service since 17 May 1990 (the date of the *Barber* judgment).

Permitted exceptions

The equal treatment rules do not apply where men and women receive different amounts of pension because of differences in State pensions ie bridging pensions, but not GMPs. The government has said that it will not issue regulations legalising differences in benefits caused by the sex-based rules for the calculation of GMPs. Although this would have solved the problem of GMPs between 1990 and 1997, it is the government's view that this would contravene Community law.

Sex-based actuarial factors

The equal treatment rule does not ban the use of sex-based actuarial factors for the calculation of employer contributions or benefits in certain circumstances. This will permit sex-based actuarial factors to be used in calculating benefits in money purchase schemes and optional benefits, eg transfer values, in final salary schemes.

The Equal Treatment Regulations

Introduction

These regulations set out the requirements both for equal access to pension schemes by men and women and for equal treatment of members once they have been admitted. The regulations permit certain exceptions to the equal treatment principle which the European Court of Justice has ruled are not contrary to Art 119 of the Treaty of Rome. Claims made before 31 May 1995 are not affected by the regulations. Some key issues for those claims were dealt with by the Employment Appeal Tribunal in a test case. This decided that the Equal Pay Act time limits of six months and two years' back service apply to claims made before 31 May 1995. This ruling is being appealed.

Time limit

The regulations import from the Equal Pay Act a time limit of six months from leaving employment or, if earlier, when the discrimination ceased for bringing proceedings to a court or an industrial tribunal. The time limit will not therefore apply where the discrimination is still continuing eg where the employee is still in the relevant employment.

The extent of the claim

The regulations preclude a claim for damages for breach of the equal treatment rule and provide instead that the claimant may be given retrospective access to the scheme for up to two years before the claim. If retrospective access is granted, then the employer must provide the necessary resources. The regulations draw a distinction between claims made before and claims made after 31 May 1995. For part-timer claims made before 31 May 1995 it seems that the employee will have to pay the arrears of his contributions as the price of getting past membership. Where the breach of the equal treatment rule was by reference to discrimination on account of age or length of service, the employer has to provide all the cost of retrospective membership. For claims made after 31 May 1995 the employer has to pay all the cost. Where the claim relates to unequal treatment of a member rather than a denial of access to the scheme, the tribunal may declare that the member's rights can be retrospective as far back as 17 May 1990, not just the previous two years as in access claims. And the employer again has to pay all the cost.

The Pensions Ombudsman

The regulations do not curtail the Pensions Ombudsman's jurisdiction. He can still in appropriate cases deal with claims from part-timers, not previously referred to a court or industrial tribunal, where their exclusion amounts to injustice resulting from maladministration or there is a dispute of law. Such cases are subject to a three year time limit, which also covers the maximum award of back service.

Maternity and family leave

The Pension Schemes Act 1993 contains the unfair maternity provisions which require a woman to continue to accrue pension benefits during maternity leave. The woman has to pay contributions by reference to her statutory maternity pay or her contractual pay, although for the purpose of assessing benefits, she is assumed to have received the normal pay for the job. Maternity leave covers absence due to pregnancy for which she receives either contractual or statutory maternity pay.

Unfair family leave provisions are also outlawed. This means that if a member is entitled to paid family leave, for example paternity leave, under his contract of employment, the period must be treated as pensionable. In this case benefits are assessed by reference to actual pay, not the normal pay for the job as with maternity leave.

For further details of the problems caused by the *Barber* decision see *'The Lawyer's Tale: 'The End is Nigh'* which follows this chapter.

The Lawyer's Tale: The End is Nigh

Archie had just returned to work on Monday morning after speaking at the Law Council of Australia Superannuation Conference in Sydney. Admittedly he had added on a couple of weeks holiday in Tasmania and Kangaroo Island. But the delights of foreign travel had abruptly given way to jetlag and the sinking feeling familiar to all who face a mountain of work after a holiday.

Conscious of this, Mike nervously reminded him of a meeting fixed for that afternoon with a new client—Professional Concerns.

'I'll sit in with you; I've prepared a note. I know's what it's all about but they're new clients and they want to see you.'

Luckily for Mike, Archie's phone rang and Mike, catlike in his ability to avoid trouble, sidled back to his desk.

And so at 2.30 pm Archie and Mike met their new clients along with their actuary and consultant. A more unlikely pair could scarcely be imagined. Tubby King, the proprietor of Professional Concerns, was unkempt with long, dirty locks of hair, a suit that bore evidence of the detritus of many previous meals and whose waistcoat left visible an embarrassingly large beer gut. His son, Lee, by contrast had blonde wavy hair and was tall and slim. But Lee at least wore a smart double-breasted check suit, even though this was rather spoilt by his white socks and grey slip-on shoes.

'We're in a spot of trouble, Mr Smithers' began Tubby. 'We run a business called Professional Concerns in Southend which acts as independent trustee of pension schemes where the employer has gone bust. Me and Lee have always been involved in the insolvency trade and so we know all the insolvency practitioners around Southend. They give us the small schemes which the big boys won't touch— anything up to about £5 million. The money's good. As long as there's a surplus, back it goes to the creditors, so everyone's happy.'

'Apart from the members, I guess' interrupted Mike, but Tubby went on unheeding 'We brought along with us Colin Bell, the actuary to the scheme and your old mate, Dave, who is the consultant.'

Colin and David grinned at Archie and Mike. Archie scowled and said icily 'Kindly state your problem, Mr King.'

'Don't take the hump, Mr S' smiled Tubby disarmingly. 'I'll get there in my own good time. You see, it's your advice we want. Your boy offered to help while you were away, but, like my Lee, he's still a bit wet behind the ears. We wanted the advice of the maestro. We've heard you on radio and TV; nothing less would do.'

No wonder Tubby was successful, Mike mused; he lays it on with a trowel. Archie visibly melted.

'Let me explain' said Mike. 'They've been advised by their local lawyer in Southend that they can't buy out benefits without applying to the court for directions. Although *Coloroll* clarifies some of the uncertainties, there are still unresolved problems about:

(a) whether Art 119 overrides the scheme's trust deed and rules;

(b) transfers in and out of the scheme for post 1990 service;

(c) the treatment of GMPs; and

(d) part-timers who might have been wrongly refused membership.'

'Our problem' broke in Tubby, 'is that we don't actually charge fees. We get commission from the insurance company when we buy out the benefits, and a percentage on whatever goes back to the creditors. Going to court is bad news. It takes time and depletes the assets and our commission. Lee, I told you not to go to that old fool in the High Street. He doesn't know what day of the week it is.'

Mike slipped into gear quickly. 'If you agree, Archie, I'll just circulate a memorandum of our advice and run through it. I expect you'll want to sign it off at the end.

First, does Art 119 override the rules? If you read paras 27 to 29 of the *Coloroll* judgment, they fudge the issue. You can interpret them either way. I'm dead against parsing the judgments of the European Court like a nit-picking Chancery hack. They're broad statements of principle. In a nutshell it seems to me and Archie that the terms of the *Coloroll* and *Avdel* judgments on levelling up are so clear that trustees should either treat Art 119 as overriding inconsistent scheme rules or, alternatively, that they are so clear as to render an application for directions an unnecessary waste of time and the members' money.'

'Eh, lad' cried Colin. 'You can't play fast and loose with the rules like that. If you level up the men's benefits, you're altering the order of priority on winding up. If the scheme's in deficit, you're robbing Petra to pay Paul. It might even have the effect of reducing the women's GMPs. What do a lot of smelly garlic eaters know about all this?'

'That's rubbish, isn't it, Archie?' replied Mike. 'Levelling up alters the liabilities; the winding up rule then applies to those altered liabilities. Plus the Pensions Act allows trustees to amend their rules retrospectively by resolution without getting consent from the employer where that's difficult to get. The Act also makes equal treatment overriding in any event.'

'Just so' said Archie smoothly. 'Next question.'

'Let's take transfers in, first' replied Mike. 'Paragraph 99 of the *Coloroll* judgment rules that the receiving scheme is obliged to increase the benefits secured by the transfer payment to make up for any inequality in the old scheme so far as post-17 May 1990 benefits are concerned. Since trustees have to do everything in their power to ensure that the principle of equality is observed, they will have to recalculate the men's benefits in these circumstances.'

'But' said David, 'that's only for bulk transfers and we haven't had any in this scheme. Plus you can always go back to the old scheme for more money.'

'Not so' replied Mike. 'There's nothing in para 99 to limit the ruling to bulk transfers. And while in theory you can force the old scheme to cough up, it may be difficult in practice. I suppose the member could claim but only if he's suffered loss.'

'I agree' said Archie. 'What about transfers out?'

'Well' Mike continued, 'for transfers you've already made, its tough on the new scheme. I think that in practice we needn't revisit transfers already made, because the transferring scheme may well be wound up before a claim could be made. But I do think that any transfers you make in the future must reflect the principle of equality.'

'Quite so' Archie crooned in a jet lagged state. 'What about GMPs?'

'People, especially actuaries, Colin, really get their knickers in a twist about GMPs. It's all quite simple. You just contract back into SERPS by paying state scheme premiums. Responsibility for the GMP component of benefits would then lie with the State. Of course you can't do this after April 1997. The residual benefits would then have to be equalised for post-Barber service. What's the problem?'

'I like this. The boy makes sense. He's got an answer to our problems, not like that old fool in Southend who has a difficulty for every solution' said Tubby with a smile.

'Well Archie, I'm sure they'll want to hear from the master about part-timers' said Mike with a grin.

Not a whit abashed Archie replied:

'I don't think I can quite match your elegance of language, Mike but my knickers are quite unfazed by part-timers.'

'He should know all about part-timers' interjected Colin. 'He's the biggest part-timer there's ever been.'

Archie continued disregarding Colin, 'I can't of course disguise from you that the European Court's rulings on part-timers were a blow and do cause problems for trustees. Nevertheless one has to keep a sense of proportion.

(1) First my view is that while trustees should make enquiries of the employer about part-timers, they don't have to be pro-active and seek out all part-timers and tell them of their potential claims.

(2) Second, a combination of national time limits and objective justification may defeat such claims. Claims by part-timers would be subject to a six month time limit from the date of leaving with a maximum award of two years' compensation.

(3) Last, the trustees should be able to rely on the missing beneficiary notices under s 27 of the Trustee Act. That protects the trustees from people who pop out of the woodwork when all the assets have gone. I would suggest that you expand the notice to refer specifically to claims from part-timers.

There is an element of risk. But that's what you get paid for, isn't it. After all, if you act in accordance with professional advice and have acted honestly and reasonably, you'll get relief from the court under s 61 of the Trustee Act.'

'We really are most grateful, Mr Smithers. You've taken a weight off our minds' beamed Tubby. 'Lee, get the chauffeur to bring the Jag to the door. We parked it downstairs.'

'You never know, Archie, it could have been parked next door to your Jag and the two of them could have had a nice chat about *Color-oll* too' said Mike.

When Tubby and Lee had gone, Colin burst out:

'There's no justice in this world, you old goat. You fooled the tax payers into funding a test case to clarify *Barber*. The result is that we've now got more problems than before and you're still raking it in. If only you'd been put down years ago, we'd never have had all this fuss and bother; the world would be a better place.'

'Did you see their gold bracelets and fake Rolexes, Archie? They positively gleamed' said David. 'Those two really put you in the shade. Don't you think you need some gold bangles and an earring or two?'

But Archie, with Mike tagging behind, was already on his way to the next meeting.

Chapter 12

Preservation and Transfers

Preserved benefits

Refund of contributions

A member who leaves a pension scheme with less than two years' qualifying service is usually only entitled to a refund of his or her own contributions; and even this right does not arise unless conferred by scheme rules. Tax at 20 per cent is deducted by the trustees together with the member's share of the contributions equivalent premium, which is payable if the scheme is contracted-out. This premium represents the cost of buying the member back into SERPS.

Preserved pension

After two years' qualifying service a member must receive a preserved pension. A member must also receive a preserved pension if the scheme accepted a transfer value from a personal pension previously taken out by the member. This preserved pension is based on pay and service at the date of leaving and is payable at the scheme's normal retirement date. In a money purchase scheme the member's preserved pension is based on the amount standing to his or her credit in the scheme at the date of leaving.

Qualifying service

Qualifying service is pensionable service under the rules of the scheme plus the actual period of service in a previous scheme from which a transfer payment has been made to the present scheme. Qualifying service also includes pensionable waiting periods. Waiting periods are periods during which a member waits to join the scheme. When qualifying service is broken by absences of a month or less or by maternity absence, or absences in furtherance of a trade dispute, the periods either side of the break are regarded as continuous.

Leaving the pension scheme but not the job

Since 6 April 1988 members have the right to leave a pension scheme even if they do not leave their job.

Revaluation

If a member left a scheme before 1 January 1986 there is no requirement to revalue his or her preserved pension. If a member left the scheme on or after 1 January 1986 but before 1 January 1991 part of the preserved pension is revalued in line with prices with a ceiling of 5 per cent. The part of the pension that is revalued in this way is the part earned by service from 1 January 1985; service before that date does not have to be revalued. If, however, the member left on or after 1 January 1991 the whole of the preserved pension has to be revalued in line with prices up to the 5 per cent limit. There is no revaluation if the member leaves within one year of the scheme's normal retirement date.

In the case of a money purchase scheme the amount standing to the member's credit in the scheme is revalued by adding to it the investment yield, for example interest or bonuses.

Transfers

The right to a transfer

Generally a member who leaves a scheme with a preserved pension can transfer the cash equivalent of the pension to a new employer's scheme or to a personal pension or to a buy out policy.

Conditions for exercising the option

The member must exercise this option in writing but can withdraw it at any time until the trustees have done all that is required of them to enter into the transfer arrangement. The member must exercise the option by the later of either six months after leaving or one year before his normal retirement date.

Calculation of transfer value

The transfer value is the cash equivalent of the member's accrued benefits. It must be calculated using methods and assumptions approved by an actuary and in accordance with the professional guidelines published by the Institute and Faculty of Actuaries. It must also be calculated in a way which is consistent with the methods and assumptions used to calculate benefits to be given in return for transfer payments from another scheme. Where it is the established custom of the trustees to award discretionary pension increases, the cash equivalent has to be increased to take this into account, unless the trustees make a direction to the contrary. But the trustees will not be able to make such a direction without specific actuarial advice including advice about whether there would be adverse funding implications if the direction were not made.

If a member leaves the scheme but not his or her job, the right to a cash equivalent is restricted to the proportion of his or her accrued rights which has arisen since 6 April 1988 unless the scheme rules permit the whole of the accrued rights to be transferred.

New employer's scheme

A new employer's scheme, in order to be able to accept a transfer, must either be a statutory scheme, or one which is fully approved by the Inland Revenue. If the scheme is not yet fully approved because, for example, it is still operating on the basis of an Interim Trust Deed, the Revenue's consent to the transfer must be obtained.

Buy out policies

If the member wishes to transfer to a buy out policy, then the policy must satisfy the requirements of the Inland Revenue and the insurance company must be authorised by the Department of Trade and Industry. The member can have as many policies as he or she wants.

A buy out policy must, so far as possible, replicate the benefits provided by the transferring scheme. This option will therefore suit someone who wishes to keep the same benefits, for example, a spouse's pension.

Personal pensions

Members can also transfer their cash equivalent to a personal pension. The member must consent in writing and the transfer value must be used to buy money purchase benefits. A personal pension gives considerable freedom to choose benefits, for example a level or an escalating pension and to have, or not have, a spouse's pension. This option will, therefore, suit someone who is not married or who wishes to retain flexibility of benefits.

Guaranteed statement of cash equivalents

The trustees of a salary related scheme must, on request, provide a member with a written statement of the amount of the cash equivalent at a 'guarantee date'. The member has a right to the amount stated if he makes an application within three months from the guarantee date.

The guarantee date must fall within three months of the member requesting the statement. However this three month period can be extended for up to a further three months if the trustees are unable to get the information needed to calculate the cash equivalent. The member must be given the statement within ten working days of the guarantee date.

A member who has applied for a guaranteed statement cannot do so again for another year unless this is permitted by the scheme rules or the trustees agree.

The guaranteed transfer value must be calculated in a way consistent with that used in the latest MFR valuation.

Cash equivalents (but not cash equivalents which have already been guaranteed) may be reduced where the latest valuation shows that the scheme is underfunded. A guaranteed cash equivalent cannot normally be reduced.

Guaranteed cash equivalents can however be adjusted where:

   (a) benefits have been surrendered, commuted or forfeited after the guarantee date;

(b) the guaranteed statement was wrong eg because of a mistake; or

(c) it is necessary to comply with the statutory order of priorities where a scheme has entered winding up.

Cash equivalents will have to be recalculated if not paid in time, whether or not the trustees have a reasonable excuse for the failure. It will only be necessary to recalculate or add interest, if the result is greater, if the trustees' failure is without reasonable excuse. The interest rate to be applied is 1 per cent above base rate.

Time limits

The time limit for giving effect to a member's request for his cash equivalent is six months from the date of request, although for salary related schemes this will only begin to run from the guarantee date. Reduced cash equivalents will continue to be allowed for members who opt out but remain in employment. OPRA may grant the trustees extensions of time for paying cash equivalents so long as they apply within the six month period. Where trustees have not given effect to a member's request within six months, they must notify OPRA. In addition if they have failed to take reasonable steps to comply with the member's request, they are liable to penalties.

Penalties

Breaches of the transfer value rules attract medium penalties—£1,000 for individuals and £10,000 for companies.

For an illustration of some of the problems that can arise on transfers readers are referred to *'The Lawyer's Tale: The Bird has Flown'*, which follows this chapter.

The Lawyer's Tale: The Bird has Flown

Paul struggled wearily through the crowds of commuters pouring out of Bank tube station as he tried to find the entrance to the Docklands Light Railway. He was due at the unearthly hour of 8.30 am to discuss the *Hill Kestrel* case with Philip and Colin at the Magnificent Mutual. He found his assistant, Gabriel, waiting for him on the platform. Although only 27, Paul was already much too grand to carry his own bags, but Gabriel had another virtue besides. Before turning to the law he had worked as a pensions administrator and, unlike Paul, knew how insurance companies worked; more to the point he also knew that pensions actuaries and lawyers did not constitute a mutual admiration society.

'I don't know why Archie didn't do this job' grumbled Paul. 'After all he used to work for the Magnificent Mutual and knows the problem backwards. How he expects me to get to Canary Wharf by 8.30 am when I didn't get to bed until 5 am this morning passes my comprehension.'

'Perhaps' replied Gabriel, 'it was a gentle hint to get you to go to bed at a less ungodly hour and to lead you away from the temptations of the West End in the middle of the night! But there's another reason, which you'll soon find out.'

The train, full of a strange mixture of men in suits and real people from the Isle of Dogs, lurched out of the tunnel and rose up into the sky to cross the tracks at Fenchurch Street. It then raced down to the aluminium and glass palaces at Canary Wharf. It was a different world, so modern and shiny and bright, so different from the City a few miles away.

The mists of Paul's hangover began to melt away in the early morning sun.

'I wouldn't mind working here, I must admit. It's much nicer than our industrial slum at Megalaw House.' Gabriel mused.

Minutes later they were wafted to the 57th floor offices of the Magnificent Mutual, cantilevered over one of the old docks, with wide, concentration-bending views from Wren's baroque palace at Greenwich up to Tower Bridge and St Pauls.

They were met by Martin, a young man dressed in the current estuarine fashion for grey slip-on shoes and white socks. He quickly took them to the boardroom to meet Colin Bell, the pensions actuary and his boss, Philip, the managing director.

'I don't suppose that senile old goat, Archie, told you what all this was about' began Colin with a braying laugh.

'It's about Hill Kestrel; that's all I know. I haven't seen Archie for ages. I've just come back from trekking in the Himalayas, and before that I was at the APL Conference.'

Philip looked at Paul very coldly. 'When I was your age, my trekking was confined to the Lake District and I was the better for it. None of this drug taking and smoking pot that you must have indulged in at Katmandu. But I haven't time to waste on your holiday except to observe that you're obviously paid too much. Colin, explain the problem.'

'Well, it all started in 1984 when we still employed the goat. You won't remember but there was no revaluation or right to a transfer value then. And so a number of insurance companies set up buy out policies; s 32 policies they were called, but for a variety of reasons trustees felt unsafe in paying transfer values to them. And so a consultancy called Hill Kestrel hit upon the idea of setting up an exempt approved occupational scheme to receive transfer values. The members were given token contracts of employment and an insurance company organised the documents, provided actuarial advice and certificates and invested the money.'

'Well, what's wrong with that?' asked Paul.

'In the beginning, nothing. It enabled members to invest their frozen deferred pensions and to escape from their old employer's scheme. But it all snowballed, the money poured in and the consultants—the middle-men—got greedy. They weren't content to rake off the commission. They sacked the insurance company and took all the money and ran to Florida. The members, not unnaturally, were upset and looked for compensation from their old scheme.'

Paul looked completely mystified and a pregnant silence ensued. Eventually Gabriel broke in 'Yes, I remember. The Hill Kestrel Scheme had one or two problems, didn't it? Like no exempt approval from the Revenue and no employment with the new employer.'

'I'm glad one of you is awake' cut in Philip with asperity. 'Like you said, Gabriel, there was no real employment with a new employer; hence no contracted-out employment and so the OPB cancelled the contracting-out certificate.'

'And' went on Colin, 'they conned the trustees into making a transfer by saying the scheme was 'approved' and quoting the Revenue reference number, when it was only provisionally approved.'

Comprehension came flooding back to Paul; coffee was getting his brain into gear; 'Archie left me a note that he had advised you that the old trustees should reinstate the members. There's no such thing as "provisional approval". You can only make a transfer to a new employer's scheme where the scheme is exempt approved or you get the specific approval of the PSO.'

'It also helps' Gabriel butted in, 'if the new employer's scheme has a real employer instead of a disembodied bird!'

'Yes, yes' replied Philip irritably. 'We know that. Archie, as you say, told us that years ago. It was wrong advice. It would have cost us money because the trustees would have looked to us to pay the cost of reinstatement. So we ignored Archie and he then left our employment.'

'We got rid of the goat' said Colin with a grin.

'He told me' said Paul, 'that he had left to better himself in the City.'

'Details, details' replied Philip. 'I understand that the Ombudsman has made a determination in the *Hill Kestrel* case and indeed has confirmed that Archie's advice was right in law.'

'Yes and no' answered Paul 'but let me explain.

First the Ombudsman did uphold the members' complaint that the transferring trustees were guilty of maladministration because they had no power to pay over the transfer value. They were accordingly ordered to reinstate the former members back into their old scheme. Like you said, Philip, since the Magnificent Mutual administered the old scheme, the buck stopped with you.'

'We will not tolerate 'wrong' advice, young man' Philip thundered. 'That's why we sent for you, not Archie.'

Paul sat forward, squared his shoulders, blinked twice and, like the rugby forward he was, went into the attack.

'For once what Archie said was spot on. You only think it was wrong because it was unpalatable and would have cost you money. But if you'd stop ranting I'll tell you the good news. The insurance company which actually set up the Hill Kestrel Scheme, although not guilty of any involvement in fraud, was according to the Ombudsman liable to pay the former scheme the cost of reinstatement. He ruled that they were the managers of the Hill Kestrel Scheme because:

   (a)   they helped to devise the scheme;
   (b)   they provided actuarial and documentation services;
   (c)   they seconded staff to the consultants; and

(d)   they provided quotations for transfer values.

The Ombudsman concluded:

> "Without the very active participation of the insurer from the outset, it would not have been possible for the scheme to be established. The application for approval was flawed in that it pretended that all the members of the scheme were to become employees of the consultants' company. The insurer knew from the outset that this was clearly untrue in reality and so colluded with the pretence instead of advising the PSO of the real intention of the scheme ... The insurer, as an established and expert pensions life office, must be taken to have been aware that the transferring trustees would not have been permitted by their rules to pay transfer values to a scheme which was not properly approvable, such transfers being contrary to PSO rules.'"

'Goody, goody gumdrops' broke in Philip with an unaccustomed smile. 'So that's all right then; they've got to foot the bill, not us. Serve them right for taking money from us.' he went on displaying the customary love of one dog for another.

'This is excellent news. Kindly confirm it by fax this afternoon. You may go now. The kitchen staff will need the room to lay the table for the directors' lunch.'

With this Martin flung open the door and the kitchen staff started to bring in the food and drink. Philip and Colin evidently sensed an air of disapproval from their visitors.

'It's not for us, you know' said Colin, 'but the directors insist on it.'

'Are you asking us to advise you' replied Paul, now beginning to enjoy himself, 'whether all this'—he indicated with a wave the serried bottles of champagne and brandy—'is a proper use of the policy holders' funds? I guess not, but before we depart and leave you to the hardship of your deliberations, I've got two further points.

The insurer argued that the complaint was out of time and was already the subject of court proceedings, debarring the member from bringing his complaint to the Ombudsman.

There was a court case but that involved a different member. The Ombudsman ruled that it would be wholly unjust that his jurisdiction should be ousted by proceedings started by someone else, to which he was not a party.

As to the time limit, the Ombudsman has discretion to extend the three year time limit for bringing claims. The Ombudsman ruled that the statutory discretion to accept the complaint out of time had been exercised by his predecessor and it did not appear to be appropriate for him to reconsider it.'

'This is daft' Colin broke in, 'What had the insurance company done wrong. It didn't make off with the money.'

'Quite right' smiled Paul. 'Although it was the consultants who were guilty of fraud, this did not preclude civil liability on the part of the insurer. The insurer was not dishonest but exercised such a lack of responsibility, such lack of control over the scheme assets and such lack of concern for the interests of the members as to justify liability, in effect for its maladministration in not preventing the loss of benefits.'

'Well, that's excellent news, although I don't know why Archie didn't tell us this years ago' said Philip. 'Martin, take them to the lift.'

'Just one final point before we go' replied Gabriel.

'It's likely that the insurance company will take this to appeal, probably on the question of time limits. Just remember that when you're tucking into your lunch. You'll certainly have to wait a bit longer to get your money and the insurer may even win on appeal, you never know. And in that case, just like Archie said ten years ago, the Magnificent Mutual will have to bear the loss.'

Paul and Gabriel had a good laugh on the way back.

'I don't know how Archie put up with those two. Do you know I even felt quite sorry for him today.' said Paul.

'They're nothing, Philip and Colin, compared to Archie's old boss, Monty Murgatroyd. He was the Chief General Manager when Archie was there. He wouldn't employ people with beards. If you wore a red tie, you were a communist, so Archie told me. He used to keep people waiting for hours outside his door. Philip and Colin are pussy cats compared to Monty Murgatroyd.'

Chapter 13

Funding and Surpluses

The minimum funding requirement

Schemes will be subject to a minimum funding requirement (MFR) that the value of their assets is not less than the amount of their liabilities. The MFR will only apply from the first actuarial valuation after 6 April 1997. But the following kinds of schemes will be excluded from the requirement:

(a) public service schemes;
(b) money purchase schemes;
(c) unapproved schemes; and
(d) schemes with only one member.

Assets and liabilities are to be calculated in the way set out in the regulations and relevant professional guidance notes. Schemes must have actuarial valuations at intervals of not more than three years, with annual certificates to check on the funding position in between. The actuary in his certificate must state whether, in his opinion, the contributions are adequate to meet the MFR. If the certificate does not say that contributions are adequate, the trustees must get a full valuation within six months.

Contributions schedule

The trustees of a scheme to which the MFR applies must maintain a contributions schedule showing the rates of contributions payable by the employer and the members and the due dates for payment. The contribution rates must be certified by the actuary. The schedule must be agreed between the trustees and the employer, but if no agreement is reached, the schedule must show the contribution rates decided by the trustees as adequate for the purpose of securing that the MFR will be met either throughout the period or, if it is not met, by the end of that period. This represents a shift in the balance of power to the trustees, who will effectively be given power to decide the employer's contribution rate at any rate for the purpose of meeting the MFR. If the trustees fail to prepare or revise the contributions schedule within 12 weeks of the MFR valuation report, they can be removed by OPRA or fined.

Reporting to OPRA

When contributions are not paid in accordance with the schedule, the trustees must notify OPRA and the members. OPRA must be notified within 30 days of the due date for payment; the members must be notified within 90 days unless payment has been made within 60 days. Any unpaid contributions, whether from the employer or the members, will then be treated as a debt due from the employer. Where the trustees think that the MFR is not being met, they must prepare a report. Failure to comply with these obligations renders the trustees liable to penalties.

Serious underprovision

Where an actuarial valuation shows that the value of the scheme's assets is less than 90 per cent of its liabilities, the employer must make good the shortfall up to 90 per cent within twelve months. But this will not apply if the actuary is of the opinion that the funding level has recovered to 90 per cent by the time he certifies the schedule of contributions. If the employer fails to make good the shortfall, the trustees must, within 14 days, notify OPRA and the members. The shortfall, if not paid within the 12 months time limit, will be treated as a debt due from the employer. Where the deficit is less than 10 per cent, the employer has five years to make it good. OPRA may extend time limits for these purposes.

In addition, there will be a five year transition period from 1997 before the five year time limit for meeting the MFR takes full effect.

Basis of valuation

Pensioner liabilities will be valued on an actuarial basis similar to the cost of buying annuities. This will be based on rates of return on gilt investments with an expense loading to reflect the cost of buy out or, for larger schemes, the cost of running off as a closed fund. Non-pensioner liabilities will be calculated by reference to cash equivalents based on UK (but not overseas) equity returns, but if the members were near to retirement there would be a much larger element of gilt rather than equity valuation. Such members would receive a larger value which would be nearer to the cost of a deferred annuity than would be the case with younger members. The MFR calculation will take account of market values on the valuation date. If the valuation takes place on a day when market conditions are extreme, the actuary can take account of changes between that date and the date the schedule of contributions is certified. For larger schemes with pensioner liabilities of over £100 million the valuation basis will allow a proportion of the pensioner liabilities to be based on UK equity returns. The MFR will look only at rights accrued to the valuation date and will exclude discretionary benefits. The MFR will not therefore ensure that members' benefits will be fully secured; that would require the purchase of guaranteed insurance annuities. But if a scheme is at least 100 per cent funded on the statutory basis, pensioners will be able to expect their pensions to be met in full, while other members will be entitled to the cash equivalent of their rights which they can transfer elsewhere.

Content of contributions schedule

In the words of the DSS Consultation Paper: *Overview of the Minimum Funding Provision*:

'The requirement for schemes to have a schedule in place is to ensure there is a clear understanding as to the payments that are due and when they are due. In addition it provides a means of enabling the funding position to be checked and monitored by the trustees. Most schemes will already have such arrangements or funding plans in place and it is not proposed that they should be required to change their arrangements simply to conform to a standard pattern or design. The rates of contributions due may be recorded as amounts or as a percentage of the payroll and due dates for payment will normally reflect whatever arrangements have been established by the employer and/or are set out in scheme rules. In preparing the schedule the actuary should take account of the proposed frequency of payment and assumptions about salary increases, membership changes etc.'

The schedule must show separately:

    (a)   the rates and due dates of contributions (except voluntary contributions) payable by or on behalf of the active members;

    (b)   the rates and due dates of contributions payable by each participating employer; and

    (c)   if separate contributions to cover expenses are made, the rates and due dates of those contributions.

The schedule must show the rates of contributions payable during the period of five years from the date on which the contribution rates are certified by the actuary.

The trustees must keep records of all contributions paid showing separately:

    (a)   the total amount of contributions paid by or on behalf of active members and the dates on which they are paid, distinguishing voluntary contributions from other contributions and showing the amount of each member's voluntary contributions; and

    (b)   the total amount of contributions paid by each participating employer and the dates on which they are paid.

The trustees must also keep records of any action taken by them to recover:

    (a)   any contributions not paid on the due date;

    (b)   the amount of any debt which has arisen from the employer's failure to secure the increase required as a result of a serious shortfall; and

    (c)   the amount of any debt that has arisen from any deficiency on the employer's insolvency.

Summary of time limits

- Schemes should have MFR valuations at intervals of no more than three years.
- MFR valuation reports should be obtained within 12 months of the effective date of the valuation. Emergency valuation reports should be obtained within six months.

- The schedule of contributions should be prepared or revised within 12 weeks of the signing of the MFR valuation report. The schedule should cover a period of five years.
- Contributions and due dates in the schedule of contributions must be agreed by employer and trustees within eight weeks of the signing of the valuation report.
- Funding certificates should be produced not later than three weeks after each anniversary of the signing of the latest MFR valuation report.
- Where a valuation reveals a scheme's funding to be less than 90 per cent of the MFR, the funding level should be made up to 90 per cent within a year and to 100 per cent within five years of the date the valuation was signed by the actuary.

Payment schedule

Money purchase schemes will be required to prepare, maintain and revise a payment schedule showing:

(a) the rates of employer and member contributions;
(b) the amount of the scheme expenses payable by the employer likely to be incurred in the scheme year; and
(c) the due dates for payment of these contributions or other amounts.

The payment schedule must show amounts payable in the scheme year. The schedule must contain separate entries for employer and member contribution rates and due dates for payment (other than voluntary contributions). But when an insurance premium is payable, the payment schedule need not contain separate entries for the employer and member contributions covered by that premium.

The matters to be shown in the schedule must be determined in accordance with scheme rules so far as applicable and otherwise be agreed between the employer and the trustees. In default of agreement between the employer and the trustees, the trustees are responsible for deciding the contents of the schedule. Trustees who fail to take reasonable steps to comply with their obligations are subject to removal by OPRA and to penalties.

The requirements relating to payment schedules do not apply to:

(a) unapproved schemes;
(b) public service schemes;

(c) one person schemes;

(d) schemes providing death benefits only; and

(e) small self-administered schemes where all the members are trustees and all decisions by the trustees are unanimous.

Reporting to OPRA

Just as with contribution schedules, if contributions are not paid by the due date, the trustees must notify OPRA within 30 days and the members within 90 days. But if payment is received within 60 days, notice need not be given to the members. Any amounts unpaid by the due date, whether payable by the employer or not, are to be treated as a debt due from the employer. It would seem therefore that the employer is being treated as a guarantor not merely of its own contributions but also those of the members, whether or not they have been paid or deducted from members' pay. The employer is liable to civil penalties if payments are not made in accordance with the payment schedule.

Surpluses

A surplus is simply an excess of the resources of the scheme over its liabilities. The Finance Act 1986 introduced a statutory test for calculating the amount of past service surplus under which it has to be calculated by reference to a set of assumptions laid down by the Government Actuary. The assumptions relate both to the value of the assets as well as the benefits. This is known as 'the prescribed basis'.

The rules for eliminating surpluses

The Finance Act 1986 lays down that unless a scheme is to lose a proportionate part of its tax exemptions, then a surplus, calculated on the prescribed basis, has to be eliminated within a five year period. For this purpose a surplus exists if the assets of the scheme exceed its liabilities by more than 5 per cent. The permitted ways of achieving this are:

(a) a refund to the employer;

(b) benefit improvements;

    (c)   a contribution holiday for the members;

    (d)   a contribution holiday for the employer; or

    (e)   any combination of these methods.

The tax charge

A refund to the employer, or a combination of methods which includes a refund, must not result in the assets being reduced to less than 105 per cent of the scheme's liabilities. A free-standing tax charge of 40 per cent is levied on a refund and has to be deducted at source by the trustees. There are no offsetting tax allowances. No payment to an employer can be made unless:

    (a)   the written consent of the Inland Revenue has been obtained;

    (b)   LPI for past as well as future service is applied to all pensions;

    (c)   the trustees are satisfied that it is in the members' interests; and

    (d)   notice has been given to the members.

Refunds of surplus to the employer

Some scheme rules prevent a refund of surplus being paid to an employer. If the trustees' consent to a rule change is required, to enable such a payment to be made, they will have to secure some benefit improvement for their members in return for giving their consent. Permitting an employer's refund would not normally be considered to be in the interests of the members. The trustees must come to some agreement with the employer about the division of the surplus between a refund on the one hand and benefit improvements on the other.

Modification orders

Some trust deeds may prevent both a refund and a rule change to permit it. Where this is the case OPRA has power to modify the rules where:

    (a)   an actuary's certificate, as calculated for Inland Revenue purposes, shows that the scheme's assets exceed liabilities by more than 5 per cent;

(b) the trustees are satisfied that it is in the members' interests that the surplus is eliminated in the way proposed;

(c) the proposals have been approved by the Inland Revenue;

(d) the scheme provides for guaranteed pension increases—limited price indexation (or LPI)—or a provision for LPI is included in the proposals.

Who Owns a Pension Scheme's Surplus

Many final salary schemes have shown a healthy surplus. This has led to renewed interest in the question of who owns that surplus. Employers usually assume it is theirs as they are expected to pay the balance of cost in a final salary scheme, but members often feel that money in a pension fund is there for the purpose of providing pensions. There have been a number of cases on this subject. Most of the cases have lent support to the view that the surplus effectively belongs to the employer.

The Hillsdown case

The question to be decided here was whether a bulk transfer payment from one scheme to another on the sale of a company should include a share of the surplus. The judge, Walton J, said that a surplus had no existence in reality but was 'what may be termed temporary surplus funding by the employing company'. There was no certainty that the surplus, if transferred, would be used for the members' benefit. And so he refused to order that the transfer payment should include a share of the surplus.

The Courage case

In this case the judge's observations on the ownership of surplus are even more encouraging to employers. He also saw surpluses as arising from what, with hindsight, is past overfunding. He said that any surplus arises from past overfunding not in proportion to the employer's and the members' contributions but by the employer alone to the full extent of its past contributions. However, having said that members have no legal right to participate in the surplus of a continuing scheme, the judge, Millett J, went on to say that they were entitled to have it dealt with by negotiation and consultation with their employers and trustees and not to be irrevocably parted from it by the unilateral decision of a takeover raider. So members have a right to be considered in relation to a surplus.

The Imperial Tobacco Pension Fund case

The Imperial Tobacco pension fund gave guaranteed increases to pensions in payment of 5 per cent or in line with the Retail Prices Index, if less. The trustees could amend the scheme rules with the company's consent. The judge, Sir Nicolas Browne-Wilkinson, decided that the power of the company to consent was not a fiduciary power, but the company was nevertheless bound to consider proposals for amendment and could not state in advance that it would not consent in the future.

In considering whether or not to give its consent, the company was bound to give effect to the implied duty to maintain mutual trust and confidence on the part of both the employee and the employer. There was, therefore, to be implied in the pension scheme a provision that the company would not conduct itself in a manner which was likely to destroy the relationship of trust and confidence between it and the members.

This is another ruling that pension benefits are 'pay' in line with the European case of *Barber v Guardian Royal Exchange*. While the judgment (like that in the *Courage* case) indicates that members have a right not to be parted from 'their surplus', it does not give them a right to the surplus. There are indications (but no more) that surplus does not necessarily belong to the company, but the judge refrained from deciding who does own it. Again, the judge stressed that members had earned their rights. But it is clear nevertheless that a company can act in its own self-interest, although it cannot act capriciously nor for an ulterior motive, for example to take back a surplus to which it is not otherwise entitled. In particular, the judgment does not require surpluses to be used for pension increases or benefit improvements. There is nothing to stop a company from taking a contribution holiday. But the case will make it much harder for a company to extract surplus from a pension scheme otherwise than by way of a contribution holiday.

The winding up cases

Next come three decisions on the ownership of surplus on the winding up of a scheme. This turns on the winding up rule. What it says on the subject will decide the issue. The trouble is that many winding up rules were vaguely and ambiguously drafted at a time when surpluses were not much in evidence.

The Icarus case

The company went into liquidation and the pension scheme was wound up. The rules gave the company discretion to use surplus to increase benefits. Any balance went back to the company. The judge, Aldous J, found that the surplus largely arose from good investment. If the company had continued, it could have taken a contribution holiday and so he concluded that the surplus was due to overfunding by the company. The liquidator, as long as he acted in good faith and considered all the facts, could pay the surplus to the creditors and use none for the members. The case therefore bears out the conventional view that a pension surplus is an employer's asset.

The Mettoy case

Here the facts were similar to those in *Icarus*. Again, the company had a discretion to use surplus on winding up for the benefit of the members. The judge, Warner J, decided that this discretion, although vested in the company, was a fiduciary or trust power. It could not, therefore, be exercised by a liquidator or receiver because of the impossible conflict of interest between the members and the creditors. In the circumstances the judge would have to exercise the discretion.

The judge stressed that the members were not volunteers. They earned their pension in the same way as their pay. He did not think it was correct to say that members' rights were satisfied when they had received the benefits laid down by the rules, and that anything more lay in the bounty of the company.

> 'One cannot in my view in construing a provision in the rules of a balance of cost pension scheme relating to surplus, start from an assumption that any surplus belongs morally to the employer'.

But tantalisingly he did not go on to say that surplus belongs morally to the members.

Davis v Richards & Wallington

This was an unusual case because, when the scheme came to be wound up it was still operating on interim documentation and there was not a winding up rule. The judge, Scott J, decided that the surplus belonged to the company because it was liable to pay the balance of cost. It was likely that all of the surplus arose from company contributions. The members paid defined contributions in return for defined benefits. This reasoning is hard to follow and contrasts sharply with the *Mettoy* case where Warner J said that members were not just entitled to receive defined benefits but had a moral claim to be considered in the distribution of the surplus.

In circumstances such as these an independent trustee now has to be appointed. The independent trustee is alone competent to exercise fiduciary powers, whether vested in the company or the other trustees. In addition, before any payment can be made to the company, surplus must be used to provide limited price indexation for all service; only any balance remaining after that may be returned to the company, or whatever the winding up rule provides.

Conclusion

So where do these cases leave employers and trustees? The indications are that judges will look closely at the factors that led to the surplus—investment performance, redundancies, employer's and members' contributions. It is impossible to draw firm conclusions, particularly from the cases about the winding up of a scheme. In a continuing scheme members can still expect to earn further benefits, while in the winding up cases the members have lost their jobs. Furthermore, only on a winding up does a surplus really exist. Before then it is only an actuarial estimate. It is likely, therefore, that in ongoing schemes the courts will lean to viewing surpluses as arising from past overfunding by the company. On winding up, it all depends on what the rules say.

Where trustees are faced with requests by an employer for a refund of surplus from an ongoing scheme, they have to act in the interests of the members. They have to consider the balance of power as between them and the company, as set out in the trust deed and rules. They must consider what will happen if they refuse the company's request; they may lose the company's goodwill which is essential for the continued running of the scheme. In these circumstances they have a duty to bargain with the employer and to seek the best deal they can for their members.

Perhaps the last word on this subject should be left to Vinelott J in the *Lucas Pension Fund* case in 1993:

'The Pension Fund, to the extent that it is in surplus (that is that the funds are more than are needed to meet accrued liabilities under the Scheme), does not in any intelligible sense belong to anyone. Members and pensioners (present and future) have an interest if and so far as the fund as a whole is capable of being applied in improving benefits or adding new benefits. They also have an interest in ensuring that the fund is retained intact, in that it represents additional security for payment of benefits and may have to be applied in improving benefits for members and pensioners in a winding up.

However, an employer has an interest insofar as a surplus in the fund can be used to relieve him of his obligation to contribute to the fund.'

For an illustration of the way in which these problems are dealt with, see *'The Lawyer's Tales: Telling it to the Colonel'* and *'Adam and Eve'* which follow this chapter.

The Lawyer's Tale: Telling it to the Colonel

A brief telephone call the previous Friday had brought young David
of Pan European Pension Services (PEPS) and Oliver of Megalaw together at 7 am at the domestic departure lounge at Gatwick en route
to Manchester. They were smartly dressed clean cut young men, colleagues together from the old days at Docs Galore.

One of PEPS major clients was the Automated Widgets Pension
Scheme where the chairman of the trustees was Colonel Braithwaite.
A year ago Colonel Braithwaite made a reverse takeover of one of his
competitors. And so although all the names had changed, the pension
scheme was in fact the larger scheme inherited on the takeover.

'I'll tell you all about it on the plane on Tuesday' said David. 'I
haven't got time now or I'll be late for cricket. I've arranged for the
file to be biked round to you so you can read it over the weekend. It's
all about a bulk transfer the trustees made last year. One of the
members is saying it's not enough. In fact I asked for my old boss, Archie Smithers, but I gather he's resting in the Caribbean, so you'll
have to do!'

'Steady on, David' cut in Oliver, bridling. 'You may have been
Archie's personal assistant but I'm certainly not. Plus I've got to be
in Newcastle on Tuesday afternoon for another meeting.'

'Don't take on so, Oliver' laughed David. 'The Colonel never liked
Archie anyway. So you've got to be in Newcastle and I'm doing a documentation seminar in Edinburgh in the afternoon. No problem; I'll
ask the Colonel to take us in the company plane from Manchester,
drop you off in Newcastle and take me on to Edinburgh. See you on
Tuesday all bright eyed and bushy tailed.'

And so the following Tuesday David filled Oliver in on the details.

'Last year Automated Widgets sold off a big subsidiary, with a
third of the group's workforce. There was the usual pension transfer
clause providing for a past service reserve transfer based on the
scheme's normal actuarial assumptions. In return the buyer agreed
to give identical benefits and year for year past service.'

'Well what's special about that?' asked Oliver.

'Nothing.' said David 'Nine months later the trustees paid over the
transfer value on the basis set out in the sale agreement. And that's
when the trouble started. One of the transferring members complained that the transfer didn't include any part of the Automated
Widgets surplus, and the trustees ought to have done this. I advised

the company and told Colonel Braithwaite that the trustees ought to get independent legal advice. And that's why we're on the shuttle to Manchester tucking into our second airline breakfast!'

The stewardess had got some spare breakfasts. Who better to use as dustbins than David and Oliver.

David continued: 'You'll have to watch out with the Colonel. He's an old military type. He doesn't like anyone to disagree with him; he can't bear to be crossed. The other trustees are Steve Huxtable, a trade union shop steward, and the personnel manager, Donna. And don't be fooled by them either. They're no pushovers. The Colonel has known them for years and they help him in his battles with the American parent company.'

When the trustees meeting started, David introduced Oliver. Oliver quickly explained the trustees duties in relation to the bulk transfer. They were not bound by the sale agreement. The rules provided for a just and equitable share of the fund to be transferred. Until recently it had been thought that a past service reserve transfer satisfied this.

It wasn't necessary to hand over a share of the surplus. Indeed if that were to be done without more, it would simply be handing over surplus to the buyer for nothing, and that would be a breach of trust.

'That's what David said at the trustees meeting which approved the transfer' said Donna.

'The problem' went on Oliver quickly, 'is that the Court of Appeal in the *Fisons* case has cast doubt on all this and suggested that, at any rate in some circumstances, a share of surplus should be included. Let me quote:

"At the heart of this case, in my opinion, lies the question
whether the employees of a company have a legitimate interest
in a surplus which exists in the company's pension fund.
Perhaps "legitimate" is not the right word to use, for it is not
suggested that the employees have a legal right to participate
directly in the surplus. More accurately, in deciding what is
just and equitable upon a division of the pension fund, should
one have regard to and evaluate the possibility that all or part
of the surplus will one day prove to be a benefit for the
employees."'

'And so David got it wrong then and we should have transferred more' said Steve.

'Just let me go on—I've not finished my quotation yet' said Oliver.

The judge, Lord Justice Staughton, went on to say that he could not altogether accept the view expressed in the *Hillsdown* case that any surplus should be disregarded; it might be of a temporary nature, there was no certainty that it would continue, and there was equally no certainty that any of the existing employees would ever benefit from it. Again to quote:

> "For my part I cannot altogether accept that view. It seems to me that there was some degree of likelihood that the Fisons fund would continue to be in surplus for the foreseeable future; and there was some degree of likelihood that the existing employees and pensioners would receive some benefit from that surplus in the future, in the form of increased pensions or other benefits. When the trustees came to consider what was just and equitable upon a division of the fund they ought to have borne these points in mind and made some evaluation of them.'"

'Have you quite finished this nonsense' the Colonel erupted. 'You're as bad as that old goat, Smithers, and a bolshie to boot.'

'Not so' said Oliver, but the Colonel shouted over him 'David brings us his solutions—you bring only the problems.'

'Colonel' rushed in David quickly trying to pour oil on troubled waters. 'It's all right. Me and Oliver discussed it all on the plane. He's got the solution; but you've got to let him spell it out to the trustees—after all he's got to earn his fees!'

'I think I can safely say that the trustees have nothing to fear' said Oliver seizing his opportunity. 'Needless to say my old colleague David gave the right advice. What happened in the *Fisons* case was caused by a sequence of events:

(a) first, the transfer value was on the total service reserve basis, considerably less than past service reserve;

(b) second, this basis was chosen because the fund was then thought to be marginally in deficit;

(c) third, between the sale and the payment of the transfer the fund increased in value dramatically;

(d) fourth, the trustees didn't take this into account when they decided to pay the bulk transfer. They could easily have afforded to pay a past service reserve transfer and still had a surplus.

And so the Court of Appeal set aside their decision. But your case is different.'

David thought it was time he had a turn: 'One, we paid a past service reserve transfer. Two, although we've got a surplus, the value of the fund fell slightly between the sale and the payment. Three, we've never used surplus for benefit improvements.'

'That's quite right' interjected the Colonel. 'We've always said that the first priority was the company. Every penny of surplus has been used to give the company a contribution holiday.

We've got a good pension scheme with good benefits; pension increases are guaranteed at 5 per cent. We haven't waited for LPI to come in. The engineering industry has been torn apart in the past decade. We've survived thanks to our pension holiday. That's right, isn't it?'

'Yes' said Steve and Donna together. 'As trustees, we couldn't have stopped the company taking a contribution holiday. Mind you, if things ever improve, we'll be looking to see some of the surplus used for the members.'

'Well, I must say' said the Colonel, 'it's a relief to get such clear and positive advice. Just draft a letter to that joker who caused all the trouble. And now we can adjourn for a quick snifter before you two catch the plane.'

While they were sitting drinking their pint sized gin and tonics, David asked the Colonel's indulgence to say one thing more.

'We could have avoided all this trouble if we'd had a properly drafted bulk transfer rule which gave the trustees power to pay cash equivalents, and the company, acting in its own interests, power to direct them to transfer a higher amount. Your old scheme rules were drafted like that but on the takeover your old scheme was merged into the other scheme. That scheme had the "just and equitable" bulk transfer rule.'

'Well' asked the Colonel, 'why didn't you change it when you did the new rules?'

'You can't just change the balance of power without so much as a by your leave' replied David.

'I explained it to you and your co-trustees when we went through the new rules last year. A change like that would not really be in the members' interests; they couldn't in the members' interests agree to it and so we left things as they were. I just didn't want anyone to think I overlooked it.'

On their way back to the airport in the Colonel's Daimler, David explained to the Colonel how his life had changed. 'In the old days people doing docs were locked in a cupboard on Monday morning and let out on a Friday when their quota had been churned out. But it's not like that anymore. People like you, Colonel, want to be advised about whether the rules protect the members properly, whether there are sufficient controls over the company and so on. I spend all my time at meetings like this. It's no longer a matter of just knocking up a quick deed of amendment.

And another thing—the clear implication of the *Fisons* judgment was that if surplus had been used in the past for benefit improvements, you'd have to pass over a share of it in the bulk transfer. One of the judges said that in some circumstances it might even have been a breach of the contract of employment for Fisons to have used up the surplus by taking a contribution holiday. That sounds precious near to saying that surplus belongs to the members and that a company can't even take a contribution holiday. That's fairly revolutionary from the old gentlemen in the Strand, isn't it? No wonder people like us are in such demand, Oliver!'

The Lawyer's Tale: Adam and Eve

'Archie' said David urgently one morning, when he saw him on the train to Cannon Street, 'I saw old Maudie Belchamber last week. She needs some legal advice about merging the pension scheme operated by her latest acquisition, the Harrogate Aerated Water Company.'

Maud Belchamber, now since the death of her brother, the Marchioness of Maidstone, owned Waters of Wells, England's leading producer of bottled water. A sprightly 75-year-old she had seen off six spouses and now enjoyed her remaining years with a succession of toyboys employed by her in various roles. Maud's six husbands had all been actuaries. As she was fond of saying 'Marry an actuary every time. They're rich and boring and they work so hard they don't worry about what you do in your spare time.'

So it was no surprise that Archie instead of asking 'what' she wanted, merely asked 'who' was required.

'Well' sighed David, the consultant to the Waters of Wells pension scheme and a buddy of Archie's, 'she says she wants someone new this time. We all know what that means!'

'I've got the very person—Adam. He was a trainee and stayed on after he qualified. He knows all about mergers but more importantly, I guess, he looks like James Dean or rather what James Dean would have looked like in an Armani navy blue suit. His sober city style of dressing conceals the steamy sultriness of the deep south. Maudie will love him!'

And so a few days later David and Adam took the M20 down to Maud's fairytale moated castle between Maidstone and Tunbridge Wells. At the petrol station Adam eased into the driving seat and notched David's silver Lamborghini up to 120 when they were back in the fast lane. With the hood down and his foot hard down on the accelerator he observed with a laugh to poor horror-stricken David:

'It would be rude to pass Brands Hatch at under a ton!'

Soon they were being greeted by Maud, resplendent in a cerise suit, her pink bouffant hair surmounted by a ruby tiara.

'Sit down beside me, my dears' she crooned in delight to Adam, who somewhat sulkily took his place beside her on the sofa. Maud went on, purring like a large ginger cat 'It's all the fault of those horrid Yorkshire tykes from Harrogate. It's quite simple: I want to put them in my pension scheme and close theirs. Dear David tells me that it's quite normal. According to Colin Bell, our actuary, their scheme has got about enough to cover the liabilities. It would just pass the MFR test.'

'Whereas your scheme, Maud,' smoothed David 'has got a large surplus. Like you, its amply covered. The problem is not in fact the tykes, Adam; its the Wells trustees or rather two of them.'

'Exactly' cried Maud, 'while I was taking a well earned rest cure at Aix in the summer, they went off behind my back and took legal advice. It all originates in these terrible member trustees this wicked government has rammed down my throat. We've landed up with old Rainey, my ex-chauffeur, as a pensioner trustee and that tiresome woman, Violet from the bottling plant.'

'They went off to a lawyer' butted in David, 'who has never been near a client, let alone attended a trustees' meeting. But he's on the conference circuit and writes for the trade press. He told the trustees that they oughtn't to let 'their' surplus be diluted by admitting the Harrogate members.'

'I guess, Maud' Adam cut in quickly 'he said you'd have to give benefit improvements to your members, not that you couldn't let them in.'

'Details, details' flashed Maud petulantly. 'Both schemes are solvent. I'm not changing the benefit structure. Harrogate will get our benefits, better benefits I might add, for future service. I don't want to run two pension schemes where one will do. I'm not doing anyone down. Why should this trigger windfall, and no doubt costly, benefit improvements for the people in the Wells scheme? There's no logic in it. Why should I put my hand in my pocket. I've already had to pull in my belt and sell the second Roller.'

Maud, like many another tycoon, often confused her pockets. Not for nothing was she a successful billionaire entrepreneur.

Maud and David looked at Adam, who blushed and gulped 'Trust law requires the Wells trustees to put their members' interests first. Having the surplus diluted by admitting a tranche of new members for whom the company does not contribute is not in their interests. In the words of Knox J in the *Hillsdown* case:

> "It would in my view constitute a breach of the implied obligation of good faith on the one hand to enlarge the class of employers and so bring in large categories of new members and at the same time decline to make contributions in respect of them for the purpose of running off a surplus which had arisen in relation to other members."'

'Hillsdown, Hillsdown' rambled Maud, 'it sounds more like an eventide home where no doubt your old boss Archie Smithers is passing his ill-deserved retirement.'

'But,' cried David '*Hillsdown* isn't about a scheme merger. Like many of the surplus cases it was unfortunate in that the judge clearly disliked the artificial device set in train by *Hillsdown* to extract surplus from a scheme, which it had acquired as a result of a takeover, to which it had never contributed and to which it was not entitled under the rules.'

'How very shocking' pontificated Maud censoriously. 'You must tell me again, David, why I can't get my hands on the Wells surplus.'

'Another time, Maud' replied David. 'I'd like Adam to tell us why we've got to give something to the Wells members, to grease their palms, before their trustees can graciously condescend to admit the Harrogate members.'

Poor Adam was between a rock and a hard place.

'I'm not sure that *Hillsdown* has got anything to do with it. I've already explained the general trust law principle which requires the Wells trustees to bargain for benefit improvements as the price of diluting their surplus. I agree that *Hillsdown* is a special case and should be confined to its basic facts:

(a) the trustees had an unfettered power to use surplus, of which they were ignorant; and

(b) *Hillsdown's* improper threats to the trustees to induce the trustees to transfer that surplus to enable a refund to be made in breach of the rules.'

At this point they were interrupted by Gorgio, Maud's 16-year-old butler, whom she had imported from Thailand to look after her domestic needs, with the menu for lunch. Maud called all her butlers 'Gorgio' regardless; she found it saved time and effort.

'It's all vegetarian, darlings' Maud cooed. 'I've felt a new woman since I went to southern India last year and met my new guru. It's just saffron rice and a few vegetables. We'll eat with our hands off banana leaf plates and wash it down with my own water.'

David and Adam looked glum and Adam battled on 'What is worrying is that part of the *Hillsdown* judgment where Knox J said:

"It is one thing for an employer to take a contributions holiday in respect of a category of existing members and quite another to introduce a large class of new members and take a contribution holiday in relation to them so as to accelerate the

effect of the contributions holiday in relation to the existing
members.""

'But' said David judicially, 'that's rubbish. If read literally that would
tend to suggest that a surplus at any given time vests for the benefit
of the members at that time. But surplus is not attributable to the
members at any particular moment. It ignores the open-ended nature of a final salary pension scheme.'

Poor Adam was having a hard time. Maud had got up to feed the
peacocks. Attention to detail was never one of her strengths.

'Dave, if only you'd let me finish' spluttered Adam. 'I agree that
Hillsdown is not an authority for saying that an employer cannot admit new members to a scheme without paying contributions for
them. But if new members were admitted for the sole purpose of ac-
celerating the contribution holiday, that could be a breach of the employer's obligation of good faith. It's all very difficult. It's not like it
was in your and Archie's day, when you just set the word processor
on autopilot and swanned off to conferences and corporate golf.'

'But' rammed on David mercilessly, 'I think you've missed the
point. It was the threat to admit new employers and new members to
achieve another objective—the refund of surplus—which was dodgy.
Me and Maud aren't doing that. We're just trying to merge two
schemes; not trying to take the surplus or make nasty threats. We'd
never do that would we, Maud?'

Maud reluctantly returned to the discussion, 'Well, I've told the
member trustees that they're out on their ear if they don't do as
they're told, if that's what you mean. What's got under their skins is
that the Harrogate boys have got LPI and we haven't. But we've always given LPI increases and they're funded for. I told them I'd be
giving LPI for all service from next year. And still they're not satisfied. So' she concluded looking malevolently at Adam, 'I want solutions. Dear David brings me his answers, not his problems.'

A beatific smile spread over Adam's face.

'It's easy peasy. I think they misheard you about LPI. It would be
your intention to introduce LPI for past and future service from 6
April next year in return for the Wells trustees agreeing to the
merger.'

'You're very innocent or very stupid, young man. That's what I just
said' grumbled Maud.

'Not quite' said David, 'but near enough. By the way young Adam
here isn't quite as innocent as he looks. He's got a lovely blonde

Latvian girlfriend. I bet he could even teach an old dog like you new tricks, Maud. We'll dictate our letter of advice to the trustees in the car on the way back to London and have it faxed through to you tonight. Why not fix the trustees' meetings for both schemes? Me and Adam will come and tell, or should I say advise, the trustees to agree to the merger.'

'But I haven't reviewed the balance of power or done due diligence' shrieked Adam.

Fortunately further discussion was pre-empted by Gorgio, flexing his muscles and banging the gong for lunch. Trays of steaming rice and little pots of spicy vegetables were brought in. Plantain leaves were set before them and they tucked in with their bare hands, washing down their food with draughts of icy water from the Waters of Wells.

'Better for you than all those chips you get in the caff at Megalaw House' opined David sanctimoniously. 'It's about time these City yuppies gave up champagne at lunchtime and started the good life, isn't it, Maud?'

Chapter 14

Pensions on Divorce

Background

Until recently, on divorce, the divorced spouse lost his or her rights to the spouse's pension payable under the scheme rules. While the courts could take account of the loss of pension rights when ordering financial provision, they did not usually do so. Since pension rights are often the largest matrimonial asset, comparing in the value with the matrimonial home, it is not difficult to see what injustice this caused.

There are three possible solutions to the problem:

(1) **Splitting the matrimonial assets**

This is what used to be done in Scotland. One party would take the matrimonial home and the other the pension fund. But if there are not enough free assets to compensate for the pension rights, it is impossible to do this.

(2) **Earmarking**

This means that part of the member's pension is earmarked or attached for the benefit of the other party. The disadvantage is that the earmarked pension does not start until the member retires and ceases when the member dies. It is a pension on someone else's life and is therefore inherently unsatisfactory. But it is the solution which is now in force.

(3) **Pension splitting**

This is the best solution and involves valuing and then splitting the pension rights on divorce, leaving the ex-spouse with his or her own cash equivalent from which to provide a pension at a time of his or her own choosing. This is the solution which is expected to be introduced at about the turn of the century.

Earmarking

The Pensions Act has clarified the courts' existing duty to take pensions into account in financial settlements, which had not always been recognised in practice. In addition the Act enables the court to order deferred maintenance to the ex-spouse when the pension comes into payment—'earmarking'. The order would be directed not just to the spouse but to the trustees or pension provider who would thus be required to pay the split pension direct to the divorced spouse. Any such order will discharge the trustees' liability in respect of the payment. The regulations:

(a) require notices of changes of circumstances to be given to the trustees;
(b) require trustees to give information about the value of pension benefits;
(c) provide for the recovery of administrative expenses for complying with court orders and providing information; and
(d) provide for the calculation of the value of pension benefits on the basis of cash equivalents.

The trustees can, if they wish, make representations to the court before an order is made.

Powers of the court

Trustees will be required to notify ex-spouses about their rights. The court may order the member to commute the whole or part of his benefits and the order will then extend to the commutation payment just like any other scheme benefits. The court may, in relation to any lump sum death benefit, require the trustees to pay part of the lump sum to the ex-spouse. These provisions apply not only to occupational pension schemes but to all kinds of personal pensions eg retirement annuity contracts and buy out policies.

The court order may require the scheme to make a payment to a former spouse from the member's pension when it becomes due. And so former spouses will not have to maintain contact with their ex-partners to ensure that they receive what the court has ordered.

Transfer to a new scheme

When a court order is in force requiring scheme trustees to make payments to an ex-spouse, that requirement will transfer automatically to a new scheme so long as the new trustees have been given notice of the order and all pension rights are transferred. The transferring trustees are required to notify the receiving scheme and give them a copy of the order. They are also required to notify the ex-spouse of the transfer and that the order automatically applies to the receiving scheme, and to give details of the receiving scheme.

If only part of the pension rights is transferred, the ex-spouse will have to be notified by the trustees and given details of the receiving scheme. He or she would then be able to apply to the court for a variation order.

Commencement date

The provisions apply to divorce proceedings started on or after 1 July 1996. They will not therefore have retrospective effect.

The ex-spouse, who will be left without income when the pension stops on the member's death, would be able to make a claim for provision from the member's estate under the Inheritance (Provision for Family and Dependants) Act 1975, so long as he or she was dependent on the member.

Clean break

In addition the government has now accepted the principle of splitting pension assets at the time of divorce—the 'clean break' principle. This is now enshrined in the Family Law Act 1996. Although this Act has now received the Royal Assent, it is unlikely that s 16 dealing with pension splitting will come into force before 2000.

Divorce in Scotland

The law in Scotland differs from English law in three ways:
  (1) Scottish courts have always had to take pensions into account in financial settlements whereas this duty has only been imposed on the courts in England and Wales since 1996.

(2) In Scotland, the pension rights to be taken into account are those that have been earned while the marriage lasted. In England and Wales all pension rights are considered whether they have been earned before or since the marriage.

(3) In Scotland, the courts have not been given any power to earmark pensions as the English courts have. The Scottish courts (like the English courts) do, however, have power to earmark lump sum payments, for example the tax-free lump sum on retirement or the lump sum death in service benefit.

If the divorce petition is brought before the Scottish courts, Scottish law applies; and similarly for England and Wales. This means that schemes will have to understand the differences between the two legal systems since they may get court orders from Scottish as well as English courts.

For an illustration of the problems, see *'The Lawyer's Tale: Doing the Splits'*, which follows this chapter.

The Lawyer's Tale: Doing the Splits

'Mike, do you remember Dora Threadgold?' said David on the line to his friend Mike, in New York. Dora, or more properly Pandora, Threadgold was the pension fund investment director for World Investment Now, known as Win.

'Yes, indeed' replied Mike with a throaty laugh. 'She's our much married friend who still claims to be 39 and has a succession of toyboys who get younger as she gets older. She's very attractive; if only I were free!'

'Well,' continued David, 'last time we saw her she had Carlo from Dagenham, an Elvis lookalike in blue suede shoes. Now he's gone off the boil and she's at last found her true love, Kevin, but for how long it lasts is another thing. He's a 17-year-old settlement clerk in the backroom from white socks country, just like Carlo, and is responsible for preparing cheques for Dora to sign. Even the daily cheque signing routine is invested with a rosy hue. In a nutshell it's off with Carlo and on with Kevin. All was going well until Carlo's lawyers read an article about s 166 of the Pensions Act and said they won't finalise the divorce until 1997.'

'I'm a bit out of the loop on the Act at the moment, but, as you know, I'm back in London on 1 September. That's only next week. So I could fit Dora and you in that week just before I go off on my honeymoon to Bermuda—my first honeymoon so far, by the way! I expect I could bone up on the Act with Archie before we meet. He's obsessed with it all, reads it in bed and totally ignores his wife, Bella. She's even threatening divorce. Though why it matters at their age, I can't imagine.'

And so fresh from the pampered luxury of BA's first class cabin Mike, along with David, sauntered into their meeting with Dora in her penthouse suite. Dora introduced Kevin to them. Kevin was surprisingly ordinary compared with his predecessor, a fresh faced young man with short hair and a fashionable shiny olive green suit.

'You must be exhausted' crooned Dora to Mike.

'Not at all. It's lovely going first class. You get dinner at Kennedy, then the stewardess gives you champagne on the plane, tucks you up for the night and you wake up to fresh coffee and orange juice. At Heathrow you have a shower and then have a proper breakfast.'

'Can we get back to reality for a moment' cut in David. 'Just talk Dora through s 166 and stop wittering on about the high life.'

'OK, OK' replied Mike. 'Well the government finally bowed to pressure and agreed to a modified form of pension splitting on divorce. Section 166 enables courts to order deferred maintenance to the ex-spouse when the pension comes into payment. The order would be directed not just to you, Dora, but also to the scheme trustees who would have to pay the split pension direct to the ex-spouse. This is deferred maintenance, known in the trade as "earmarking".'

'Will this earmarking be of an amount of money or a percentage of Dora's pension?' asked David.

'The exact way in which it will work is not clear yet. There are the usual regulations to:

(a) require notice to be given of changes in the circumstances of the parties;

(b) require trustees to give information about the value of pension benefits;

(c) provide for the trustees to get back from the divorcing spouses their costs of complying with the new rules, and for supplying information; and

(d) provide for pension benefits to be valued on the cash equivalent basis.'

'Well, well' said Dora, snappily tossing her peroxide curls. 'That's easy; I'll just take my money out of the company scheme into a personal pension, won't we, Kev, so Carlo won't be able to touch our nest egg.'

'Not so fast' broke in David. 'Section 166 says that in the event of a transfer, the order would bind the new provider.'

'But how would Carlo know if I did a transfer? After all, he's as thick as three planks, unlike Kev, which is why we have such a deep, intellectual relationship, don't we darling?' she gushed.

'Well, you have a point there' gasped Mike in disbelief. 'But if the new scheme has been given notice of the court order, it will apply to the new scheme, so they'll have to give effect to it.'

'As I understand it,' butted in David, 'the problem with earmarking is that Carlo would have part of your pension, Dora, so it would be paid for your life, not his. So Carlo would be dependent on your whims.'

'I don't follow you' said Dora tetchily.

'Well, you could retire early, and he would get less; you could retire late and he would be left hanging around; you could die and he'd get nothing.'

'So when I reach putting out to grass time, I could jump off Beachy Head and Carlo would get nothing. In any event I'll never make 65. I like this. I could even contemplate Beachy Head if necessary.'

'That's not quite true' interjected Mike rather boringly. 'Carlo, if he thought you hadn't made reasonable provision for him, could make a claim on your estate under the Inheritance (Provision for Family and Dependants) Act 1975. An ex-spouse who is a dependant can claim the protection of this Act. Plus the court will have power to require the trustees to pay the lump sum death benefit to Carlo.'

'What if Dora allocated part of her pension to me?' asked Kevin, making everyone jump in surprise.

'I'm afraid that would probably breach the court order and would be ineffective' replied Mike.

'Darling,' said Dora, 'I could eat you, even when you say nasty things.'

'I think someone else is going to eat him on Saturday so I'm afraid it's paws off, Dora' David cut in quickly.

Dora ignored this tactless interruption: 'When does all this come into effect?'

'The rules apply' said David seizing his chance, 'to divorce proceedings started after 1 July 1996.'

'What happens if I have more than one divorce?' asked Dora. 'Kevin darling, just run down to the bookies and put a fiver on the date of the next election and drop in at Sainsburys on the way back for some pate and champagne. We always seem to be running out of life's little necessaries.' As Kevin ambled off, she continued 'We don't want to wash our dirty linen in front of the children.'

'We don't know yet.' Mike pontificated, lounging back with his hands in his pockets. 'But since pension rights will be valued on a cash equivalent basis, the percentage split should stay the same. So Carlo would get 50 per cent of your *present* cash equivalent, although it would, of course, be payable in the future by way of pension. Kevin would get 50 per cent of the cash equivalent built up during your marriage (or perhaps since you started living together?) and so on. Members would build up slices of cash equivalents earned during "matrimonial (or equivalent) pensionable service". What a prospect! No doubt there will be rich pickings for us lawyers!'

'You can be married and "cohabit" with someone else, as you lawyers would say,' said Dora sarcastically, 'I usually have, I must admit, more than one relationship on the go. I used to weekend with poor Carlo while indulging Kevin in the week. I expect that will add to the bill.'

'Just so' replied Mike diplomatically.

'I've just had an idea' said David, sensing that Dora was getting both bored and angry with the advice she was receiving. 'Why don't we change the scheme rules so that on divorce, just like bankruptcy, the entitlement to the pension ceases and the trustees are given a discretion to pay the pension to the member or to the member's dependants. That way there would never be a "payment in respect of any benefits under the scheme due to the party with pension rights"—to quote s 166 of the Act. The entitlement would evaporate on divorce.'

'But' said Mike, 'you've ignored another bit which says that nothing in the rules applies to the court exercising these powers in respect of any benefits under a pension scheme which a party to the marriage has or is likely to have. Furthermore,' he continued pompously, 'while the existing law, and indeed s 92 of the Act, allows forfeiture on bankruptcy and in certain other cases, forfeiture of pensions is not generally allowed, and certainly not on divorce.'

'We mustn't argue in front of the client, Mike. All I'm saying is that there will be a big market for divorce-proof pensions. Whoever succeeds in putting the lid back on Pandora's box will reap a rich reward.' David explained with a grin.

'By the way how is Archie? I hear he's just back from a lecture tour in Canada and the States.'

'Yes,' replied Mike 'the amazing thing is they liked him, you know; just like the Aussies. It's sad. When he came back, he said he felt revitalised and would carry on till he was 150. You should have seen the faces of Oliver and the rest of the team' said Mike.

Quick as a flash David replied: 'You should remind him of that other great leader who was convinced she was immortal and would carry on until the 21st century. She got the order of the boot soon afterwards.'

Chapter 15

Accountability of Trustees

There are a number of ways in which trustees can be held account-able to members of their pension schemes.

Internal dispute resolution

Company pension schemes have to have a procedure for dispute res-olution. The procedure is in two stages. The first stage requires a named person to give a decision about a complaint, normally within two months. The complainant must be told that, if he is dissatisfied, he has the right to refer the matter within six months for reconsider-ation by the trustees. If the decision, at the first stage, is not given within two months, an interim reply must be sent immediately ex-plaining the reasons for the delay and the expected date for giving the decision.

The second stage requires the trustees, if the complainant is not satisfied, to reconsider the matter. This means the trustee body as a whole, unless the scheme rules permit the trustees to delegate this task to a sub-committee of the trustees. The time limit for the com-plainant to go to the second stage is six months from being notified of the decision at stage one. The trustees will have two months to deal with the complaint. If the trustees' decision is not given within two months, an interim reply must be sent immediately explaining the reasons for the delay and the expected date for giving the decision—just as with the first stage. The complainant must be told that OPAS is available to assist in connection with difficulties that the trustees have been unable to resolve and that the Ombudsman can investi-gate and decide any complaint which is referred to him.

The list of possible complainants includes:

(a) active, deferred and pensioner members of the scheme;

(b) the spouse or dependants of a deceased member;

(c) prospective members;

(d) anyone who has ceased to be in any of these categories in the last six months; and

(e) anyone who claims to be in any of these categories.

Complainants may be represented by someone else on their behalf.

Complaints must be in writing, give full particulars of the complaint and be signed by or on behalf of, the complainant. The complainant must give his full name, address, date of birth and National Insurance number. If the complainant is represented by someone the complaint must contain details of the representative's name and address. If the complaint is made by the spouse or dependant of a deceased member, details of their relationship with the deceased member must be included.

The notice of the decision must set out the decision itself together with a reference to any legislation or scheme rule relied on and where a discretion has been exercised, a reference to the scheme rule conferring the discretion. It must also state that if the complainant is not satisfied with the decision it can be referred to the trustees.

Disputes which have gone to the Ombudsman or to a court or an industrial tribunal are excluded from the procedure.

The trustees will be liable for medium penalties—maximum fine of £1,000 for individuals and £10,000 for companies—if they fail to take reasonable steps to implement arrangements for the resolution of disputes.

As part of the basic information about the scheme which has to be given automatically to all prospective members, if practicable before they join the scheme, and if not, within two months of joining, details of the dispute resolution procedure and of the named first stage contact point must be given.

The register

The register of personal and occupational pension schemes offers a tracing service to enable members to investigate and claim their pension rights from their former schemes. The register is open to public inspection without charge. This is a valuable source of information to help members trace deferred pensions in old schemes.

The Pensions Advisory Service

The Pensions Advisory Service (OPAS) was founded in 1983 to advise members of occupational pension schemes about their rights. Under powers given by the Pension Schemes Act 1993 the Secretary of State for Social Security funds OPAS. The role of OPAS embraces both personal and occupational pension schemes. OPAS has a London office at 11 Belgrave Road, London SW1V 1RB, but it also operates on a regional basis through a network of voluntary advisers. The services of OPAS are free.

The Pensions Ombudsman

The Pension Schemes Act provides for a Pensions Ombudsman who is able to investigate complaints about maladministration or disputes, whether of fact or law. His decisions are legally binding; an appeal is permitted only on questions of law. The Ombudsman is able to make people give evidence and produce documents. His awards are enforced like a court order. The Ombudsman produces an annual report.

So members have a free and effective method of redressing their grievances. They are not faced by the uncertainty, delay and expense of the High Court. This means that trustees have to be able to demonstrate that they have acted fairly and properly.

The Ombudsman's jurisdiction has been extended to cover:
  (a) complaints alleging maladministration by the scheme administrators;
  (b) complaints by the employer or the trustees alleging maladministration by the employer or another person;
  (c) complaints by the employer or the trustees of one scheme alleging maladministration of another scheme; and
  (d) any dispute of fact or law between the employer or the trustees and another person responsible for the management of the scheme or the employer or the trustees of another scheme.

Thus the Ombudsman will be able to deal with complaints between trustees and the employer and with disputes between two schemes, and with complaints against administrators.

The Ombudsman, when he holds an oral hearing, can pay travel and subsistence expenses and compensation for lost earnings to the complainant. He can also order the payment of interest if benefits are paid late.

The Ombudsman can also direct employers and trustees to pay compensation to members for distress and inconvenience.

The Ombudsman will not be able to make *findings of fact* relating to compliance with the following statutory duties:

(a) member-nominated trustees;
(b) repayment of surplus to the employer;
(c) restriction on employer-related investments;
(d) appointment of professional advisers;
(e) requirement to keep books and records;
(f) MFR and contributions schedules; and
(g) requirement for money purchase schemes to keep payment schedules.

But the Ombudsman will be able to rely on OPRA's findings in making his own determinations where a member claims to have suffered injustice as a result of the non-compliance.

The Ombudsman will not be able to deal with complaints or disputes where both stages of the scheme's internal dispute resolution procedure have not been completed. But there is an exception where the procedure has been tried and the Ombudsman is satisfied that there is no real prospect of a decision being given within a reasonable time and that it is reasonable for him to investigate the case.

The Compensation Scheme

The Pensions Act sets up the Pensions Compensation Board and Scheme. It covers schemes where the employer is insolvent and:

(a) the value of the assets has been reduced as a result of an offence involving dishonesty;
(b) in the case of a salary related scheme the value of the assets is less than 90 per cent of the liabilities; and
(c) it is reasonable that members of the scheme should be compensated.

The maximum amount payable will be 90 per cent of the loss or the amount needed to restore the scheme to 90 per cent funding. The Board will need to satisfy themselves that there are reasonable grounds for believing that funds have been dishonestly removed.

This represents a less stringent test than that applied in criminal cases. No individuals will be named by the Board or otherwise identified by them as being responsible for the losses. The actions of the Board will not, therefore, prejudice any criminal proceedings taken by prosecuting authorities and payment of compensation will not be dependent upon a criminal conviction.

The Act provides for payments on account, but these will not cover lump sum benefits. The Board can recover compensation payments which with hindsight should not have been paid except if it would result in the scheme being in a worse position than if interim payments had not been made.

The Compensation Scheme does not benefit individual members directly but indirectly they will benefit as a result of their scheme being restored to 90 per cent funding.

OPRA

The Pensions Act has set up a new regulator for occupational pension schemes. It will be the 'policeman' charged with supervising the statutory duties placed on trustees, employers and their advisers by the Pensions Act and the Pension Schemes Act 1993.

OPRA may prohibit a person from being a trustee of a scheme who is in serious or persistent breach of any of his statutory duties. OPRA may also suspend a trustee while considering a prohibition order against him. Before making a prohibition order OPRA must give one month's notice to the person concerned inviting representations, and to the other trustees. It is an offence to act as a trustee while suspended or prohibited, but any actions taken by such a person are not invalid merely because of the order. A prohibition order will have the effect of removing the person as a trustee or, in the case of a suspension order, from acting as a trustee.

Where a trustee is subject to a prohibition order or disqualified, OPRA may appoint a new trustee. OPRA may also appoint a trustee:
  (a) to secure that the trustees as a whole have the necessary knowledge and skill for the proper administration of the scheme;
  (b) to secure that the number of trustees is sufficient for the proper administration of the scheme; or
  (c) to secure the proper use of scheme assets.
The order appointing the trustee may provide for his fees to be paid

out of the scheme and for his powers and duties to be exercisable to the exclusion of the other trustees.

OPRA may order the winding up of schemes where:

(a)   the scheme ought to be replaced by a different scheme;

(b)   the scheme is no longer required; or

(c)   it is necessary to protect the interests of the members.

OPRA may apply to the court for an injunction if it is likely that someone will misappropriate scheme assets. OPRA may apply to the court for a restitution order if a power to make a payment to the employer has been wrongfully exercised or if the trustees have made unlawful loans or provided financial assistance to the employer.

Schemes are required to disclose to members the existence of OPRA in the scheme booklet.

OPRA may impose civil penalties of up to £5,000 in the case of individuals and £50,000 in the case of companies for breaches of their statutory duties by trustees, employers and their advisers.

In addition it may initiate criminal proceedings against employers, trustees and their advisers in the more serious cases. Appendix 2 contains a summary of the duties and sanctions imposed by the Pensions Act. Trustees will not be able to be indemnified out of the scheme's assets for these fines or penalties, nor are they allowed to take out insurance at the expense of the scheme covering fines or penalties.

OPRA is not meant to be used as a method of resolving individual disputes. The function of OPRA is to act as a regulator to enforce the observance of the duties imposed on trustees and employers by the Pension Schemes Act 1993 and the Pensions Act. But there will be an inevitable overlap between the functions of OPRA and the Ombudsman. Basically the Ombudsman will deal with individual disputes while OPRA will deal with complaints about the way in which a scheme is being run.

The levy

A levy is imposed on schemes to pay for OPRA, the register, the Ombudsman, OPAS and the Compensation Scheme.

Whistle blowing

If the actuary or auditor has reasonable cause to believe that any duty relevant to the administration of the scheme is not being complied with and the failure is likely to be of material significance to OPRA, he must report it immediately to OPRA. Such disclosure will not amount to a breach of any professional duty.

Any adviser, other than the actuary or auditor, and any trustee and anyone involved in the administration of the scheme may (not must) whistle blow in the same circumstances as the actuary or auditor. Such disclosure will not amount to a breach of any professional duty. Matters covered by legal professional privilege are, however, exempted from the whistle blowing requirement.

'The Lawyer's Tale: The Whinger's Charter' which follows illustrates how some of these protections for members will work in practice.

The Lawyer's Tale: The Whinger's Charter

Adam slid unobserved into his room at Megalaw House at 10 am one morning. He thought he had escaped detection and would have time to adjust his aching head to the day's work. But just as he had settled himself comfortably, obscured by files and papers, for a 10 minute doze, he was brutally awakened by Paul; they had both been out playing football the night before followed by a few drinks before dancing the night away in their latest club down in Docklands.

Unlike Adam, however, Paul survived, and indeed seemed to thrive, on only a few hours' sleep.

'Adam, you know you're due to see Sir Hector Grandison at 11 am to talk about what he calls the "tiddy bits" in the Pensions Act—dispute resolution, statement of investment principles, appointing advisers etc etc. You'd best look sharp. You've got to be out at Colindale in under an hour, but you've got the journey to bone up on the details. Did you know, by the way' he concluded inconsequentially 'that your eyes look like they've been pickled in vinegar!'

With a head, splitting laugh and a hearty slap on the back that almost knocked Adam to the floor, Paul continued on his way. Adam struggled back into his overcoat, picked up the Megalaw Plain English Guide to the Pensions Act and headed for St Paul's tube station. By a stroke of good timing, he met David, the scheme's pension consultant, just as he drove up to Anglo Metals House in his silver Lamborghini, soaking poor Adam as he splashed his way through the puddles.

In honour of the Pensions Act, Sir Hector had recruited a new pensions manager, a comfortable motherly lady of 35 called Sheila. She immediately took poor Adam under her wing, taking pity on his bedraggled appearance.

'Let's just get you undressed and dried before I take you in to see Sir Hector.' With that she deftly removed his overcoat and jacket and gave him a modified form of blanket bath.

'It's not nice to drive so fast in the lake that the car park has turned into and soak your friend' she smoothed at David, to make him feel guilty.

'Now let's see what we've got on the agenda for this morning—dispute resolution, statement of investment principles and professional advisers. Not a lot, which is lucky because his lordship is off on Concorde this evening to New York and he's got a full day before him.'

Moments later they were ushered into Sir Hector's baronial board-room where Sheila efficiently ran through the reason for the meeting.

'We've dealt with member-nominated trustees, decided to remain contracted-out on a salary related basis by reference to the new benchmark reference scheme. Colin Bell, our actuary, is satisfied he can give his certificate of broad equivalence and he's said that we'll have no problems with the MFR. So that leaves the odds and ends to sort out before April. First on the agenda is setting up a procedure for internal dispute resolution.'

'That's easy' growled Sir Hector staring through his pince-nez at Adam as if he was something the cat had brought in. 'We don't have disputes. Never have and never will, I wouldn't have got where I am today if I'd had disputes. If people don't like it, they can always leave. "If you don't like this hole, find a better one" as my old mother used to say.'

'But, Sir Hector' soaped Adam unctuously, 'the Pensions Act isn't designed to catch good employers like you. Nevertheless,' he floundered on, 'every scheme has got to have an internal dispute resolution procedure in place. If you don't, you and your co-trustees will be liable to medium level penalties—up to £1,000 for an individual and £10,000 for a company. The only schemes to be exempt from the requirement are one member schemes and schemes where all the members are trustees.'

'And what pray,' thundered Sir Hector, 'does this nonsense involve?'

'Well,' gulped Adam struggling, 'the procedure is basically in two stages. The first stage will require someone to give a decision about the complaint, normally within two months. You could nominate Sheila for this purpose. If the member is not satisfied, he can require the trustees to reconsider it. He's got six months to make the second application and the trustees will normally have two months to deal with the complaint. If either the first named contact point or the trustees can't give their decision within two months, they must write immediately explaining the reason for the delay and the expected date for giving the decision.'

By this time Adam was on the home straight because Sir Hector was taking a conference call from Chicago.

Adam ploughed on 'At the second stage the complainant must be told that OPAS (the Pensions Advisory Service) is available to assist members and beneficiaries in connection with unresolved disputes and also that the Pensions Ombudsman may investigate and determine any complaint or dispute of fact or law in relation to a scheme. What's more members have to be told about the scheme's internal dispute resolution procedure in the scheme booklet as part of the basic information about the scheme.'

By this time Adam was on autopilot and he hadn't, rather dangerously, noticed that Sir Hector had finished talking about the price of hogs' bellies and was listening once again with thunderous attention.

'I've never heard such dangerous nonsense in my life' roared Sir Hector. 'First, I don't have disputes. Second, if I have to tell my members that there's a procedure for resolving disputes, it'll only encourage them to have disputes. Third,' he continued ticking off his stubby fingers, menacing poor Adam, transfixed like a rabbit in the headlights, 'I've got to tell them that if they don't accept Sheila's ruling, they can appeal to me.'

There were, in fact, other trustees but Sir Hector swept this aside in his furious onslaught.

'Fourth, in the unimaginable event that they are not satisfied by me, I've got to tell them about OPAS and the Ombudsman. Now who on earth are they? No don't tell me' he rumbled, 'OPAS are a bunch of dissatisfied do-gooders who've got nothing better to do than meddle in other people's affairs. At least they've got no teeth whereas I hear that the Ombudsman can, and does, whack people hard. That's all quite right and proper of course for the bad schemes. Indeed I hear that he's even ordered Her Majesty's Government to repay £200 million they swiped out of the National Bus Scheme. When you've got crooks, then, of course, you need the appropriate penalties.'

Seeing his chance David butted in 'According to the DSS, Sir Hector, the mere fact of having a dispute resolution procedure will mean that, in future, everything will be just dandy and there'll be nothing more for OPAS or the Ombudsman to do.'

'Pshaw' or words to that effect riposted Sir Hector. 'Got their heads in the sand and their feet off the ground. In fact it's just the opposite. All this little piece of bureaucratic nonsense will mean is a culture of disputes—a veritable dispute resolution industry. If a troublemaker (and by definition anyone who makes a complaint is a troublemaker) doesn't like my ruling, and he's told all about OPAS and the Ombudsman, he'd be a fool to himself if he didn't take advantage.'

'Before we get on to the other items on the agenda, Sir Hector, perhaps Adam will tell us what happens if Sheila rules in favour of the member; does this bind the trustees?' burbled David a tad maliciously.

'Thanks, Dave, for that interesting question' maundered Adam while desperately thinking of the answer. But he was saved by Sir Hector.

'We won't waste time on hypothetical questions. The trustees will obviously choose as their first port of call someone sensible like Sheila. You wouldn't find in favour of the member without consulting me first, would you, my dear? But nonetheless it's a good point, David. Best choose a sound fellow, like Sheila, for the first stage. The last thing you want is one of these fresh-faced wet-behind-the-ears pinkos in the Human Resources Department. Have we done that subject now?' he concluded looking at his watch.

'You haven't told us who can complain, how they should make their complaint, whether they can have someone represent them or how Sheila and the trustees should deal with a complaint' rubbed in David.

'Yes, do tell us all' syrupped Sheila who had obviously taken a fancy to Adam. 'What should I do with all those 14-page letters in green ink?'

Adam thought of saying that Anglo-Metals didn't have any complaints but then second, better, thoughts prevailed. Luckily Sir Hector was back to pork bellies in Chicago.

'Authorised complainants include:

(a)   active members, deferred members, pensioners and their dependants;

(b)   prospective members;

(c)   anyone who has left the scheme in the last six months; and

(d)   anyone who claims to be in any of the previous categories.

Complainants can nominate a representative to act for them. Applications have got to be in writing ...'

'This is all most interesting, but another time' interrupted Sir Hector. 'I've got to go to New York and you still haven't told us about the statement of investment principles or about appointing our advisers.'

Quick as a dog after a rabbit David opined:

'Sir Hector, the written statement of investment principles is a complex document covering:

(a)   the minimum funding requirement;

(b)   the kinds of investment to be held;

(c)   the balance between different kinds of investment;

(d)   risk;

(e)   expected return; and

(f)   realisation.

I'd best get Colin Bell to do the first draft. With due respect to Adam, it's something for the actuary and the fund manager, not the lawyers. By the way I happen to have handy a specimen form of internal dispute resolution procedure with some guidance notes for Sheila plus suitable wording for the scheme booklet.'

Smoothing on he continued 'I know how valuable your time is, Sir Hector, so I have taken the liberty of bringing with me the new forms for appointing the scheme actuary, the auditor, consultants and the fund manager. Since trustees don't have to have a legal adviser, I didn't bring one along for Megalaw. If you would just sign them on behalf of the trustees at your convenience, Sheila can send them back to me.'

On their way back to the City in the warmth and luxury of David's Lamborghini, Adam sulkily shook his James Dean quiff at David. Quick as a flash, sensing danger, David said 'Would you like me to drop you at the station or would you like to take a turn at the wheel back to the City? Incidentally, how is my old boss, Archie? Down and out, Jagless and in his eventide home?'

'Not yet' smiled Adam, 'he's lecturing in South Africa at the moment. It's his rivals, who put about those stories of his retirement, who need your sympathy, not Archie. Like Mark Twain, the rumours of his death are greatly exaggerated.'

Chapter 16

The Liability of Trustees

Breach of trust

If trustees do anything that is wrong, it is called a breach of trust. If they cause loss to their members by not acting in accordance with the rules or by carelessness or fraud, they are personally liable and the trust assets can be claimed to make good the loss. Trustees thus face heavy responsibilities when they take on their duties. Not only are they responsible for their own breaches of trust, they are liable for the breaches of trust committed by their fellow trustees. Trustees can also be called to account by the Pensions Ombudsman where they have been guilty of maladministration.

Liability of trustees

Trustees can also face liability to the Inland Revenue, for example, on the 20 per cent tax due on employee refunds or for the 40 per cent tax charge on payments of surplus to the employer. Trustees must also comply with the rules on insider dealing. If they act on the basis of unpublished price-sensitive information in marketable securities, they will commit a criminal offence.

Corporate trustees

Sometimes trustees form a limited company to act as trustee, partly on the grounds of administrative convenience but also to limit their liability as trustees. It is doubtful, however, if there is any significant difference in the liabilities of the directors of such a company and the liabilities of individual trustees.

Penalties and sanctions

The Pensions Act gives full effect to the recommendation of the Pension Law Review Committee that every duty should carry a sanction. There is a bristling array of civil penalties and criminal sanctions for a whole host of new offences. OPRA may impose civil penalties of up to £5,000 in the case of individuals and £50,000 in the case of companies for breaches of their statutory duties by trustees, employers and their advisers.

The civil penalties range from low—a maximum fine of £200 for individuals and £1,000 for companies—to medium—£1,000 for individuals and £10,000 for companies—to high—£5,000 for individuals and £50,000 for companies. Most of the duties imposed on trustees and employers by the Pensions Act attract penalties for their breach, but the most serious offences attract criminal sanctions.

In the Magistrates courts, summary conviction can result in a fine and in the Crown courts, conviction can lead to imprisonment for up to two years and an unlimited fine.

Examples of criminal offences are non-compliance with the regulations on self-investment by trustees or fund managers who agreed to the investment, and the failure by the employer to hand over to the trustees employee contributions deducted from their pay within 19 days of the end of the month in which the deduction is made without reasonable excuse.

A table of sanctions showing the full range of the new civil and criminal penalties is contained in Appendix 2.

Protection for trustees

It is not possible to give an exhaustive list of all the situations in which a trustee could be held personally liable for a breach of trust. However, examples include the following:

(a) payment of the wrong amounts of benefits;
(b) payment to the wrong beneficiary;
(c) late payment of benefits;
(d) investments outside the trustees' powers;
(e) failure to review investments;
(f) wrongful delegation of powers;

(g) failure to collect the employer's contributions; and

(h) payment of a transfer to an unsuitable (eg unapproved)
     scheme.

In spite of this frightening array of possibilities, it is unusual for a
trustee to be made personally liable for a breach of trust. Trustees
are protected by the Trustee Act 1925 and usually by the provisions
of the trust deed. Under s 61 of the Trustee Act 1925, if it appears to
the court that a trustee is, or may be, personally liable for any breach
of trust, but that he has acted honestly and reasonably and ought
fairly to be excused, the court may relieve him from personal liability
for the breach.

The practical problem for trustees is that they will have to wait for
the court order before they know whether they are safe. It is dependent on the exercise of the court's discretion and so it is impossible to
know in advance if a trustee will be relieved.

The trust deed may include what is known as an 'exclusion clause'
or an indemnity clause. An exclusion clause will contain words to the
effect that a trustee will not be liable for any breach of trust except
when committed through his own wilful default or personal conscious
wrongdoing. While, at first sight, this type of provision might be seen
to afford complete protection, there is the danger that a court might
decide that such a clause did not exclude liability for negligence. It
certainly would not exclude liability for fraud or reckless conduct.

An indemnity is a provision for a trustee to be indemnified either
by the employer or out of the fund. An indemnity from the employer
only gives protection while the employer is solvent. This does not apply to an indemnity out of the fund.

Even if trustees decide that they are sufficiently protected whilst
the scheme is continuing, they might feel it prudent to take out indemnity insurance in the event of the scheme winding up.

Trustees' Indemnity Insurance

The trust deed and rules should be checked to ensure that the trustees have express power to take out insurance. Similarly, if the
trustees want to pay premiums out of the fund they need express
power. Alternatively the employer can pay the premiums direct.

The Pensions Act prevents trustees from being indemnified
against the various civil penalties which it imposes out of the assets

of the scheme or by insurance effected at the expense of the scheme. It does not, however, prevent the employer from giving such an indemnity or from effecting insurance against these liabilities.

Before a meaningful decision can be made upon whether to insure, an estimate has to be made of the amount of cover required and of the premium to be charged for that cover. Trustees' indemnity insurance is expensive and is really only necessary for schemes in winding up where, once the trustees have completed the winding up and parted with the assets, they have nothing further to protect them from any unforeseen claims.

In normal circumstances with an ongoing scheme it is unlikely that any trustee or director of a corporate trustee would be liable for a breach of trust in the absence of dishonesty or recklessness. The trustees would have the protection of the exclusion clause or indemnity in the trust deed and would often be able to demonstrate that they had acted on professional advice. If a trustee is dishonest or reckless it is unlikely that any indemnity in the trust deed and rules would protect him. Equally any insurance policy makes it quite clear that a dishonest trustee would not be protected, even though the other trustees and the fund would be.

It is necessary therefore to weigh up the likelihood of a dishonest or reckless breach of trust being committed by one of the trustees which depletes the assets of the fund and set this against the cost of the premium. In a well run scheme the risk of this occurring is usually so unlikely as to make the premium too expensive in practice. In an ongoing scheme therefore trustees' indemnity cover is usually considered unnecessary and not worthwhile or appropriate.

'The Lawyer's Tale: Putting up Your Umbrella' which follows, discusses trustees' indemnity insurance.

The Lawyer's Tale: Putting Up Your Umbrella

'Hi, Archie, I'm on my car phone' announced David one morning breaking into Archie's daydreams about his forthcoming visit to Australia.

'You remember Colonel Braithwaite from Automated Widgets, don't you?' he continued.

'Of course' replied Archie sharply. 'Why do you suppose that I could forget one of my most important clients? You're not suggesting I'm off my trolley, are you?'

'Not completely—at any rate yet' said David with a laugh. 'But that's the point; he's not "your" client, is he, Archie? In fact he's ours, plus he can't stand you!'

'Yes, yes' said Archie testily. 'Do get on, David, I take it you have a point to make; you're not just filling in time on the M25, are you?'

'As a matter of fact I do have a point. Did you get out of bed the wrong side today by any chance.' He pressed on quickly without waiting for a reply. 'The Colonel has now sold Automated Widgets. PEPS are only just hanging on as consultants by a whisker. I couldn't go to the last trustees' meeting and they decided to call in some local insurance brokers to advise the trustees on indemnity insurance. Like you, Archie, I'm not a great fan of that, even more so when its being peddled by our competitors. I actually asked Oliver to come with me to the next trustees' meeting but he's going to be serving Queen and Country under canvas on Salisbury Plain. So I'll take Paul instead.'

Paul was the latest recruit at the Employee Benefits Group at Megalaw. He was a stocky young man with short fair hair and the self-assurance of one many years his senior. He had a nice manner and was good at handling Archie. The trouble was that when he was humouring Archie like a nurse with a difficult patient, it sometimes showed a little obviously.

'Paul is fine, but I don't let him go out by himself just yet, you know, David' replied Archie.

'Don't worry your remaining grey hairs over that' laughed David. 'I'll be there for starters plus he's a big boy. I heard him speak at a conference recently. You must let him spread his wings, Archie. I'll have Paul, if you don't mind.'

Archie did mind. He wasn't used to David overruling him. He was used to being the boss. That was the trouble. 'I suppose I must do what I'm told. I'm not your boss any more, I know.'

And so two days later David and Paul were racing up the M1 to Milton Keynes in David's silver Porsche. 'You're not going to whinge about my driving, like your colleagues, I hope' said David as the speedometer needle hovered on the 100 mark.

'No' laughed Paul, 'but then I've got a bit more padding than them.'

When they got to the meeting Colonel Braithwaite introduced the other trustees. The Colonel was now the independent chairman, there were two company appointees and two trustees appointed by the members. As the Colonel said 'We're Goode boys now. We haven't waited for the law to catch up with us. Our two new member trustees are worried about personal liability. They say that the company trustees are covered by their Directors and Officers Policy. But that leaves the rest of us out in the cold. So we asked Mr Blenkinsop here to come and advise us.'

Mr Blenkinsop was not cast in the mould to advise the Colonel. He was in his mid 30s, wore a shiny green double-breasted suit and a pony tail. 'Well, Colonel' he began in a Geordie accent, 'you must get yourself and the two lads covered double quick. It's not fair that you should bear this weight of personal responsibility when the management trustees are sitting pretty. I've got some brochures here plus proposal forms. I suggest you have a dekko at them, then sign your names. I'll fill in the rest and send the invoice to the company. Then you can sleep easy in your bed tonight.'

'I'm sure you're right' said the Colonel looking at him with distaste over the top of his half-moon glasses. 'But not so fast.'

At this point David, one of the Colonel's favourites, butted in:

'Like you say, Colonel, oughtn't we to start off at the first tee before we get to the 19th? Wouldn't it be a good idea if Paul, as the trustees' lawyer, gave us the background first?'

'Capital' the Colonel replied beaming. 'Here's your chance, young man.'

'There are all sorts of things that can go wrong with a pension scheme' Paul started off 'but it is almost unheard of for a trustee to be made personally liable for a breach of trust. Let's just consider some of the various methods of protecting trustees:

(1) The Trustee Act 1925 gives the court power to relieve a trustee from personal liability for breach of trust if he has acted honestly and reasonably and "ought fairly to be excused". But you can't be sure how the courts would react, especially if a trustee has been negligent.

(2) Much better is an exclusion clause in the trust deed. This will exonerate the trustees unless the breach of trust is caused by wilful default. Alternatively the trustees may have an indemnity from the company and from the assets of the scheme, but this won't cover the new penalties imposed by the Pensions Act. The employer's indemnity is of course only as good as the employer.'

'That is a point you should bear in mind, Colonel,' said David, 'seeing that you no longer own the company.'

'(3) Third, there is, as Mr Blenkinsop says, insurance. I've checked that your rules allow you to take out insurance at the expense of the scheme. By the way, did you check that too, Mr Blenkinsop?' asked Paul with a twinkle in his eye. He went on quickly:

'But there are problems with insurance:

(a) how much and how affordable is the premium?

(b) will there be an excess for which you will remain personally liable?

(c) how much cover should you buy? Remember that there isn't the capacity in the market to cover the £700b worth of pension scheme assets in this country.

(d) last what cover does the policy provide and are there any exclusions?

You'll usually find that losses caused by pre-existing circumstances—circumstances you knew or should have known of when you took out the policy—are excluded. That's the real rub. The Maxwell trustees had in fact got indemnity insurance. But since one of the proposers was Kevin Maxwell, it didn't do much good.'

The Colonel's attention span was beginning to wane. David spotted this 'While we are digesting this advice, Colonel, might I suggest that as it's now past 12 pm, I should ring for the champagne.'

'Excellent' replied the Colonel. The company trustees looked aghast. 'When I ran the company' he continued, 'I made it a rule never to allow drink on the premises. That, of course, meant beer and spirits. Champagne, on the other hand, when the sun is past the yard arm, aids concentration. Winston Churchill always fancied Pol Roger. If that was good enough for him, it's good enough for us.'

Mr Blenkinsop saw his opportunity 'What you've overlooked, Paul, is the loss to the scheme—not the trustees' liability. You've got your trustees' hat on. I agree that the trustees might rely on the indemnity in the rules but if someone makes off with the assets, they've got to be made good. Otherwise the members suffer. So the company has got to pick up the tabs. You didn't think of that, did you?' he sneered.

'There are, as you say, two points' replied David. 'What you need to ensure is that the scheme doesn't suffer a loss and that, if it does, the trustees are not personally liable. As Paul said, there are a number of difficulties about insurance. If I may say so, before any meaningful decision can be made, an estimate has to be made of the amount of cover required and of the premium to be paid. Indemnity insurance is expensive. Since it will not protect trustees against fraud, any more than an indemnity would, you really have to weigh up whether it's necessary. It is necessary for schemes in winding up, because once the trustees have parted with the assets, they've got nothing to protect them against unforeseen claims.'

'Like David says,' jumped in Paul, 'in normal circumstances with an ongoing scheme, it's unlikely that any trustee would be liable for breach of trust in the absence of dishonesty or recklessness. The trustees would be protected by the indemnity and would often be able to show that they had acted on professional advice. If one of the trustees was reckless or dishonest, no policy or indemnity would cover him, even though, I admit, the fund and the other trustees might be protected.'

'To sum up, Colonel' David weighed in, seeing that the Colonel was looking anxiously at his watch, 'it's necessary to assess the likelihood of a dishonest or negligent breach of trust by one of the trustees which depletes the scheme's assets and set this against the cost of the premium. In a well run scheme, like yours, the risk of this occurring is usually so unlikely as to make the premium not worthwhile.'

'I was going to suggest' continued Paul, 'that the trustees commission PEPS and ourselves to do a review of your administrative controls and security procedures and report at the next trustees' meeting. We'll also produce costings for the premiums for various levels of cover. Our friend with the fake Rolex doesn't seem to have done this.'

'I've always had a healthy respect for David, but you too, Paul, seem up to scratch. It's a good job that that half-witted old goat, your employer, manages to get such good assistants; that's his only virtue as far as I can see' said the Colonel with an approving smile. 'Your recommendation is carried.'

The other trustees obediently nodded.

'Could I just finish with three minor points before we break?' Paul asked.

'(1) First, Goode thought there was neither need, nor capacity in the insurance market, for trustees to be insured or bonded.

(2) Second, the management trustees shouldn't assume that their Directors and Officers Policy covers them for trustees' liability. We must check this.

(3) Last, since technically you're not trustees but directors of a trustee company, any policy you take out must be taken out by you as individuals. A corporate trustee doesn't fall within the definition of a "private policyholder" and wouldn't therefore be protected by the Policyholders Protection Act if the insurance company goes bust.'

But it was too late. The Colonel was leading the way to the directors dining room.

As Paul remarked on the way back to London 'Life's not fair, is it? The Colonel thought I was an expert but luckily Archie and I had been through it all with a fine toothcomb yesterday. Blenkinsop can't help his accent; a draft, however it's pronounced, is the same when it's typed, isn't it?'

David, concentrating on the heavy motorway traffic, just laughed. 'Never trust a man with a pony tail.'

Chapter 17

Delegation, Conflict and Disagreement

Delegation

Trustees are given wide powers by the Trustee Act 1925 and by the scheme rules to delegate certain of their powers and duties. Nevertheless they remain in control. Principal areas of delegation are the appointment of a secretary, actuary, auditor, solicitor, bank and investment manager.

Choosing agents

Trustees can pay their agents reasonable remuneration for their services and they must exercise care in selecting and choosing them. As long as they do this, and exercise a reasonable degree of supervision, they will not be responsible for the agent's acts or defaults.

Rules of delegation

The way in which investment management is delegated has been dealt with in Chapters 5 and 6. Sometimes trustees delegate certain discretionary powers, like paying lump sum death in service benefits, to a committee or to local managers or committees. If the rules do not authorise this, the trustees will remain responsible for the acts of their delegates. And so scheme rules commonly set out extensive powers of delegation by trustees and authorise them to appoint committees to deal with certain matters. They often also deal fully with the appointment, payment and removal of agents such as actuaries. The reason for this is not to bestow these powers (this has already been conferred by the Trustee Act) but to make it clear who has the power.

Conflicts of interest

Trustees of pension schemes are often directors of the employing company or, at any rate, employees and they will probably be members of the scheme as well. The rules will probably say that the fact that a trustee is a member and an employee will not invalidate any decisions taken by him or her. The Pensions Act confirms that member trustees may exercise their discretionary powers even though this benefits or may benefit them as members of the scheme.

Trustees are not negotiators

In exercising their powers and carrying out their duties, trustees must be aware of conflicts of interest. When they are acting as trustees of the pension scheme, they must pay no regard to their other responsibilities, for example, as trade union officials or directors of the employer. Since the primary duty of trustees is to administer the scheme in accordance with the rules, conflicts of interest should not cause problems very often. Trustees do not usually have a negotiating role and thus it is not usually part of their duties to seek benefit improvements or contribution holidays for their members. If, faced with a conflict, a trustee is in doubt about what to do, he or she can either abstain or else seek professional advice. Trustees should also consult their members in appropriate cases.

Disagreement

Decisions of the trustees may, unless the scheme provides differently, be taken by a majority of the trustees. This will not apply to trustees appointed by OPRA with special powers, statutory independent trustees appointed on insolvency or to the requirement for unanimity for removal of a member-nominated trustee. Where decisions are to be taken by a majority, the trustees can specify a quorum for decisions unless the scheme provides otherwise. In addition, notice of meetings at which majority decisions may be taken must be given to each trustee to whom it is reasonably practicable to give notice, except where it is necessary as a matter of urgency to make a decision. The notice must, unless the trustees agree otherwise, specify the date, time and place of the meeting and be sent to the last known address of each trustee at least 10 working days in advance.

Readers are referred to *'The Lawyer's Tale: Splitting the Apple'*, which follows this chapter, for an illustration of how such problems may be resolved.

The Lawyer's Tale: Splitting the Apple

It had been a bad morning for Colin Bell, the deputy pensions actuary at the Magnificent Mutual Life Assurance Society. He had been
asked to produce costings for deferred pensions for the members on
the winding up of the Cox's Orange Pension Scheme. No one likes
winding up pension schemes, least of all insurance companies. It is a
scheme lost—not a scheme gained. He got his assistant John Tom-
kins to work out the figures. As an actuary, Colin would not of course
dirty his own hands with menial work like that. What emerged was
that the cost of buying out the benefits was of the order of £700,000.
That left a surplus of about £900,000. Under the winding up rule the
trustees had discretion to augment benefits up to Revenue limits.
Anything left over had to be paid back to the company.

What was disturbing both Colin and John was that the company—
Cox's Orange—had just been taken over by a French company, based
in Normandy, called Golden Delicious. It was they who had instigat-
ed the winding up of the scheme.

'We'll have to write to the trustees giving them the figures and give
them various costings for benefit improvements to mop up the surplus. We'd better suggest we go and see them to discuss it all' said
Colin.

'That would be excellent,' said John 'their head office is in Rouen.
We will go on a Thursday and come back the following Monday.'

A letter was duly despatched to Rouen. A week later a curt reply
was received. It announced that Golden Delicious had removed the
old company-appointed trustees of the pension scheme and substitut-
ed two Golden Delicious employees in their place. What's more a copy
of the deed in faultless legal English was enclosed. The letter went
on to instruct the Magnificent Mutual to buy out the members' benefits with deferred annuity policies and to pay a cheque for the balance to the company. In the same post came a letter of complaint
from one of the trustees who had been so summarily replaced.

'Well there goes our weekend in Normandy' said Colin to John
when he showed him the two letters.

'I don't like this and Philip will like it even less.' Philip was the
senior pensions actuary and was Colin's and John's boss. 'You know
how he hates any kind of complaint.'

'But it isn't a complaint about the Magnificent Mutual' replied
John. 'It's not our fault. We've just got to do what we're told.'

'I'm going to have a word with Archie Smithers. I feel a touch of the wobblies about this' said Colin. Archie was the Society's lawyer who ran the documents department. He and Colin were old friends.

So off he went in search of Archie. And, as so often before, he failed to find him. Nor did he find young David, Archie's assistant. He was away on holiday. He did, however, manage to track down Donna, their secretary and Matthew, the latest recruit to the docs department. Matthew was a newly qualified lawyer who thought he would give pensions a whirl. He was small and earnest and sometimes felt life's burdens weighed heavily upon him.

'Where is the old goat then?' cried Colin. 'I don't know why we pay him and Dave. They just set the word processor on autopilot and go away.'

'Archie is at a conference and David is on holiday so I'm in charge of the shop today. You needn't worry about the documents; all is going quite smoothly in their absence.' replied Matthew, a touch frostily.

Colin gave a great baying laugh. 'I know that. Donna does the documents—we all know that. It's just that when they're not here, their uselessness becomes embarrassingly obvious.'

'Well, in that case, I'm sure I don't know why you're wasting my time now' snapped Matthew.

'Don't take on so, lad' said Colin jovially. 'We don't usually need a pension lawyer. Some people don't even think they serve any purpose at all.'

Poor Matthew was not equipped for this kind of banter. Colin went on 'Read this winding up rule, lad' he said, 'plus a couple of letters and tell me if I've got a problem.'

After a few minutes, Matthew looked up and said that the new trustees were now in place, the pension scheme was terminated and the trustees had resolved to buy out the members' scale benefits and pay the surplus to the company.

'What you don't seem to have done is to point out to them' Matthew continued, 'that the repayment of the surplus to the company will attract a free standing 40 per cent tax charge. Nor have you reminded the trustees that they have a discretion to augment the members' benefits up to Revenue limits. You might also have pointed out to them that on a winding up the members' benefits should be revalued in line with prices with a limit of 5 per cent before surplus can be repaid to the company.'

'Proper little know-all, you are for sure' replied Colin. 'Just draft me a reply and I'll fax it through to Rouen.'

The fax was sent off and back came a curt reply confirming the previous instructions. With great daring, Matthew drafted a further fax for Colin pointing out that the trustees duties were to look after their members. They had an unfettered discretion to augment benefits. How could it be in the members' interests to pay over the whole surplus to the company?

Back came an even curter fax thanking the Magnificent Mutual for their unsolicited advice. Golden Delicious had taken its own legal advice. The trustees had a discretion; how they exercised it was their affair. They were not accountable to the Magnificent Mutual. A cheque by return was required. To make matters worse, in the same post came a letter from the members who said they were consulting the Pensions Advisory Service and threatened to take the Magnificent Mutual to court if their benefits were not augmented.

'I've had enough of this' said Colin to Matthew later that day. 'We'll have a go at sorting out this mess first thing tomorrow.'

And so the next day Colin, John and Matthew sat down in a conference room to brainstorm the problem through.

'I formulated some propositions at home last night' started Matthew 'First that deed appointing the new trustees is a bit dodgy. If it was signed after the wind up started, it could be invalid as the company's power may cease on winding up. Even if that were not the case, the deed might be set aside as being a misuse of a fiduciary power. A power to appoint and remove trustees can't be exercised to secure some ulterior objective like benefiting the company. It can only be used to further the members' interests.'

'Well' said John, 'they only put their own stooges in because they wouldn't cause trouble; so the deed is no good then?'

'The problem' replied Matthew, 'is proving it.'

'You're a real iffy lawyer, aren't you?' said Colin. 'Get to the point.'

'Secondly' continued Matthew 'the trustees—whoever they are— have got to act in the interests of the members. It's difficult to see how giving the surplus to the company is in the members' interests. In most cases where the trustees have an unfettered discretion, they should use the surplus to augment benefits up to Revenue limits. Only what's left after that should be paid to the company. Of course there may be situations where it would not be right to use all the surplus in that way. It all depends on the facts.'

'Get on with it, lad' said Colin testily, 'we haven't got all morning.'

'Thirdly' went on Matthew 'the exercise by trustees of a discretionary power can only be set aside if it was made for an improper motive, or if they didn't make proper enquiries before reaching their decision, or if their decision is so capricious that no reasonable trustee could have reached it. It's this last ground that looks as if it were the case here.'

Colin and John had had enough of this legal monologue. 'It's all a matter for the trustees, not us' said Colin. 'They've made their decision, right or wrong, and we've got to do as they tell us. If we don't, then whatever we may feel, we'll end up in court.'

'Not so fast' cried Matthew pink with excitement. 'Archie rang me up last night and I checked through these points with him. He added one final proposition 'As administrators of the scheme the Magnificent Mutual stand in the same position as the trustees themselves. They owe fiduciary duties to the members. They are in the American terminology "plan fiduciaries". And so if they did what the trustees ordered, and it was a breach of trust, the Magnificent Mutual would also be in breach and could be ordered to repay the money.'

There was an awful silence while this sank in.

'To be safe, we would really have to apply to the court for directions as to how to proceed' said Matthew rubbing his hands gleefully at the prospect.

'It all comes of sending Archie to those foreign pension conferences' muttered Colin darkly. 'He picks up strange ideas. I knew no good would come of them.' With that he rose to his feet, turned on his heels, nearly knocking down John in the process and they marched out leaving Matthew high and dry.

'How much would it cost' Colin asked John, 'to provide LPI—RPI indexation with a ceiling of 5 per cent?'

'Oh, about £500,000' said John. 'Mind you that's only a quick approximation.'

The following week Archie had returned from his holiday and he and Matthew were summoned to an 8 am meeting with Colin and John by Philip, the senior pensions actuary. Apparently he wanted to be put in the frame about the Cox's Orange pension scheme and had an early morning window in his diary.

The meeting started off—after a half hour delay—while Philip did his telephone calls—with Colin and John giving their progress report.

'We tracked down the Finance Director of Golden Delicious in Maidstone where the English factory is. So me and John went to see him. We also saw the old trustees and all seven members of the scheme. We got it all sorted out and we then had a long French lunch with wine and Calvados and cigars in the boardroom. We had a lovely day, didn't we John? And what's more we agreed a £50,000 winding up fee for the Magnificent Mutual.'

'However did you sort all that out?' asked Archie with a touch of irritation in his voice.

'It was all quite easy' replied Colin. 'We told the Finance Director that if he wanted the lot, we'd have to apply to the court for directions. And we told the members that if they wanted the lot, the same thing would happen. A fair old chunk of the surplus would be wasted on the lawyers. So why didn't we act like sensible folk and split it down the middle. So everyone agreed and we all had lunch.'

'I am sorry to put a spanner in the works' said Archie, 'but if there was a breach of trust, your precious agreement wouldn't rule out a claim by a contingent member such as a spouse.'

'Pack it in' said Colin, 'I thought you were paid to solve problems—not to invent them.'

'It just goes to prove how right I am about rules' observed Philip. 'Everything must be cut and dried. The trustees should never be given unfettered powers. They are only spending someone else's money. The rules should have required the company's consent before they could augment benefits. That way the problem would never have arisen. Thank you, Matthew, for your contribution and congratulations to Colin and John for solving the problem. As for you, Archie, just make sure our rules give defined benefits and that trustees never have an unfettered discretion.'

Chapter 18

Merger and Winding Up

Merger

As a result of takeovers or company reorganisations, an employer
may end up with two or more pension schemes. It would save time
and money in terms of administration costs if the schemes were
merged. Sometimes one person may be a trustee of both schemes.
There are two points to consider.

Is a merger authorised?

Do the rules give the trustees power to bring about a merger? If not,
they should be altered so as to facilitate the merger. If the merger is
to be effected by a winding up of one of the schemes, no express power
in the rules may be necessary.

Should the trustees agree to the merger?

Even if it is authorised, should the trustees agree to the merger? This
depends on whether it is in the interests of their members. It must
be remembered that for this purpose members include not just active
members but also pensioners and those with preserved pensions,
who have left the employer's service but retained the right to a pension from the scheme when they retire. Questions of the benefits to
be offered by the new scheme and of its solvency will arise. The trustees can only agree to the merger if it is in the interests of the gener-
ality of their members and if their rights and expectations in the new
scheme are no less favourable overall than their rights and expectations in the old scheme. There must also be enough money in the new
scheme, after the merger has taken place, to provide adequate security for the members' rights and expectations. Trustees may have to

take account of a surplus or deficit in their own scheme or the new scheme. This will affect the security of their members' benefits.

Bulk transfers

Bulk transfers of members from one scheme to another should not take place without getting members' individual consents, unless the actuary to the transferring scheme certifies that the transfer credits to be acquired for each member under the new scheme are broadly no less favourable and are not as likely to be significantly less secure than the member's accrued rights, calculated by reference to projected final pensionable earnings. The actuary must also certify that no member of the transferring scheme will receive substantially inferior benefits in the new scheme. Where there is an established custom of providing discretionary pension increases, this has to be taken into account. To avoid members complaining afterwards that the merger was not in their interests, it is often a good idea to get individual consents. Since scheme membership is voluntary, there is not a lot of point in effecting bulk transfers of members without their consent, if they then opt out of the new scheme.

Winding up

The events which cause a scheme to be wound up are set out in the winding up rule. Sometimes it is a notice from the employer, or the employer's insolvency; sometimes the trustees can decide it is no longer possible to continue the scheme.

Statutory order of priority

The Pensions Act lays down the order of priority for the allocation of scheme assets where a salary related scheme subject to the MFR is being wound up. Assets must first be applied in satisfying the following liabilities in the following order:
  (a) benefits attributable to members' voluntary contributions including those transferred from another scheme;
  (b) pensions in payment including pensions payable to the pensioner's dependants on his death;

(c)   accrued benefits, including refunds of contributions; and

(d)   future increases to pensions in payment and accrued benefits. Liabilities for this purpose are only those covered by the Minimum Funding Requirement ie cash equivalents. And so schemes which are solvent on this basis may still be in deficit because the cost of buying out benefits in full cannot be met.

There is a transitional priority order for schemes that start to wind up during the ten year period after April 1997. During that period, liability for pension increases is placed above liability for accrued benefits (other than contracted-out benefits).

Continuation as closed scheme

Where scheme rules require a scheme to be wound up, the trustees may decide not to do so, but that no new members should be admitted. They may also decide that no further contributions are to be paid or that no new benefits should accrue.

If the trustees decide to continue the scheme as a closed scheme, they may fix the priority category and amount of liabilities as at a date between the date of deferring winding up and the date winding up starts. They will have to record their decision and notify the members. Trustees of schemes where the employer is still solvent will not be able to make use of the power to defer winding up.

Surplus on winding up

When an event occurs to trigger a winding up, the assets are realised and applied to secure scheme benefits in the statutory order of priorities. Great care must be taken to apply the assets in the right order. Any surplus that there may be must be dealt with as directed by the scheme rules. If the surplus has to be or is, in the exercise of the trustees' discretion, paid over to the employer, a fixed tax charge of 40 per cent has to be deducted from the payment by the trustees, who must then account for the tax to the Inland Revenue. But before any payment out of the scheme can be made to the employer, all pensions must be guaranteed to increase in line with the rise in the Retail Prices Index with a limit of 5 per cent—LPI or limited price indexation. Trustees may well have a discretion to augment benefits up to

Inland Revenue limits, either with or without the employer's consent. Professional advice, especially advice from the actuary, will be needed before deciding how to exercise these powers.

If a final salary scheme has a deficit on winding up, the amount of the deficiency is due from the employer as an ordinary (unsecured) debt. This will not, of course, do the members much good if the employer is insolvent. If the winding up of the scheme is caused by the employer's insolvency, an independent trustee will have to be appointed. This will avoid the problems caused by the potential conflicts of interest that otherwise might arise.

For an illustration of the difficulties that can arise in this area, readers are referred to *'The Lawyer's Tale: The Revaluation Factor'*, which follows this chapter.

The Lawyer's Tale: The Revaluation Factor

Archie Smithers was having a harassing morning. The day started badly with two internal meetings; never Archie's favourite way of passing the time. Then he faced an unusually large post. Every time he made any progress the phone rang. Archie's replies got terser and terser, even by his standards of brevity.

His tenth caller that morning was young David from Pan European Pension Services, PEPS for short. Donna, Archie's secretary, smiled when she put David through. 'At least he won't bite my head off this time' she thought. It was well known that David was always able to twist Archie round his little finger.

'I've got a nice job for you, Archie, that should keep you out of your eventide home for a bit longer. PEPS Trustees Ltd is the sole trustee of the Amalgamated Carpetweavers Pension Scheme. It's the old story. The company went down last year with debts of £4m. The pension scheme has a surplus of about £1m and the liquidator wants to get his hands on it. Although PEPS Trustees is the trustee, the scheme is administered by our old friends, the Magnificent Mutual. Me and John Watson, the scheme administrator, and Colin Bell, the actuary, need a spot of advice.'

And so a meeting was fixed for the following week in Archie's office on the 57th floor of Megalaw House.

'I don't know how you can concentrate with such a spectacular view' said John Watson.

'Give over' interjected Colin in his broad Lancashire vowels and loud bookie suit, 'he's not been capable of concentrated thought for the past ten years.'

Luckily they were all old friends from their days together at the Magnificent Mutual. David explained that unusually, although the Magnificent Mutual had always looked after the scheme, the company had some time ago asked PEPS Trustees to be the independent trustee of the scheme. And so the liquidator had not needed to appoint an independent trustee when the company went down. Under the winding up rule, the trustee had an unfettered discretion to dispose of surplus.

'My directors, Archie, have decided to use the surplus to revalue benefits in line with the RPI. According to Colin that will just about use up the surplus.'

'So' asked Archie, 'what's the problem?'

'Well,' replied David, 'the problem is that the liquidator is saying that all that is required is LPI; everything else belongs to him. He is quoting the *Thrells* case in support. But that's not the way I read the *Thrells* judgment. What do you think?'

'*Thrells*?' said Archie. 'That sounds like a disease. I'm not quite sure I follow you.'

'Eh' interrupted Colin, 'he's never heard of the case.'

Archie smiled: 'Not so, but I'm going to ask my latest recruit, Mike, to remind us what it was all about.' Mike was a curly-haired Geordie, who came into the room at Archie's bidding.

'Before I get on to *Thrells*, Archie,' started Mike, 'can I just remind you that if the trustees have exercised a discretionary power, then normally the courts will not interfere. In the words of Michael Platt when he was the Pensions Ombudsman:

"I do not see it as my function to intervene here. The only instances where I would consider an investigation would be when the trustees' exercise of discretion had been in breach of a scheme rule or had been so arbitrary and irrational that no reasonable person would, on the facts of the case, have exercised discretion in that way."'

'Yes, yes' said Colin testily. 'We know that. You may be a beginner Mike, but the rest of us are not.'

Mike reddened and quickly went on 'The interest of the *Thrells* case lay simply in the judge telling us the relevant factors to take into account and then how he actually exercised the discretion which the trustee gave up in his favour.

But to start at the beginning. The power of altering the rules was vested in the company. The liquidator asked the court if he could change the rules to remove the trustees power to dispose of surplus on winding up. The judge ruled that the winding up provisions could not be amended once winding up had started.

Next, the liquidator argued that LPI was not required before surplus could be paid to the company. LPI is required for any pension which *commences or has commenced under the pension scheme* before any payment of surplus can be made to an employer. Since winding up had commenced, all pensions would be secured by annuities or transfer payments. Therefore no member's pension would commence *under the scheme*. The judge viewed this literal interpretation of the Act as absurd:

"When payment is triggered by winding up, the pensions

which are to have the benefit of LPI are those which were
payable under the scheme, whether actually or prospectively,
at the time the trigger was pulled."'
'Eh, lad, get to the point' cut in Colin. 'We can't sit here all day. What
did the judge say about exercising the trustees discretion.'

Mike grinned. 'I can't help going round the mulberry bush. It was,
after all, Archie who trained me. If I may be allowed to continue. The
judge itemised the relevant factors:

(1) **The scope and purpose of the power to augment**

There would be no point in giving the trustees power to augment
benefits if they were not meant to exercise it.

"When a scheme so provides, members have a reasonable
expectation that if the scheme funds permit, the trustee will
exercise that power to the extent that is fair and equitable."

If the members were not to benefit from surplus, there would be no
point in giving the power.

(2) **Source of surplus**

Here the judge refused to conclude that

"all the surplus should be regarded as unintended surplus
arising from the company's contributions in which members
can have no reasonable expectations to share."

(3) **Size of surplus**

Presumably the larger the surplus, the greater the possibility of
making a refund to the company.

(4) **The financial position of the company**

The judge noted that

"overfunding can be said in one sense to have been at the
expense of the creditors. They will suffer severe loss by the
failure of the company to meet its obligations to them."

(5) **The needs of the members**

The judge merely observed that he had no evidence about this. It
seems odd that if he thought this was a relevant factor, he didn't ask
for any evidence before coming to his decision.'

At this point David looked at his watch. 'I realise you boys are on time
charges but this is ridiculous. I knew all this before I came, Archie.
What did the judge actually do—that is what the liquidator is on
about.'

Mike looked a bit deflated, so Archie came to his rescue. 'He gave
LPI on all pensions in payment and in deferment and gave the balance to the creditors.'

'Exactly' cried David. 'That's what it's all about. The liquidator is saying that *Thrells* is authority for giving LPI—not RPI. Therefore, the balance after LPI belongs to him.'

'But that's absolute rubbish' replied Mike. 'If the trustees in their discretion decide on RPI, then their decision cannot be questioned in the absence of bad faith. In *Thrells* the judge merely exercised his discretion by granting LPI in the circumstances of that particular case. It's not an authority for saying that trustees must give LPI to the members but no more.'

'Well' said David. 'It's all very well. But the liquidator is threatening to take the trustees to court if they award RPI. Let's cut the cackle; what should we do?'

'Oh' cut in Archie. 'That's easy. We'll get an opinion from Sir Obadiah Thom QC. That'll shut the liquidator up. I'll fix up a consultation with him next week.'

And so the following Friday found them ensconced in Lincoln's Inn in Sir Obadiah's chambers. Sir Obadiah was never one to waste words, and, given the size of his fees, this was no doubt some small consolation.

'Mr Smithers' opinion is of course quite correct as one would expect from such an experienced solicitor of his standing.'

'Actually I thought it was my opinion' said Mike very quietly.

'You have to bear in mind' continued Sir Obadiah, disregarding Mike, 'that *Thrells* was just another in the line of cases on winding up. It said nothing about the ownership of surplus in a continuing scheme. It mainly laid down guidelines for trustees to consider in the exercise of their discretion. As long as trustees observe these guidelines, how they exercise their discretion is a matter for them alone; neither the court nor the Ombudsman will interfere. The fact that the judge himself awarded only LPI is interesting but neither here nor there.'

'But how do we get the liquidator off the trustees' back?' asked David. 'My trustees don't want to give RPI if they end up in court.'

'Ah' replied Sir Obadiah, 'that's easy. Just write him a letter saying:

(a) the trustees have considered the facts;

(b) the trustees have been advised about *Thrells*;

(c) the trustees in the exercise of their discretion have decided to give RPI; and

(d) last but not least, the trustees have had the benefit of being advised by an eminent firm of pension lawyers whose advice has been confirmed by me.

Be so good in addition as to tell them that the trustees propose to distribute the assets seven days after the date of your letter. If the liquidator disagrees he will have to apply to the court and face the prospect of paying the trustees' costs if he loses.'

With those words ringing in their ears, they went off to lunch at the River Room at the Savoy. It was Archie's birthday and his friends had decided to give him lunch.

'After all,' as John observed, 'even lunch at the Savoy is a drop in the ocean compared with Sir Obadiah's fees. And what's more, you were right after all, Archie.'

'Eh, John, come on, come on' said Colin. 'It's the boy, Mike, we should thank. I don't think Archie had even heard of the case.'

'That's only to be expected of you, Colin' replied Archie. 'So I won't bother to argue but it does make me think. For years we've drafted winding up rules and fudged the issue by giving trustees discretion to dispose of surplus. And why? It's caused nothing but trouble. Trustees don't know what to do and, not unnaturally, insolvency practitioners always want to get the surplus for the creditors. The truth is that we didn't know what we were doing. We got it all wrong.'

'At last, he's seen the light and confessed' said David laughing. 'What should we have done?'

'It's all quite simple. After providing for accrued benefits we should require surplus to be used to treat pensions, whether in payment or in deferment, just like GMPs; in other words earnings indexation in deferment and prices indexation in retirement, the balance to the company. That would stop all those silly arguments and would strike a fair balance between the members and the creditors.'

'Oh, do stop rambling' cried Colin. 'Give him another glass of Chardonnay and let's stop talking shop.'

Appendix 1

Glossary of Terms

This Appendix reproduces some of the definitions contained in *Pensions Terminology*—4th edition, published by the Pensions Management Institute and the Pensions Research Accountants Group.

ACCRUED BENEFITS—The benefits for service up to a given point in time, whether vested rights or not. They may be calculated in relation to current earnings or projected earnings. Allowance may also be made for revaluation and/or pension increases required by the scheme rules or legislation.

ACCRUED RIGHTS—A term sometimes used to describe accrued benefits. The term is given specific definitions for the purposes of preservation, contracting-out and the Disclosure Regulations.

ACTUARIAL ASSUMPTIONS—The set of assumptions as to rates of return, inflation, increase in earnings, mortality, etc, used by the actuary in an actuarial valuation or other actuarial calculations.

ACTUARIAL DEFICIENCY—The excess of the actuarial liability over the actuarial value of assets on the basis of the valuation method used. If an actuarial report refers to a surplus or deficiency, it must be studied to ascertain precisely what assets and liabilities have been taken into account. In a stricter sense, the terms surplus and deficiency might be used in relation to the results of a discontinuance valuation.

ACTUARIAL SURPLUS—The excess of the actuarial value of assets over the actuarial liability on the basis of the valuation method used. See notes under actuarial deficiency.

ACTUARIAL VALUATION—An investigation by an actuary into the ability of a pension scheme to meet its liabilities. This is usually to assess the funding level and a recommended contribution rate based on comparing the actuarial value of assets and the actuarial liability.

ADDED YEARS—The provision of extra pension benefits by reference to an additional period of pensionable service in a defined benefit scheme, arising from the receipt of a transfer payment, the paying of additional voluntary contributions or by way of augmentation.

ADDITIONAL VOLUNTARY CONTRIBUTIONS—Contributions over and above a member's normal contributions, if any, which the member elects to pay to the scheme in order to secure additional benefits, either added years or money purchase. See also free standing additional voluntary contributions.

APPROPRIATE PERSONAL PENSION SCHEME (APPS)—A personal pension scheme or free standing AVC scheme granted an appropriate scheme certificate, enabling its members to use it for the purpose of contracting-out.

AUGMENTATION—The provision of additional benefits in respect of particular members, normally where the cost is borne by the pension scheme and/or the employer.

BULK TRANSFER—The transfer of a group of members, not necessarily with their consent, from one pension scheme to another, usually with an enhanced transfer payment in comparison with an individual's cash equivalent. The PSO must be consulted about any such transfer payments.

BUY BACK—A term used to describe the payment of a type of state scheme premium by means of which a member's rights to SERPS are fully reinstated.

BUY OUT—The purchase by pension scheme trustees of an insurance policy or bond in the name of a member or other beneficiary, in lieu of entitlement to benefit from the scheme, following termination of the member's pensionable service. *Sometimes also used to refer to the purchase of an insurance policy in the name of the trustees.*

CASH EQUIVALENT—The amount which a member of a pension scheme may under the Pension Schemes Act 1993 require to be applied as a transfer payment to another permitted pension scheme or to a buy out policy.

CENTRALISED SCHEME—A pension scheme operated on behalf of several employers.

COMMUTATION—The giving up of a part or all of the pension payable from retirement for an immediate cash sum.

CONTRACTED-OUT REBATE
  (1) The amount by which the employers' and employees' National Insurance contributions are reduced in respect of employees who are contracted-out by virtue of their membership of an occupational pension scheme.
  (2) The equivalent payment made by the DSS as minimum contributions to a personal pension scheme.

CONTRIBUTION HOLIDAY—A period during which employers' and/or members' contributions are temporarily suspended, normally when the fund is in surplus. The term is sometimes used loosely when contributions continue to be paid but at a reduced rate.

DEFERRED PENSIONER—A person entitled to preserved benefits. Sometimes referred to as a deferred member.

DEFINED BENEFIT SCHEME—A pension scheme in which the rules specify the benefits to be paid, and the scheme is financed accordingly.

DEFINED CONTRIBUTION SCHEME—An alternative term for a money purchase scheme.

DEPENDANT—A person who is financially dependent on a member or pensioner or was so at the time of death or retirement of the member or pensioner. For PSO purposes a spouse qualifies automatically as a dependant and a child of the member or pensioner may always be regarded as a dependant until attaining the age of 18 or ceasing to receive full-time educational or vocational training, if later.

DISCONTINUANCE VALUATION—An actuarial valuation carried out to assess the position if the scheme were to be discontinued and the trustees were to wind it up in accordance with the requirements of the trust instrument. The valuation may take into account the possible exercise of any discretion to augment benefits.

DYNAMISATION/DYNAMISM
  (1) A term sometimes used to describe escalation or indexation.
  (2) Also used to describe index linking of earnings, either for calculating scheme benefits, or for determining final remuneration for the purpose of PSO limitations.

EARLY LEAVER—A person who ceases to be an active member of a pension scheme, other than on death, without being granted an immediate retirement benefit.

ESCALATION—A system whereby pensions in payment and/or preserved benefits are automatically increased at regular intervals and at a fixed percentage rate. The percentage may be restricted to the increase in a specified index.

EX GRATIA BENEFIT—A benefit provided by the employer which he is not legally required to provide.

EXEMPT APPROVED SCHEME—An approved scheme other than a personal pension scheme which is established under irrevocable trusts (or exceptionally, subject to a formal direction under s 592(1)(b) of the Income and Corporation Taxes Act 1988) thus giving rise to the tax reliefs specified in the Income and Corporation Taxes Act 1988.

EXPRESSION OF WISH—A means by which a member can indicate a preference as to who should receive any lump sum death benefit. The choice is not binding on the trustees, and as a result Inheritance Tax is normally avoided.

FINAL REMUNERATION—The term used by the PSO for the maximum amount of earnings which it will permit to be used for the purpose of calculating maximum approvable benefits.

FREE STANDING ADDITIONAL VOLUNTARY CONTRIBUTIONS (FSAVC)—Contributions to a pension contract separate from a company pension scheme effected by an active member of that scheme. Benefits are secured with a pension provider by contributions from the member only.

FREE STANDING AVC SCHEME—A scheme established by a pension provider to accept free standing additional voluntary contributions.

FUNDING—The provision in advance for future liabilities by the accumulation of assets, normally external to the employer's business.

FUNDING PLAN—The arrangement of the incidence over time of payments with the aim of meeting the future cost of a given set of benefits. Possible objectives of a funding plan might be that, if the actuarial assumptions are borne out by events:

(1) A specified funding level should be reached by a given date.
(2) The level of contributions should remain constant, or should after a planned period be the standard contribution rate required by the valuation method used in the actuarial valuation.

GUARANTEED MINIMUM PENSION—The minimum pension which an occupational pension scheme formerly had to provide as one of the conditions of contracting-out (unless it is contracted-out through the provision of protected rights). For an employee contracted-out under any occupational or personal pension scheme an amount equal to GMP is deducted from his/her benefits under the State scheme.

INDEXATION
  (1) A system whereby pensions in payment and/or preserved benefits are automatically increased at regular intervals by reference to a specified index of prices or earnings. The term is also occasionally used in relation to index linking of final pensionable earnings or final remuneration: see explanation under dynamisation.
  (2) It is also in common use as a method of investment management where the objective is to produce a return equal or close to that of a chosen stock market index.

INTEGRATION—The design of pension scheme benefits to take into account all or part of the State scheme benefits which the member is deemed to receive. One form of integration involves a State pension disregard.

LOWER EARNINGS LIMIT (LEL)—The minimum amount, approximately equivalent to the basic pension, which must be earned in any pay period before National Insurance Contributions are payable.

MANAGED FUND—An investment contract by means of which an insurance company offers participation in one or more pooled funds. Also used to denote an arrangement where the scheme assets are invested on similar lines to unit trusts by an external investment manager.

MEMBER—A person who has been admitted to membership of a pension scheme and is entitled to benefit under the scheme. Sometimes narrowly used to refer only to an active member. For some statutory purposes the term 'members' may include employees who are prospective members.

MINIMUM CONTRIBUTIONS
  (1) Contributions payable to a personal pension scheme or to a free standing AVC scheme by the DSS in respect of a member who has elected to contract-out. The contributions consist of

a partial rebate of National Insurance Contributions, together with the 2 per cent incentive where applicable.

(2)   The term, minimum contributions could also be used in respect of any minimum amount which a member is required to contribute in order to be a member of an occupational or personal pension scheme, or in order to make additional voluntary contributions.

MONEY PURCHASE—The determination of an individual member's benefits by reference to contributions paid into the scheme in respect of that member, usually increased by an amount based on the investment return on those contributions.

NET RELEVANT EARNINGS—Earnings from self-employment or non-pensionable employment after deducting losses and certain business charges on income, used in determining the maximum contributions to a retirement annuity or personal pension scheme which qualify for tax relief. With effect from tax year 1989/90 net relevant earnings have been restricted by the earnings cap. The maximum contribution below the cap is currently 17.5 per cent of net relevant earnings with higher percentage limits for persons aged over 35, if contributing to a personal pension scheme, or 50, if contributing to a retirement annuity.

NOMINATION—The naming by a member of the person to whom he or she wishes any death benefit to be paid. The scheme documentation will indicate whether this is binding on the trustees or merely for their consideration. In the latter case (which is the more common) the term expression of wish is to be preferred.

NON-CONTRIBUTORY SCHEME—A pension scheme which does not require contributions from its active members. Not to be confused with a contributory scheme where contributions are suspended during a contribution holiday.

OCCUPATIONAL PENSION SCHEME—An arrangement organised by an employer or on behalf of a group of employers to provide pensions and/or other benefits for, or in respect of, one or more employees on leaving service or on death or retirement.

PENSIONABLE EARNINGS—The earnings on which benefits and/or contributions are calculated. One or more elements of earnings (eg overtime) may be excluded, and/or there may be a State pension disregard.

PENSIONABLE SERVICE—The period of service which is taken into account in calculating pension benefit. The Pension Schemes Act 1993 gives the term a statutory definition for the purposes of preservation, which also applies for the purposes of the revaluation and transfer payment requirements of the Act.

PERSONAL PENSION SCHEME (PPS)—Usually used to mean a scheme approved under Chapter IV of Pt XIV of the Income and Corporation Taxes Act 1988, under which individuals who are self-employed or in non-pensionable employment, nor in an occupational pension scheme, make pension provision usually by means of unit trust or deposit account contracts. The Pension Schemes Act 1993 uses a slightly different definition which excludes a scheme open only to the self-employed but also includes a free standing AVC scheme.

PRESERVATION—The granting by a scheme of preserved benefits, in particular in accordance with minimum requirements specified by the Pension Schemes Act 1993.

PRESERVED BENEFITS—Benefits arising on an individual ceasing to be an active member of a pension scheme, payable at a later date.

PROTECTED RIGHTS—The benefits under an appropriate personal pension scheme or a money purchase contracted-out scheme, deriving respectively from at least the minimum contributions or minimum payments, which are provided in a specified form as a necessary condition for contracting-out. The term may also be used in a general sense to describe rights given to certain members on change of rules or change of pension scheme which are superior to those of a new entrant.

QUALIFYING SERVICE—The term defined in the Pension Schemes Act 1993 denoting the service to be taken into account to entitle a member to short service benefits. The current condition is for at least two years' qualifying service. If a transfer has been received from a personal pension scheme, the member is treated immediately as being entitled to short service benefits.

RELEVANT BENEFITS—The term used in the Income and Corporation Taxes Act 1988 and the Practice Notes to describe the types of benefits which are within the tax regime governing occupational pension schemes.

The full definition is set out in s 612(1) of the Act and covers any type of financial benefit given in connection with retirement, death or termination of service. The definition does not include benefits provided only in the event of accidental death or disablement during service.

RETAINED BENEFITS—Retirement or death benefits in respect of an employee deriving from an earlier period of employment or self-employment. In some circumstances retained benefits must be taken into account in the maximum approvable benefits.

REVALUATION
(1) The application, particularly to preserved benefits, of indexation, escalation or the awarding of discretionary increases. The Pension Schemes Act 1993 imposes revaluation in the calculation of guaranteed minimum pensions and of preserved benefits other than guaranteed minimum pensions.
(2) An accounting term for the revision of the carrying value of an asset, usually having regard to its market value.

SECTION 32 POLICY—The term used widely to describe an insurance policy used for buy out purposes, where the member chooses the insurance company.

The term came into use as a result of s 32 of the Finance Act 1981, which gave prominence to the possibility of effecting such policies (now contained in s 591 of the Income and Corporation Taxes Act 1988).

SEGREGATED FUND—An arrangement whereby the investments of a particular pension scheme are managed by an external investment manager independently of other funds under its control. Often used to indicate an individual portfolio of stocks and shares in contrast to a pooled fund.

SELF-ADMINISTERED SCHEME—A pension scheme where the assets are invested, other than wholly by payment of insurance premiums, by the trustees, an in-house manager or an external investment manager. Although on the face of it the term self-administered should refer to the method of administering contributions and benefits, in practice the term has become solely related to the way in which the investments are managed.

SELF-INVESTMENT—A term used to describe the investment of a scheme's assets in employer-related investments.

A 5 per cent limit is imposed on employer-related investments by the Pensions Act (with certain exemptions). The PSO imposes separate restrictions on self-investment by small self-administered schemes. Requirements as to disclosure and reporting of self-investment are laid down by the Disclosure Regulations.

SERVICE—A period of employment with one or more connected employers.

SHORT SERVICE BENEFIT—The benefit which must be provided for an early leaver under the preservation requirements of the Pension Schemes Act 1993.

TRANSFER PAYMENT—A payment made from a pension scheme to another pension scheme, or to an insurance company to purchase a buy out policy, in lieu of benefits which have accrued to the member or members concerned, to enable the receiving arrangement to provide alternative benefits. The transfer payment may be made in accordance with the scheme rules or in exercise of a member's statutory rights under the Pension Schemes Act 1993.

TRANSFER VALUE—The amount of the transfer payment, usually based on actuarial advice, which the trustees are prepared to make to another pension scheme or an insurance company.

UPLIFTED 60ths—Benefits in excess of 1/60 of final remuneration for each year of service to the extent permitted by the PSO in an approved occupational pension scheme.

UPPER BAND EARNINGS—Earnings between the lower earnings limit and the upper earnings limit on which the additional pension is calculated. Also used in the calculation of a guaranteed minimum pension.

UPPER EARNINGS LIMIT (UEL)—The maximum amount of earnings (equal to approximately seven times the lower earnings limit) on which National Insurance Contributions are payable by employees.

VESTED RIGHTS

    (a)   For active members, benefits to which they would unconditionally be entitled on leaving the scheme;

    (b)   for deferred pensioners, their preserved benefits; and

    (c)   for pensioners, pensions to which they are entitled including where appropriate the related benefits for spouses or other dependants.

WAITING PERIOD—A period of service specified in the rules which an employee must serve before being entitled to join the pension scheme or to receive a particular benefit. In some pension schemes the waiting period before being entitled to join may automatically count as pensionable service. Not to be confused with qualifying service.

Reproduced by permission of The Pensions Management Institute

Duties and Sanctions Imposed by the Pensions Act

Duty	Sanction	Section
Serious or persistent breach of statutory duties under the Act and in relation to registration, transfer values, information and the levy	Prohibition order	s 3(2)
Non-compliance with OPRA directions	Prohibition order and civil penalty	s 15(4)
Employer opt-out proposals: failure to give effect to statutory consultation procedure	Civil penalty on employer	s 17(5) s 19(5)
Member-nominated trustees: failure to comply	Prohibition order and civil penalty	s 21(1) & (2)
Acting as trustee while actuary or auditor	Criminal offence—fine or imprisonment—and prohibition order	s 28(1) & s 28(4)

Duty	Sanction	Section
Acting as trustee while disqualified	Criminal offence—fine or imprisonment	s 30(3)
Indemnifying trustees for fines or civil penalties	Prohibition order and civil penalty Criminal offence—fine or imprisonment—for trustee indemnified	s 31(3) s 31(4)
Decisions by majority: failure to give notice	Prohibition order and civil penalty	s 32(5)
Statement of investment principles: failure to comply	Prohibition order and civil penalty	s 35(6)
Choosing investments: failure to obtain advice	Prohibition order and civil penalty	s 36(8)
Payment of surplus to employer: non-compliance with requirements by trustees	Prohibition order and civil penalty	s 37(8)
Payment of surplus to employer: exercise of power by someone other than trustees	Civil penalty	s 37(9)

Duty	Sanction	Section
Employer-related investments: failure to take reasonable steps to secure compliance	Prohibition order and civil penalty	s 40(4)
Employer-related investments: trustee or manager who agreed to decision	Criminal offence— fine or imprisonment	s 40(5)
Placing reliance on professional advisers not appointed by trustees	Prohibition order and civil penalty	s 47(3)
Failure to appoint auditor, actuary or fund manager	Prohibition order and civil penalty	s 47(8)
Failure to disclose information to trustees by employer Failure to disclose information to advisers by trustees	Prohibition order and civil penalty Prohibition order and civil penalty	s 47(10) & (11) s 47(10) & (11)
Failure to whistle blow: auditor or actuary	Civil penalty Disqualification order Criminal offence— fine or imprisonment—acting while disqualified	s 48(7) s 48(8) s 48(12)
Receipts, payments and records: non-compliance	Prohibition order and civil penalty	s 49(6) & (7)

Duty	Sanction	Section
Non-payment of employee contributions to trustees	Criminal offence—fine or imprisonment	s 49(8)
Dispute resolution: non-compliance	Civil penalty	s 50(6)
MFR: non-compliance	Prohibition order and civil penalty	s 57(7)
Schedules of contributions: non-compliance	Prohibition order and civil penalty	s 58(8)
Non-payment of scheduled contributions: failure to notify OPRA and members	Prohibition order and civil penalty	s 59(4)
Non-compliance with MFR: failure to report	Prohibition order and civil penalty	s 59(4)
Serious underprovision: failure to report	Prohibition order and civil penalty	s 60(8)
Preferential liabilities on winding up: non-compliance	Prohibition order and civil penalty	s 73(6)
Excess assets on winding up: non-compliance	Prohibition order and civil penalty	s 76(6)
Excess assets remaining after winding up: non-compliance	Prohibition order	s 77(5)

Duty	Sanction	Section
Compensation scheme: failure to obtain recoveries by trustees	Prohibition order	s 81(6)
Schedules of payments—money purchase schemes: non-compliance non-payment by employer failure by trustees to notify OPRA and members	Prohibition order and civil penalty Civil penalty Prohibition order and civil penalty	s 87(5) s 88(3) s 88(4)
Failing to produce a document to OPRA, delaying or obstructing an OPRA inspector or failing to provide information to OPRA	Criminal offence—fine	s 101(1) & (2)
Knowingly or recklessly providing OPRA with false or misleading information	Criminal offence—fine or imprisonment	s 101(5)
Altering, concealing or destroying a document required by OPRA	Criminal offence—fine or imprisonment	s 101(6)
Disclosing restricted information	Criminal offence—fine or imprisonment	s 104(3)

Duty	Sanction	Section
Failing to produce a document to the Compensation Board	Criminal offence—fine	s 111(1)
Knowingly or recklessly providing the Compensation Board with false or misleading information	Criminal offence—fine or imprisonment	s 111(4)
Altering, concealing or destroying a document required by the Compensation Board	Criminal offence—fine or imprisonment	s 111(5)
Failing to provide statement of guaranteed entitlement to the amount of the cash equivalent	Civil penalty	s 153(4)
Supplying the Registrar with false or misleading information	Criminal offence—fine or imprisonment	s 155

Appendix 3

Steps to be Taken to Comply with the Pensions Act

(1) Member-nominated trustees
- Employer to decide about opt out proposals; or
- Trustees to make proposals for their own selection procedure; or
- Trustees to use prescribed default procedure.

(2) Investment
- Prepare statement of investment principles.

(3) Advisers
- Appoint fund manager, actuary and auditor; and
- Prepare terms of appointment for advisers.

(4) Administration
- Open scheme bank account if necessary; and
- Keep proper records, books, accounts and minutes.

(5) Internal dispute resolution
- Set up internal dispute resolution procedure; and
- Disclose details to members.

(6) Indexation of pensions
- LPI required for pensionable service or contributions after 6 April 1997; and
- Decide whether employer to bear extra cost or to reduce future accrual rate or increase members' contributions.

(7) Minimum funding requirement
- Obtain MFR valuation; and
- Prepare schedule of contributions or payment schedule.

(8) Contracting-out
- Review present arrangements;
- Decide whether to (or to continue to) contract-out; and
- Decide whether to retain GMP liabilities or buy-back into SERPS.

(9) Transfer values
- Extend right to cash equivalents to pre-1986 leavers;
- Arrange for guaranteed statements of cash equivalents; and
- Review policy on discretionary benefits in calculating transfer values and get actuarial advice before directing that they are to be disregarded.

(10) Disclosure
- Amend booklets to provide details about:
  — whether admission is subject to employer's consent;
  — AVC arrangements;
  — the definition of pensionable earnings;
  — accrual rates;
  — whether, and if so on what conditions, survivors' benefits are payable;
  — arrangements for estimates of, or guaranteed statements of, entitlement to cash equivalents;
  — how transfer values are calculated;
  — internal dispute resolution procedure and a named contact point; and
  — details of OPRA's jurisdiction.

Details of pensions increases in the past 10 years will no longer be required.

- Amend early leavers' statements to provide details of:
  — guaranteed statement of entitlement to cash equivalent;
  — availability of actuary's report to trustees about treatment of discretionary benefits in transfer values (where they are disregarded).
- Amend trustees' annual report to provide details of:
  — the names of the directors of corporate trustees;
  — custodians;
  — whether discretionary benefits are included in the calculation of transfer values and, if so, the method of assessing their value;

- whether the accounts have been prepared and audited in accordance with legal requirements;
- if the auditor's statement is negative or qualified, the reasons why and when it is likely to be resolved;
- whether the trustees have prepared a statement of investment principles and, if so, that a copy is available on request;
- the trustees' policy on custodianship; and
- an investment report containing:

- a statement about whether the investments are in line with the statement of investment principles, and, if not, why not and when it will be put right;
- a review of investment performance during the year and also for a longer period of between three to five years against objectives (eg percentage increase in the fund); and
  - any statement made on the resignation or removal of the actuary (previously only the auditor).

But schemes will no longer have to disclose whether the OPB's leaflet on principles of trusteeship has been made available to the trustees.

(11) Generally

- Review trust deed and rules and balance of power;
- Arrange for trustee and potential trustee training;
- Review indemnities for trustees; and
- Review administration procedures generally.

Member-nominated Trustees

The requirement for member-nominated trustees

The trustees must ensure that arrangements are made for some of the trustees to be nominated and selected by the members in accordance with the appropriate rules. The requirement does not apply if the employer has proposed arrangements which are approved under the statutory consultation procedure or to certain kinds of scheme including:

- schemes where the trustees consist of all the members;
- small self-administered schemes;
- schemes where an insolvency practitioner has been appointed in relation to the employer, but in that event any existing member-nominated trustees will continue in office so long as they are members, regardless of their term of office, and the independent trustee (who is required to act in such circumstances) may fill a vacancy;
- schemes with one member;
- unapproved schemes;
- certain industry-wide schemes for non-associated employers;
- schemes providing death benefits only;
- certain paid up insured schemes;
- wholly insured schemes where the insurance company is the sole trustee; and
- certain executive schemes for directors where the employer is the sole trustee.

The number of member-nominated trustees must not fall below the minimum except:

- for the first six months after the requirements take effect;
- while the employer's opt out proposals are being considered and for six months after the failure of the opt out proposals;

- for the period for which the arrangements last where there is a vacancy because there were not enough nominations; and
- for six months (or the remainder of his term of office) where a trustee has ceased to be a trustee otherwise than because his term of office has ended.

The Pensions Act draws a distinction between the arrangements and the appropriate rules.

The arrangements

The arrangements must provide that:

- anyone nominated and selected in accordance with the appropriate rules becomes a trustee automatically;
- a member-nominated trustee can only be removed with the consent of the other trustees;
- where a vacancy is not filled because not enough nominations are received, the vacancy is either to be filled or left open until the next election;
- member-nominated trustees will remain in office for not less than three nor more than six years;
- the number of member-nominated trustees must be at least two or (if the scheme has less than 100 members) at least one, and at least one-third of the trustees; and
- if a member-nominated trustee who was a member of the scheme when he was appointed ceases to be a member (not just ceases to be an employee), he ceases to be a trustee.

The arrangements must not provide for:

- a greater number of member-nominated trustees than is required to satisfy the statutory minimum unless the employer agrees;
- the functions of member-nominated trustees to differ from those of any other trustee, except for independent trustees appointed on insolvency or trustees appointed by OPRA with special powers; or
- anything which can or should be done by the appropriate rules.

The appropriate rules

The appropriate rules are rules:

- which do what is authorised or required by the Act and nothing else; and
- approved under the statutory consultation procedure or, if no such rules are approved, are the prescribed rules.

The appropriate rules must:

- define the procedure for filling a vacancy as a member-nominated trustee and may provide for the conditions for filling such a vacancy;
- provide for a member-nominated trustee to be eligible for re-selection;
- where a vacancy for a member-nominated trustee is not filled because there are not enough nominations, provide for deciding the next period in which anyone may be nominated and selected in accordance with the rules; and
- provide that, where the employer requires this, anyone who is not a member must have the employer's approval to qualify for selection.

Corporate trustees

A corporate trustee has the same duties in relation to the selection of member-nominated trustees and the employer opt out proposals as individual trustees. The member-nominated 'trustees' are called member-nominated directors. Broadly the same rules apply to member-nominated directors as apply to member-nominated trustees. Where the corporate trustee is a trustee of two or more schemes and:

- either it is connected with the employer; or
- the corporate trustee is the sole trustee or the other trustees are also companies;

then the schemes are treated as one scheme and the members are treated as members of that scheme. But the corporate trustee can decide to treat each scheme separately if:

- only two schemes are involved; and
- it is the sole trustee or the other trustees are also companies.

The trustees' proposals

The Act allows trustees to put forward selection rules to suit the circumstances of their scheme. It is these rules which will lay down who is eligible to be a trustee and who is eligible to select trustees. Members from different locations may wish to have trustees chosen from each site; some schemes may want to have a pensioner trustee. Any of these options is possible so long as the rules put forward by the trustees have members' approval under the statutory consultation procedure.

The statutory consultation procedure

The statutory consultation procedure means the procedure for obtaining members' views. Approval under the statutory consultation procedure must be given by the members as a whole. This means the active and pensioner members, and such of the deferred pensioners as the trustees decide. The trustees might, for example, decide not to consult those deferred pensioners with whom they have lost contact. But they must not pick and choose capriciously which of them should be consulted.

The notice and general statement

The trustees must give each of the members, ie active and pensioner members and such of the deferred pensioners as they decide to consult, notice in writing specifying that the trustees are required to make arrangements for the selection of member-nominated trustees and to implement appropriate rules.

General information about arrangements

The notice must specify in general terms the arrangements the trustees are proposing to make, and in particular:
- the total number of trustees;
- the number of trustees to be selected by the members;
- the number of trustees to be selected by the employer or anyone else;
- whether if there are not enough nominations for a member-nominated trustee the vacancy is to remain open or is to be filled, and, if so, the procedure for filling it; and
- the proposed term of office.

The proposed rules

The notice must specify the rules including particulars about:
- any eligibility conditions for member-nominated trustees;
- whether nominations must be seconded, and, if so, by how many;
- where a vacancy is not filled because there are not enough nominations, the next period in which people may be nominated and selected; and
- the selection procedure where the number of persons nominated exceeds the vacancies.

The approval procedure

The notice must state:
- that the appropriate rules must be approved by the members;
- whether they are being balloted at the outset or whether they are being given a time within which to object and that they will be balloted only if the rules are rejected;
- how objections are to be made and the time for objection (not less than one month);
- the date of the ballot, if applicable, the procedure to be used, whether or not it is to be a secret ballot, and the last date for voting (not less than one month from the notice);
- where the trustees have decided to consult the deferred pensioners, their decision;
- where members are being given a time within which to object, that if objections by less than 10 per cent (or 10,000 if less) of the members are received the rules will be treated as approved; and
- where the members are being balloted at the outset or if objections by at least 10 per cent (or 10,000 if less) are received, that the rules must be approved by a ballot by a majority of those voting and that the trustees, or the employer if opt out arrangements are proposed, will give notice of the result of the ballot.

So long as objections to the proposed rules are only made by less than 10 per cent (or 10,000 if less) of the members, the rules will be treated as approved; otherwise a ballot will be held. Where there is a ballot, the rules must be approved by a majority of those voting. Alternatively if agreement on the trustees' proposals is not reached, the trustees can either present fresh proposals and go through the hoop again or opt for the procedure of last resort—the prescribed rules. Trustees and, if appropriate, the employer should keep records because OPRA can investigate members' complaints that the procedure has not been followed properly.

The employer's opt out proposals

The requirement for member-nominated trustees will not apply if:
- the employer gives notice to the trustees;
- the employer has made a proposal for continuing the present arrangements, or adopting new arrangements, for choosing the trustees;
- these arrangements are approved under the statutory consultation procedure; and
- the employer notifies the trustees of the approval giving details of the arrangements.

The trustees are responsible for implementing the new arrangements. The arrangements for choosing the trustees include for this purpose everything relating to:
- the continuation in office of the present trustees;
- the selection of new trustees and the terms of their appointment; and
- any special rules about decisions to be made by particular trustees.

Schemes will thus be free to have whatever arrangements they want so long as they meet with members' approval.

Statutory consultation procedure—employer's opt out proposals

This is similar to the procedure to be adopted by the trustees except that:
- the employer has to give notice to the trustees;
- the employer (rather than the trustees) must give the notice to members specifying the alternative arrangements;
- the notice must state that, unless the employer's proposals are approved, the trustees must arrange for the selection of member-nominated trustees; and

- the employer's notice must state the total number of trustees, the proposed procedure for the selection of trustees, their term of office and any difference in the functions of any of the trustees and whether any existing member-nominated trustees should remain or not. In the case of a corporate trustee the notice must set out any special rules for decisions to be made by individual directors.

If objections are made by less than 10 per cent (or 10,000 if less) of the members, the proposals will be treated as approved; otherwise a ballot will be held, unless the employer presents fresh proposals.

Where the employer proposes a continuation of the *existing* arrangements and this is not rejected, it has immediate effect. But where either:

- the employer's proposals (new or existing) are rejected; or
- the employer proposes *new* arrangements, which are approved

the trustees have six months to implement either their own arrangements (where the employer's proposals were rejected) or to give effect to the employer's new arrangements (where they were approved). Meanwhile the existing rules of the scheme stand and the employer's notice suspends the requirement for member-nominated trustees.

Proper records must be kept by the trustees, and the employer if appropriate, of the steps taken by them to comply with the statutory consultation procedure. Notice must be given to each member in writing by post or by personal delivery or leaving it at his last known address.

Alternatively some other procedure for giving notice may be followed which the trustees are satisfied is adequate to draw members' attention to it, for example a notice on a noticeboard coupled with a reference drawing attention to it in payslips or a pensions newsletter.

The prescribed rules

These are supposed to be the rules of last resort, where the trustees and the members cannot agree about selection procedures; but there is nothing to stop them being used from the beginning if the trustees want to. They are designed to be quick to implement, easy to operate and avoid unnecessary cost.

- The trustees must give written notice to the active members specifying in general terms the proposed arrangements and giving the same information as would be required if the trustees were proposing their own arrangements;

- The trustees must invite nominations by a specified date (not less than one month after the notice is given);
- Anyone may be nominated but non-members must be approved in writing by the employer;
- Nominations must be made by an active member and supported by another active member;
- Nominations must be made by written notice to the trustees with the consent of the candidate;
- If the number of candidates does not exceed the vacancies, they will become member-nominated trustees;
- If the number exceeds the vacancies, the trustees must ballot the active members;
- Each member may vote for only one of the candidates and vacancies will be filled by the candidates who get most votes (a tie being resolved by drawing lots);
- Within 14 days of the last day for nominations the trustees must give written notice to the active members specifying:
  — the procedure to be used for the ballot and whether or not it is to be secret;
  — the last day for voting (not less than 14 days nor more than one month from the date of the notice); and
  — the arrangements for overseeing the ballot, counting the votes and declaring the result;
- If the arrangements provide for a vacancy caused by insufficient nominations to be filled, further nominations may be made and members may be selected;
- If the arrangements provide for the vacancy to be left open when there are not enough nominations, nominations may not be made without the trustees' consent until the original term of office expires.

Transitional provisions

The employer has been able to give effect to the new requirements from 6 October 1996. Written notice must be given to the trustees. Unless members approve the employer's alternative arrangements, the latest possible time for having member-nominated trustees is April 1998, one year after the Pensions Act came into force. If the employer gives the trustees written notice that it does not intend to make opt out proposals before 6 May 1997, it will lose the right to do so until the next time round.

Penalties

An employer who makes an opt out proposal but fails to give effect to the statutory consultation procedure will be liable to a penalty of up to £5,000 for an individual or £50,000 for a company.

If the arrangements, whether for member-nominated trustees or for the employer's opt out proposals, are not made or implemented or the appropriate rules are not implemented, any trustee who fails to take reasonable steps to secure compliance is liable to removal and penalties of up to £5,000 or £50,000 in the case of a company.

Ballots

Schemes can choose whether to conduct the statutory consultation either with a ballot at the outset or by a process of objection followed by a ballot. Employers will therefore be able to test the water to find out members' views before committing themselves to a ballot. The arrangements for a ballot are to be decided by those who conduct it. There are no requirements for independent scrutineers or even secrecy. Ballots will be decided by a simple majority of those voting.

How long will the arrangements last?

The approval of the rules ceases to have effect:
- after six years; or
- if a relevant event has occurred, six months after the trustees give notice that they consider that it would be detrimental to the interests of the members for the arrangements to continue; or
- when new rules are approved or the existing ones are approved again.

A relevant event is:
- a bulk transfer into or out of the scheme; or
- a change of any of the participating employers; or
- a 100 per cent takeover of any of the participating employers by a non-participating employer.

Advantages and disadvantages of the procedures

	The trustees' proposals	The employers proposals	The prescribed rules
Possible advantages	Pensioners involved Tailor made arrangements Opportunity to re-present No automatic ballot	Pensioners involved Tailor made arrangements Opportunity to re-present No automatic ballot Employer can control process Existing arrangements can continue	Cheap and cheerful Quick and easy Avoids cost of repeated communications with members No pensioner or deferred pensioner involvement
Possible disadvantages	Pensioners involved Possible involvement of deferreds Risk of rejection Pensioners can vote		No tailor made arrangements No pensioner or deferred pensioner involvement Automatic ballot if more nominations than vacancies No opportunity to re-present

Schemes with an entrenched independent trustee, if they want to go on as they are, will have to get the employer to make the necessary opt out proposals for approval by the members under the statutory consultation procedure. Employers who dislike the idea of member trustees will have to present opt out proposals if they think they will not be rejected by the members. Schemes which wish to qualify the purity of 'one person one vote' by creating constituencies eg based on sites or to have a pensioner trustee, will have to propose suitable arrangements for approval by the members.

Schemes that do not wish to risk alienating their pensioners or deferred members will also have to make proposals for approval by their members. However, the prescribed rules, involving only the active members, will no doubt prove attractive to small schemes and to schemes that wish to avoid pensioner trustees. The likely outcome is that schemes which now have member trustees, although not complying with the strict letter of the Pensions Act, and schemes with entrenched independent trustees, will wish to continue their present arrangements; the employer will therefore make proposals for members' approval. But schemes which make no pretence at having member trustees, and in particular small schemes, will probably go down the route of the prescribed rules, avoiding pensioner involvement and the risk of rebuff by them.

Checklist

(1) If the employer wishes to make opt out proposals:
- should the present arrangements continue?
- should there be new arrangements?
- are deferred pensioners to be consulted?
- notice to the trustees must be given.

(2) If the employer does not wish to make opt out proposals or its proposals are rejected:
- the employer's approval for non-member trustees must be obtained;
- the employer's approval for more than the minimum number of member trustees must be obtained;
- terms of office for member trustees must be fixed;
- should vacancies be filled or left open?
- should the prescribed rules be used or should trustees propose their own selection procedure?

(3) If trustees wish to propose their own procedure:
- are deferred pensioners to be consulted?
- what is to be the selection procedure eg pensioner trustee, eligibility conditions, seconding etc?
- should there be a ballot at the outset?
- how is a ballot to be conducted eg constituencies, open or secret?

(4) If there is an entrenched independent trustee:
- does the employer propose to continue the present arrangements?

(5) What training should be given to trustees and prospective trustees?

Timetable

- Effective date for new requirements is 6 April 1997.
- Transitional provisions take effect from 6 October 1996.
- Employer opt out:
  — initial notice to trustees before 6 May 1997;
  — in the case of a second or subsequent notice, where the employer's previous proposals had been approved, the notice to the trustees must be given not more than 12 nor less than six months before approval of the current arrangements expires;
  — six months to obtain members' approval.
- Trustees' proposals—six months from 6 April 1997 or rejection of employer's proposals.
- Members to have at least one month to object or to vote.
- Casual vacancies are to be filled within six months or, if less, the remainder of the term of office.
- Renewal of arrangements to be undertaken:
  — every six years; or
  — if a relevant event has occurred, six months after the trustees give notice that they consider that it would be detrimental to continue; or
  — when the current arrangements expire.

Index